The political thought of the Liberals and Liberal Democrats since 1945

MANCHESTER
1824

Manchester University Press

The political thought of the Liberals and Liberal Democrats since 1945

edited by Kevin Hickson

Manchester University Press
Manchester and New York

distributed in the United States exclusively
by Palgrave Macmillan

Published by Manchester University Press
Oxford Road, Manchester M13 9NR, UK
and Room 400, 175 Fifth Avenue, New York, NY 10010, USA
www.manchesteruniversitypress.co.uk

Distributed in the United States exclusively by
Palgrave Macmillan, 175 Fifth Avenue, New York,
NY 10010, USA

Distributed in Canada exclusively by
UBC Press, University of British Columbia, 2029 West Mall,
Vancouver, BC, Canada V6T 1Z2

British Library Cataloguing-in-Publication Data
A catalogue record for this book is available from the British Library

Library of Congress Cataloging-in-Publication Data applied for

ISBN   978 07190 7948 1 *hardback*

First published 2009

18 17 16 15 14 13 12 11 10 09 10 9 8 7 6 5 4 3 2 1

The publisher has no responsibility for the persistence or accuracy of URLs for any external or third-party internet websites referred to in this book, and does not guarantee that any content on such websites is, or will remain, accurate or appropriate.

Typeset
by Action Publishing Technology Ltd, Gloucester
Printed in Great Britain
by TJ International Ltd, Padstow

Contents

List of tables and figures

Tables

Figures

Acknowledgements

I would like to thank first and foremost all of the contributors to the book. The quality of the work is, I believe, very strong throughout and all of the contributors have approached their work with enthusiasm.

I would particularly like to thank Duncan Brack, who has allowed me to pester him from the early stages of the book through to its completion without complaint. He has been a tremendous source of advice. Duncan and Mark Garnett both provided detailed comments on the first draft of my introduction.

I would also like to thank Tony Mason and his staff at Manchester University Press, who have been strongly committed to the book.

Finally I would like to thank Brian Davies, Lee Miles and Jon Tonge for their support and encouragement and the students on my third year undergraduate module, British Political Ideologies, over the past two years for making me think.

Kevin Hickson
Hurleston

Notes on contributors

Duncan Brack is editor of the *Journal of Liberal History* and Chair of the Liberal Democrat Federal Conference Committee. He was formerly Director of Policy for the Liberal Democrats. He has published widely on the Liberal Democrats, most notably as editor and contributor to *Reinventing the State: Social Liberalism for the 21st Century* (edited with Richard Grayson and David Howarth, 2007).

Alan Butt Philip is Jean Monnet Reader in European Integration in the School of Management at the University of Bath. He is Convenor of the John Stuart Mill Institute and has published widely on the Liberals and Liberal Democrats and on aspects of European integration. He has been a Liberal or Liberal Democrat candidate on five occasions in Westminster elections and three times for the European Parliament.

Vincent Cable has been the Liberal Democrat MP for Twickenham since 1997. He was Acting Leader in 2007 and is now Deputy Leader and Shadow Chancellor. He previously worked as a lecturer in economics at Glasgow University, in the Kenyan Treasury, the UK Diplomatic Service and as Chief Economist for Shell. His recent publications include *The World's New Fissures: The Politics of Identity* (1995); *Globalisation and Global Governance* (1999); and *Public Services: Reform with a Purpose* (2005).

Matt Cole lectures at the London School of Economics for the Hansard Society. He completed his PhD at the University of Birmingham on the post-war Liberal Party and has published in a number of journals. He is the author of *Democracy in Britain* (2006) and is currently writing a biography of the Liberal MP Richard Wainwright.

Russell Deacon is Reader in Welsh Governance and Modern Political History and Head of Humanities at the University of Wales Institute, Cardiff. He is Chair of the Political Studies Association Liberal Studies Group.

Roy Douglas is Emeritus Reader at the University of Surrey. He has published a substantial number of works on the history of the Liberal and Liberal Democrat parties and his publications include *The History of the Liberal Party 1895–1970* (1971) and *Liberals: A History of the Liberal and Liberal Democrat Parties* (2005).

Mark Garnett is Lecturer in Politics at the University of Lancaster and previously taught at the University of Leicester. He has published widely on British politics. His recent publications include *Exploring British Politics* (with Philip Lynch, 2007) and *From Anger to Apathy: The British Experience 1975–2005* (2007).

Richard S. Grayson is Senior Lecturer in British and Irish Politics and Head of the Department of Politics at Goldsmiths, University of London. He was previously Director of Policy at the Liberal Democrats and Director of the Centre for Reform. He has published widely on the Liberals and Liberal Democrats including *Reinventing the State: Social Liberalism for the 21ˢᵗ Century* (edited with Duncan Brack and David Howarth, 2007).

Kevin Hickson is Lecturer in Politics at the University of Liverpool and previously taught at the universities of Manchester, Salford and Southampton. He has published several books on British politics including *The Struggle for Labour's Soul: Understanding the Political Thought of the Labour Party* (edited with Raymond Plant and Matt Beech, 2004) and *The Political Thought of the Conservative Party Since 1945* (edited, 2005).

David Howarth has been the Liberal Democrat MP for Cambridge since 2005 and was previously the Leader of Cambridge City Council. He was Reader at Cambridge University and since becoming an MP has held several frontbench positions; he is currently the Shadow Solicitor General. His publications include, *Reinventing the State: Social Liberalism for the 21ˢᵗ Century* (edited with Duncan Brack and Richard Grayson, 2007).

Bruce Pilbeam is Senior Lecturer in American Studies at London Metropolitan University. He has published widely on British and American politics in a number of scholarly journals and with the book *Conservatism in Crisis* (2003).

Andrew Russell is Senior Lecturer in Politics at the University of Manchester. He was the joint author of *Neither Left nor Right? The Liberal Democrats and the Electorate* (2005, with Ed Fieldhouse).

Steve Webb has been the Liberal Democrat MP for Northavon since 1997 and has held several frontbench positions since 1999. He was the Chair of the election manifesto team and is now Shadow Secretary of State for Work and Pensions. He previously worked as an economist at the Institute of Fiscal Studies and was Professor of Social Policy at the University of Bath.

1   *Kevin Hickson*

Introduction

In comparison to the two major parties – Conservative and Labour – the Liberals/ Liberal Democrats have been relatively neglected by academics.[1] The reason for this may seem fairly obvious. The last Liberal Prime Minister lost office in 1922 and the Liberal Party ceased to be a major force in British politics by the end of that decade. What academic attention there has been has tended therefore to focus on the earlier periods of the Party's history, while the post-1945 period suffers from comparative neglect.[2] Such a feature of the academic literature has had two effects. Firstly, the role of the Liberals in the development of policies after 1945 is neglected. As a number of commentators point out in this volume, debates in the Party have sometimes had an impact on the policy-making of governments and Liberal MPs like David Steel have promoted important social reforms. Secondly, there has been only a very limited analysis of the political thought of the Liberal and Liberal Democrat parties. This is so even in more recent studies of the Liberal Democrats, which have tended to focus on the electoral and political strategies of the Party.[3] Such a focus is important and is included in this volume. However, a one-dimensional view of politics stressing either political and electoral strategy on the one hand or ideology on the other is simplistic and misleading. It is necessary to examine how one element both shapes and is shaped by the other.

Hence, the rationale for this book is clear. There are very few accounts in the academic literature of the ideology of the Liberals and Liberal Democrats. The last major study of the Liberal Party was published in the early 1980s and was edited by Vernon Bogdanor.[4] A number of studies of the Social Democratic Party appeared after its formation and the definitive study was that written by Ivor Crewe and Anthony King,[5] although there was little on the SDP–Liberal Alliance. The only major studies of the Liberal Democrats have been those edited by Don McIver and Richard Grayson.[6] In contrast, there have been a number of works published recently by those within or close to the Liberal Democrats advocating a particular ideological direction – the works associated with David Laws MP representing the clearest advocacy of classical liberalism and the recent book *Reinventing the State* being the clearest social liberal response.[7] These books include contributions from a number of those who have contributed to this book and can be used as primary

texts for a study of contemporary Liberal Democrat ideology. However, there is no
volume which seeks to address the ideology of the Liberals and Liberal Democrats
as a whole since 1945, which this book does.[8]

One major theme of this volume is how liberal political thought and practice
from the pre-1914 era has impacted on the developments of the Liberal and Liberal
Democrat parties since 1945. Liberalism is usually discussed in terms of classical
and social, or new, forms of liberalism and the distinction rests largely on the definition of freedom. Therefore a central aim of this introduction is to outline these
terms, which are then developed in a number of the chapters in the book. A further
aim is to relate the political ideology of Liberalism/Liberal Democracy to Liberal-
ism/Liberal Democracy as a political and electoral strategy.

Liberalism as an ideology

In analysing Liberalism as an ideology there are close links with liberalism as a
tradition of political thought. The Party has often contained elements of both 'classical' and 'social' liberalism and many of the internal Party debates can be
understood as a tension between these two traditions.[9] Many of the contributors in
this volume use the terms classical and social liberalism and the first section is dedi-
cated, in part, to an analysis of these traditions and how they have evolved in the
Liberals and Liberal Democrats since 1945. It is therefore important to outline
these positions here.

Both classical liberalism and social liberalism are concerned with the promotion
of individual freedom. However, freedom is a contestable concept and the debates
within liberalism can essentially be seen as a contestation of the core liberal value
of individual freedom. For classical liberals, freedom is best defined as a *negative*
term, as freedom from external constraint. This implied a reduced, although not
necessarily a minimal state. The role of the state should be limited as it could act
as a restriction on personal liberty – through taxation or regulation of what should
be private activities. The market was seen as a way of extending personal liberty.
However, the market could also act to undermine individual liberties, especially
through the exploitation of the consumer through monopolistic or oligopolistic
behaviour. Therefore, the state could be permitted to have a role in regulating the
market so as to ensure competition and choice. Similarly, the state could act against
the coercive pressures present within society through the promotion of social diversity and civil rights. The state's role in the alleviation of absolute poverty could also
be interpreted from a classical liberal viewpoint as a way of eliminating a barrier to
the exercise of liberty, as Roy Douglas has attempted to do in this volume.
However, in general terms the role of the state is more likely to act as a restraint on
freedom and from a classical liberal perspective ought always to be limited.

The social liberal viewpoint, which developed in theoretical terms from the late
nineteenth century and underpinned many of the policies of the Liberal Government of 1906–14, marked a more positive view of the state. For social liberals the
individual citizen was not free if they lacked sufficient resources in order to exer-

cise their liberty. To the classic question posed by social liberals – Is the individual free to dine at the Ritz? – the classical liberal would say that they were so long as no-one was barring their access. For social liberals, this was an absurdity since the answer to the question would surely depend on whether the individual possessed enough money to pay the bill. Hence, a strongly positive definition of freedom was developed – that freedom involved the capacity to act. In turn this led Liberals to advocate state intervention to alleviate poverty. Hence, the Liberal Government elected in 1906 was very different in character from that of Gladstone's governments at the end of the nineteenth century and, as Richard Grayson discusses in detail, the social liberal viewpoint has continued to have a significant following since 1945.

However, it would be a mistake to subsume all political discussion in the Liberals and Liberal Democrats to such a distinction. This is so for several reasons. The first, as this book makes clear, is that there are a number of issues that cut across the classical–social liberal distinction, including constitutional reform, questions of social morality and the relationship between Britain and the rest of the world. Even in the field of political economy, where this distinction is easier to maintain, there are issues such as the environment that cannot be understood within the classical–social liberal divide. Hence, such issues are dealt with in a separate section of the book.

The second reason why we should be careful in making a rigid distinction between social and classical liberalism is that many in the Party do not conform easily with one or other of these ideological positions. One particular feature of this book is the emphasis placed on the 'centrists' within the Party. The centre is defined as the pragmatic element of a party, one which seeks to promote party unity, loyalty to the leader and to eschew the ideological polarities of left and right – in this case social and classical liberals. It is argued by Mark Garnett that the centre became increasingly important from the 1970s when the number of Liberal MPs increased. This brings us to the relevance of political and electoral strategy.

Political and electoral strategy

This is not the place to discuss in any depth the history of the Liberals and Liberal Democrats, which in any case has been done elsewhere.[10] Instead a brief outline of their history can reveal some interesting features of the political ideology and the electoral and political strategy of the Liberals and Liberal Democrats. The years after the end of the Second World War marked a period of crisis for the Liberal Party, and with only a handful of MPs it looked as if the Party would collapse. However, as Garnett comments, the ethos of independent radicalism ensured that the Party continued and sometimes had a direct impact on policy, such as with the liberal law and order measures of the mid-1960s when for instance David Steel introduced the abortion law reform. In the 1970s, in the face of economic crisis, the support for the Liberal Party increased in terms of votes and although the larger Liberal vote was never reflected fully in terms of seats in the House of Commons, there were more Liberal MPs. For a while after the departure of the 'Gang of Four' from the Labour Party and the creation of the Alliance between the Liberals and the SDP it looked as if there might be a fundamental realignment of British politics. However, the challenge of the Alliance was finally seen off in the 1987 General Election. This was followed by a merger of the majority of the two separate parties under the new leadership of Paddy Ashdown. His leadership led to the close association of the Liberal Democrats with the 'New' Labour Party of Tony Blair. Any hopes of an alliance were removed by the large Labour landslide in 1997 and many Liberal Democrats became more critical of the close association of their Party with Labour. The subsequent leadership of Charles Kennedy marked a more critical attitude towards New Labour, especially, but not exclusively, on Iraq. However, Kennedy's leadership also marked a consolidation of the Liberal Democrat's position on the centre left. The period from the formation of the Alliance through to the end of Kennedy's leadership was a period of expansion for the Party and it was clearly identified as being on the centre left.

At the time of writing the position is rather different.[11] The 2005 General Election could be viewed as a further breakthrough in the sense that the number of Liberal Democrat MPs increased to 62, an increase of 11 from 2001, and the share of the vote increased by 3.9% to 22.6%. However, many commentators and some in the Party regarded the result as only a limited success since the Labour Government had lost support over Iraq and the Conservative opposition was unpopular, and in such circumstances they had expected that the Liberal Democrats could have done better than they did. Given that circumstances would likely be less favourable to the Liberal Democrats at the time of the next general election – the change in leadership of both parties and the changed international context would likely count against them – this may well have been the last chance for a bigger breakthrough. The leadership issue 2005–7 could be explained in terms of personalities – the alcohol-related problems of Kennedy and the issue of Menzies Campbell's age – but it could also be seen as a struggle over the future ideological and strategic direction of the Liberal Democrats.

In the run-up to the next general election, the Liberal Democrat leadership has three choices.[12] The first is to continue to be an essentially left-of-centre party, seeking to win seats from Labour. In 2005, the Liberal Democrat Party won 16 seats from Labour and it is second to Labour in 10 of the most marginal seats it has to win for a further electoral advance. The Party had improved its position in 2005 by being seen to be a left-of-centre party, proposing to abolish tuition fees, impose a 50% rate of income tax on those earning over £100,000 per year and pledging to withdraw troops from Iraq. The second choice is to continue to appeal to wavering Conservative and Labour voters by appearing to be neither left nor right. The final strategy, proposed by some in the Liberal Democrats, is to move to the right so as to challenge the Conservatives. There is some evidence to support such a strategy. Of the 25 most marginal seats, the Liberal Democrats challenge the Conservatives in 15, and moreover the Conservatives are second to the Liberal Democrats in 42 seats and provide a serious challenge to them in 17 seats. The revival of the Conservatives under David Cameron – at least at the time of writing – is therefore a significant challenge to the Liberal Democrats.

Such a strategic outlook may suggest that ideology is determined by pragmatic deliberations. It is certainly the case that strategic considerations are important in conditioning the future ideological direction of the Liberal Democrats. If it is argued that the electoral advances made by the Party have been made by being a left-of-centre alternative to the Labour Government since 1997 then a more social liberal ideology would seem more appropriate. If the case is made successfully that the Party should seek to challenge the Conservatives then a shift to the right would result. However, it is this uncertainty over the most viable electoral strategy for the Liberal Democrats that means that strategic considerations do not simply determine the ideological direction of the Party. The reality, in which political strategy and political ideology interact, is more complex.

Structure of the book

This book has a similar rationale and the same structure as two earlier books on the political thought of the political parties: *The Struggle for Labour's Soul: Understanding Labour's Political Thought Since 1945* and *The Political Thought of the Conservative Party Since 1945*.[13] All of these books seek to identify the main ideological traditions and to examine a range of cross-cutting themes and issues within the same chronological framework. In addition, the books seek to do two extra things. The first is to place emphasis on the centrists of each party and not just to look at the more familiar territory of left and right. The second feature of the books is in seeking to break down the divide between academia and practitioners (journalists and politicians).

The book is divided into three parts. The first part outlines the main ideological traditions present with the Liberals and Liberal Democrats since 1945. Three positions are identified: classical liberalism, the centre and social liberalism. The second part discusses a range of cross-cutting themes and issues. Those identified as being crucial within the ideological development of Liberalism and Liberal Democracy are constitutional reform, decentralisation, political economy, social morality, internationalism and political strategy. In terms of constitutional reform, Matt Cole discusses three issues, namely electoral reform, parliamentary reform and judicial reform. The emphasis on constitutional issues is a central feature of the ideology of Liberalism and Liberal Democracy, as evidenced by the fact that the discussion of these issues is picked up by Russell Deacon, who discusses devolution and the emergence and impact of community politics. The theme of decentralisation is developed by Duncan Brack in relation to reform of public services and his discussion of political economy also includes an account of the environment as a core feature of Liberal and Liberal Democrat policy debate. Bruce Pilbeam then discusses issues of social morality stressing the presence of liberal and non-liberal themes within the Liberals and Liberal Democrats. The final policy area is that of internationalism, which includes a detailed discussion of the issue of European integration and the relations between Britain and the wider world. The inclusion of a chapter on political strategy here is important for the reasons outlined above – the interplay of strategic and ideological considerations in the shaping of Liberal and Liberal Democrat thought and policy. The final part allows for the expression of ideological statements by MPs representative of each of the positions outlined in part I of the book. Vince Cable seeks to defend the classical liberal position, David Howarth presents the case of the centrists for party unity and Steve Webb outlines what a modern-day manifestation of social liberalism would look like.

One final issue should be addressed directly in the introduction. That is the position of the Social Democratic Party. Some readers may object that the SDP should be seen as a separate position in its own right, representing a distinctive ideological tradition. However, the book deals with the political thought of the Liberals and Liberal Democrats since 1945. Since the period in which the SDP existed was only a very small proportion of these years (1981–88, excluding the Owenite rump) then it clearly does not represent a continuous force within the Liberal Party. Indeed, Liberals did not refer to themselves as social democrats, which was seen as the ideology of the Labour Party. This is not to deny that the SDP was insignificant – although its precise significance is still a matter of debate – but rather that it does not warrant inclusion as a separate strand of the Party's thought. Instead, I have asked all contributors to examine the significance of the SDP in their respective area of enquiry. Hence, there is not a separate chapter on the SDP, but rather the SDP is included in all of the chapters in parts I and II of the book.

Notes

1 I use the term Liberals/Liberal Democrats as the easiest label to describe the various manifestations of the Party. The Party was called the Social and Liberal Democrats just after the merger with the Social Democratic Party before becoming the Liberal Democrats. Also, some Liberals refused to merge with the SDP and continued to call themselves the Liberal Party. However, in broad terms the use of Liberals/Liberal Democrats is correct and is widely recognised. Similarly, the book makes a distinction between Liberal(ism) and liberal(ism) to distinguish between the Party and its ideology on the one hand and the wider liberal set of ideas on the other.

2 The best histories of the Liberals and Liberal Democrats are: C. Cook, *A Short History of the Liberal Party 1900–2001* (Palgrave, Basingstoke, 2002, 6th edition); D. Dutton, *A History of the Liberal Party the the Twentieth Century* (Palgrave, Basingstoke, 2004) and R. Douglas, *Liberals: A History of the Liberal and Liberal Democrat Parties* (Continuum, London, 2005).

3 Especially, A. Russell and E. Fieldhouse, *Neither Left nor Right? The Liberal Democrats and the Electorate* (Manchester University Press, Manchester, 2005).

4 V. Bogdanor (ed.), *Liberal Party Politics* (Oxford University Press, Oxford, 1983).

5 I. Crewe and A. King, *SDP: The Birth, Life and Death of the Social Democratic Party* (Oxford University Press, Oxford, 1995).

6 D. McIver (ed.), *Liberal Democrat Politics* (Harvester Wheatsheaf, Hemel Hempstead,

1996) and R.S. Grayson, *Political Quarterly*, 78:1 (2007).

7 P. Marshall and D. Laws (eds), *The Orange Book: Reclaiming Liberalism* (Profile, London, 2004); J. Astle, D. Laws, P. Marshall and A. Murray (eds), *Britain After Blair: A Liberal Agenda* (Profile, London, 2006) and D. Brack, R. Grayson and D. Howarth (eds), *Reinventing the State: Social Liberalism for the 21ˢᵗ Century* (Politico's, London, 2007).

8 Although an important contribution is that by D. Brack and E. Randall (eds), *Dictionary of Liberal Thought* (Politico's, London, 2007).

9 The term 'classical liberalism' is preferred to both 'economic liberalism' and 'market liberalism' as both of these neglect the non-economic aspects of classical liberalism.

10 See in particular, Dutton, *A History of the Liberal Party* and Douglas, *Liberals*.

11 The following discussion draws on the relevant sections of A. Geddes and J. Tonge (eds), *Britain Decides: The UK General Election, 2005* (Palgrave, Basingstoke, 2005).

12 See E. Fieldhouse and D. Cutts, 'The Liberal Democrats: steady progress or failure to seize the moment', in Geddes and Tonge (eds), *Britain Decides*.

13 R. Plant, M. Beech and K. Hickson (eds), *The Struggle for Labour's Soul: Understanding Labour's Political Thought since 1945* (Routledge, London, 2004) and K. Hickson (ed.), *The Political Thought of the Conservative Party Since 1945* (Palgrave, Basingstoke, 2005).

Part I

Positions

Classical liberalism

What is 'classical liberalism'?

As with so many terms in politics, there appears to be no authoritative definition of 'classical liberalism' and neither the noun nor the adjective is always used in the same way. Ramsay Muir, sometime MP, President of the National Liberal Federation and chief Liberal apologist in the desolate 1930s, declared liberalism to be 'the belief in freedom of thought, freedom of enterprise, freedom of intercourse and freedom in government'.[1] That view appears to have been held by most people who considered themselves Liberals before his time, and in that sense it was 'classical'. So, classical liberalism pivots on the idea of personal liberty. As a general rule a person is a better judge of how his or her interest can be served than somebody else acting, or claiming to act, on his or her behalf. To the classical liberal, there ought to be a 'presumption of liberty'. On occasions, no doubt, that presumption may be overturned by overwhelming considerations to the contrary; but there is always a heavy burden on the shoulders of the person or government which seeks to do so.

Other ideas are closely linked with the idea of liberty. The classical liberal is usually internationalist in outlook. The notion that some people are superior or inferior to others because they happen to have been born in a different country, or to have skin of a different colour, or adhere to a different religion, is seen to be not just wicked but absurd. The idea that government should be democratic, and should correspond closely with the will of the governed, is held by most people who consider themselves classical liberals. Although from ancient times to the present, majorities have frequently decided to support illiberal actions, one recalls Churchill's words, that 'it has been said that democracy is the worst form of government except all those other forms that have been tried from time to time'.[2] As far back as the General Election of 1865, Gladstone had declared that liberalism requires 'trust in the people qualified by prudence', a message which greets the visitor to the National Liberal Club under the bust of the Grand Old Man in the entrance.

Some have caricatured the economic aspects of classical liberalism as pure *laissez-faire*, but this wrong. 'I know of no Liberal economist,' wrote Jo Grimond, 'who has ever held the extreme *laissez-faire* doctrine. I know of no Liberal philosopher who has regarded the individual as completely atomized.'[3] All Liberal governments interfered in various ways with the completely free economy, moved, one hopes, by the desire to make people more free in other respects.

As with other political ideologies, classical liberalism may involve apparent contradictions. What defines a person as a classical liberal or otherwise is often intentions rather than the actual policies supported. A person who favoured British entry to the European Economic Community because he saw this as a step towards the general liberalisation of world commerce and human life was acting as a classical liberal; but so also was a person who opposed entry because he considered that it would have the opposite effect. In the same way a person who favoured entry because he wished to see Britain as part of an introspective group of prosperous western nations with high barriers against outsiders was not a classical liberal; nor was a person who opposed entry because he wanted Britain to exclude foreign goods.

To give another example, many people who would consider themselves classical liberals believe that extreme disparities of wealth and poverty derive from past violations of classical liberal principles, and consider that measures of state intervention should be adopted which on their face appear illiberal in order to rectify those disparities – what might be called 'social liberalism' – while other classical liberals have taken the opposite view. Thus social liberalism might be considered the negation of classical liberalism, or it might be considered a natural development from classical liberalism. On another view, the two ideas are consistent, but separate. Again, some consider that war against evil and tyrannical regimes, with its necessary horrors and illiberalities, is sometimes justified on the principle that the end might justify the means, while others take a strictly pacifist line.

Classical liberalism has never been the exclusive preserve of any political party. There has been, however, a distinct correlation between support for classical liberalism and support for the Liberal Party and its successors. In a book published in 2001, not long after his accession to leadership of the Liberal Democrats, Charles Kennedy declared his belief in

> above all ... a commitment to the liberty of the individual, a course which the other parties cannot lead – Labour has a strong authoritarian streak, while the Conservatives tend to equate liberty with rampant market forces.[4]

Nearly all of the Liberal and Liberal Democrat leaders, and the popular organs of the Parties too, have repeatedly affirmed similar opinions. To put it in somewhat different terms, the classical liberal differs from what we might call the 'classical socialist' in that while both are concerned to build a society corresponding more closely with ideas of natural justice, the classical liberal's first response is to look for some restriction to remove, and the classical socialist's first response is to look for some new restriction to impose. The classical liberal differs from what we might call the 'classical Conservative' in that while both view new developments in the restrictionist direction with suspicion, the classical Conservative tends to accept them once they are in place, while the classical liberal still seeks to remove them.

The background

Although any political party is likely to contain people with very disparate ideas and objectives, the Liberal Party had been forced to define its position more formally than most in the dozen years before 1945. It was necessary to explain both to existing members and to outsiders why they should support a party which had declined so much in recent times and seemed to have no prospect of forming the government in the foreseeable future. This involved showing that its policies and principles would prove immensely beneficial, and were very different from those of its larger rivals. It was also necessary to explain how and why 'official' Liberals who were opposed to the National Government differed from Liberal Nationals who carried the Liberal name, had recently belonged to the Liberal Party, and yet who were also members of that government.

Two important pre-1939 pronouncements sought to make those points clear. A book, *The Liberal Way*, bearing the hallmark of Ramsay Muir, was published in 1934, with the express authority of the National Liberal Federation. It laid down Liberal policy on a comprehensive range of subjects. In his Foreword, Muir concentrated on five of these which were of particular contemporary interest: peace and the League of Nations; the removal of tariff barriers; unemployment; political liberty; and free enterprise versus state control.[5] When the National Liberal Federation was succeeded by a new body, the Liberal Party Organisation, in 1936, the preamble to its constitution laid down underlying principles, including the words 'in all cases it sets freedom first'. Such words were indeed classical liberalism, stated in an extreme way.

In the early 1940s, the Liberals eagerly endorsed the proposal to introduce what would today be called 'welfare state' legislation, which seemed a natural development from legislation of the pre-1915 Liberal Government. The most prominent proponent of that policy was Sir William Beveridge. Originally a non-Party economist, Beveridge headed two famous wartime enquiries. The Reports, *Social Insurance and Allied Services* (1942) and *Full Employment in a Free Society* (1944) attracted huge public interest, though official government responses were non-committal. Beveridge later joined the Liberal Party, and in 1944 was returned as Liberal MP for Berwick-upon-Tweed. Thereafter he was lionised by the Liberal Party, which adopted his proposals with enthusiasm. Was this 'classical liberalism'? The answer is largely a matter of definition. In one sense his proposals were not, because they implied new rules which people would be required to obey. In another sense they were, and Beveridge himself characterised them as part of a struggle for emancipation from the 'five giants': want, ignorance, disease, squalor and idleness.

1945

The 1945 General Election was held in extraordinary conditions. For the previous five years a Coalition Government led by Winston Churchill had been in office. Throughout that period, the leader of the Liberal Party, Sir Archibald Sinclair, had been Secretary of State for Air – technically not a member of the War Cabinet, but regularly invited to its meetings. Several other Liberals held junior government office.

A 'Party Truce' existed, by which seats which became vacant at by-elections were not contested by rival parties. No party leader broke the 'truce' in letter or in spirit, but there is plenty of evidence that big changes were taking place in public opinion during the wartime period. Many people in the second and third ranks of the Liberal Party, and of the Labour Party too, were becoming restive. At the end of the European war the coalition broke up, and a general election was held in which the parties made their separate appeals to the electorate. The Liberals were able to advance 306 candidates for the 628 seats: just under half, indeed, but very substantially more than at any election since 1929. A high proportion of those candidates were young ex-service people.

General election manifestos provide some indication of what a party is thinking, though they must be considered with some caution because they tend to focus on topical questions rather than long-term policies. The Liberal Manifesto of 1945[6] could be regarded as more or less consistent with classical liberalism. Free trade was clearly affirmed. The Liberals, one might say, could hardly do anything else. If the man in the street had been asked to name a particular Liberal policy in 1945, free trade would probably have come first to his mind. There were elements of classical liberalism elsewhere. The 1945 Liberals laid some emphasis on 'remov[ing] taxes on the prime necessities of life'. They accepted a responsibility 'to safeguard and enlarge civil liberties'. They pressed for the establishment of a more democratic electoral system.

Whether 1945 Liberal policies were wholly consistent with classical liberalism or not, the 1945 General Election was a disaster for the Liberals. Labour won a convincing overall majority. Just twelve Liberal MPs scrambled home, not one of them in an urban area. For a time the Liberals expected a by-election in Sinclair's remote constituency, in which case he would have had a good chance of returning to parliament. In fact the by-election never came. The Liberal MPs chose Clement Davies of Montgomeryshire as their Chairman, but a considerable time elapsed before it was clear that Sinclair would not get his by-election opportunity, and Davies became generally acknowledged as leader of the Party.

1945–50

After the 1945 General Election, many outsiders expected the Liberal Party to disintegrate. An official Party statement, issued almost immediately after the results were published, took a very different view. Their task would be 'to rebuild the movement, strengthen their organisation and prepare to retrieve their defeat at the earliest opportunity'.[7] The fact that disintegration did not occur is due to two main factors: the continuing loyalty of most of the Party 'notables' and long-term activists, and the influx of many new people, mostly quite young, who had been unknown before the war, and brought vigour, imagination and organisational skill to the Party. In her Presidential address to the Liberal Party Organisation in March 1946, Asquith's daughter, Lady Violet Bonham Carter, declared that the Liberal defeat was not due to the country's rejection of liberalism but failure through lack of funds and machinery to put forward an effective alternative to the government.

Among the new people, three names stand out. Frank Byers was a young MP, who became Chief Whip in 1946. Philip Fothergill and Edward Martell were not, and would never become, MPs. All three were convinced, like Lady Violet, that the failure of the Liberal Party in recent years was not due to the inadequacy of Liberal policies, classical or otherwise, but to failures of organisation and the absence of a sound financial basis. These failures were not irremediable in the future. This view was generally accepted by the Party, and in the later 1940s great attention was given to remedying them. This necessarily involved strengthening or re-establishing Liberal constituency organisations throughout the country and giving them a sense of purpose. In particular they were encouraged to recruit new members and estab-lish sound finances, with the immediate aim of advancing a Liberal candidate at the next election, and supporting that candidate by an organisation not inferior to that of the other parties. There was a mood of extreme, not to say wild, optimism. In August 1946 the Party Executive adopted a plan for development at all levels, which was stated to be designed to secure a Liberal majority government at the next general election.[8]

Soon any remote chance of such a result disappeared. After the West Islington contest of September 1947 there was not a single parliamentary by-election at which the Liberal candidate polled the 12.5% of votes which was then necessary to save his electoral deposit. At Camlachie, Glasgow, in January 1948 the Liberal ran sixth of six candidates. After a further disaster in the more hopeful territory of North Croydon a couple of months later, no Liberal candidate stood at all in succeeding by-elections.

Why was the Liberal Party performing so badly? The simple answer is that its organisation was still incomparably weaker than that of the other parties, most of its leading figures were unknown to the general public, and it did not have much access to the 'media' – which, in the 1940s, meant the newspapers and radio. But there was more to it than that. Public interest was focused partly on international affairs, where there was little difference between the three parties, and partly on domestic economic questions where there was – or seemed to be – a great deal. The Labour Government pursued simultaneously policies which appealed strongly to many Liberals, and policies which most Liberals found repellent. The idea of greater social equality, and the associated ideas of a welfare state, had a strong appeal, and was related to one idea of what classical liberalism meant in a contem-porary context. At the same time, Labour was pursuing economic policies which were very different from classical liberalism by any interpretation of the term. Nationalisation of monopolies, and particularly of 'natural monopolies', did not upset Liberals; but they were upset at the idea of nationalising enterprises like steel and road haulage where strong competition existed, and there seemed little reason for the change outside what was popularly called 'doctrinaire socialism'. There was also a growing feeling that wartime controls in rationing and other matters were being continued not so much because they were still required in the early post-war period but because they were considered good in themselves by people who believed passionately in state economic planning, which could hardly be reconciled with any kind of classical liberalism. As time went on, it began to look as if the positive and attractive features of Labour's economic policy were being developed less and less, the negative aspects more and more.

On the other hand, Liberal antipathy to Conservatism had been very strong in 1945. The Conservatives were blamed for pre-war international policies which were considered, rightly or wrongly, to be responsible for the genesis of the war, and for the fact that Britain came close to losing that war. They were blamed for the economic misery and social inequality of the pre-war period and for the trading policies of protection which ran so violently against classical liberalism. But had all that changed? The Conservative Party was very much in the hands of Winston Churchill. In his most liberal days, Churchill had always had a streak of Toryism; but in his Conservative days he also had a streak of liberalism. When he declared his wish to 'set the people free'; when he and his party railed against 'controls' which seemed of little benefit to most Britons, this struck a chord among believers in classical liberalism. No doubt some of this 'new Conservatism' of the Churchill era was playing cynically for Liberal votes. But there was another aspect as well. Was Churchill also trying to change the Conservative Party, to make it much more consistent with classical liberalism and to give it a strong social conscience?

And so, by the end of the decade, people who had considered themselves Liberals in 1945 – whether senior members of the Party or rank-and-file voters – were being torn in different directions. Some saw no prospect of preserving classical liberalism except through the Liberal Party. Some felt that the Labour Government's apparent belief in greater social equality and in 'welfare' compensated for defects in its other economic policies. Some felt that the Conservative Party had been 'liberalised'. Liberal activists were constantly having the depressing experience of encountering voters whom they nicknamed 'Liberals but', who told them, 'I am a Liberal but I am voting Conservative to get the Socialists out', or 'I am a Liberal but I am voting Labour to keep the Tories out'.

Meanwhile, the Party's spokesmen were compelled to talk and act as if they might form a government in the foreseeable future, even though the ordinary voter could see that this was nonsense. When the next general election came in 1950, they fielded 475 candidates. While their 1945 manifesto had been a general statement of policies, that of 1950 looked like an appeal to the country to return a Liberal Government. Official Liberal attitudes, as expressed in their manifesto, had shifted, if anything, further in the direction of classical liberalism. Free trade was again clearly affirmed. There were calls for reduction in government spending and in economic controls. There should be no further nationalisation, but more legislation was required to control private monopolies. The electoral system should be more democratic, and there should be more equality of educational opportunity.

But the results of the 1950 General Election were even worse for the Liberals than those of its predecessor. Most of their candidates forfeited their deposits, and they were down to nine MPs. The Labour Government scraped home with a tiny majority, and it was a fair guess that another election would follow soon. Liberal finances, both nationally and in most constituencies, were at a desperately low ebb, and there could be no question of the Party fighting again on a field remotely comparable with that of 1950. Every outside pressure was certain to be put on people who had voted Liberal in 1950 to switch to another party.

The 1950s

After the 1950 General Election, the Labour Government seemed to have lost its way. No major new kinds of legislation appeared to be contemplated and leading Labour politicians were very visibly at loggerheads with each other. Meanwhile the Conservatives, still with Churchill as their leader, were making considerable headway. A year and a half later, another general election was held. The Liberals were down from 475 candidates to 109, mainly for reasons of finance. The most they could ask for in their manifesto was 'a strong Liberal Party in the next House of Commons'. Broadly, the actual policies they proposed were similar to those of 1950.

Another disaster supervened. Only six MPs were elected instead of nine. Five of those MPs had had no Conservative opposition, and a glance at the voting figures makes it clear that some of the five would have had little chance of election if the Conservatives had chosen to stand. It really did look as if the Liberal Party was on its last legs. In the next few years a number of former Liberal MPs, including Lady Megan Lloyd-George, Dingle Foot, Wilfrid Roberts, Edgar Granville and Sir Geoffrey Mander seceded to the Labour Party.

Other leading Liberals appeared to be moving in the Conservative direction. Lady Violet Bonham Carter had acquired great prestige as President of the Liberal Party Organisation during the wartime period, and we have seen her initial eagerness for the Party to reconstitute itself thereafter. Perhaps significantly, she was not a candidate in 1950, but in 1951 she stood in the closely-fought Yorkshire constituency of Colne Valley. She had no Conservative opponent, and positive support from Churchill. Many suspected at the time, and Lady Violet later confirmed, that if she had been offered a suitable post by Churchill in an otherwise Conservative administration, she would have accepted.[9] In the event she was not elected and so the question did not arise; but if matters had turned out otherwise, it is difficult to avoid the conclusion that the Liberal Party would have been shattered, perhaps irretrievably so. Clement Davies was actually offered a post in Churchill's Cabinet, but – on the advice of colleagues – he properly refused, even though he must have known that this would be his last opportunity to hold public office. In two northern towns, each composed of two constituencies, arrangements were made – tacit in one case, explicit in the other – that the Liberal would have a straight run against Labour in one constituency, and Conservative in the other.

Remarkably, the Liberal organisation in the country did not disintegrate after 1951. One important factor was the continued presence of a number of members who were classical liberals, and who were disposed to argue that, whatever the weaknesses of the Liberal Party, there was no hope of pursuing Liberal principles through any other party. Some of those people were middle-aged or elderly, mainly inveterate free traders. Others were much younger and had only entered active politics since the war.

These young activists, and some of the veterans too, were disposed to link free trade with Land Value Taxation (LVT) as integral parts of the same ideology. LVT had its roots in the ideas of acknowledged classical liberals like David Ricardo and Richard Cobden, with a strong addition from the teachings of the American land reformer Henry George. Supporters argued that the overriding reason why nineteenth-century free trade had not destroyed primary poverty was that it had not been associated with reform which would 'free the land'. They were becoming increasingly the mainstay of the Liberal Party at the local level, particularly in the London area. Unless one believed that liberalism had something unique to offer, there seemed little reason to devote time and energy to the Liberal Party.

Several important changes took place in the middle and later 1950s. In the 1955 General Election the Liberals, still with six seats, broke even, instead of exhibiting a further decline. There was widespread emphasis on at least one aspect of classical liberalism, for free trade was mentioned in 66% of Liberal election addresses.[10] In 1956, Clement Davies resigned the leadership and was succeeded by Jo Grimond. A few weeks later, Sir Rhys Hopkin Morris, who of all Liberals MPs could best be called a classical liberal, died. At the by-election which followed in Carmarthen early in 1957, Lady Megan Lloyd-George, now firmly ensconced in the Labour Party, captured the seat, and the Liberals were reduced to five MPs – the lowest figure ever. In the following year, however, another by-election, this time at Torrington in Devon, resulted in a Liberal gain by Mark Bonham Carter, and restored the Liberal numbers.

It looked as if the drift of people who would have considered themselves classical liberals towards Conservatism had stopped, and the fact that Lady Violet Bonham Carter's son Mark captured what was for practical purposes a Conservative seat, with the eager support of his mother, was significant. The 'Suez expedition' pursued by Eden's Government in late 1956 had shocked many Liberals who had been coming to think that the Conservative Party was 'liberalised', and even resulted in a few Conservatives transferring to the Liberals. At the same time, the intense fear of a future Labour Government pursuing a policy of full-blooded socialism, which had been very real in the early 1950s, was beginning to abate. The current leader of the Labour Party was Hugh Gaitskell. He was not a classical liberal, but he also was not a doctrinaire socialist.

But what was happening to classical liberalism within the Liberal Party while all this was going on? Jo Grimond stands out among Liberal leaders of the twentieth century, with the exception of Herbert Samuel and perhaps Charles Kennedy, as a man deeply interested not just in the nitty-gritty of politics, but in underlying principles. This was important, for he arrived at a moment when the Liberal Party was as clay in the potter's hands, and the Party's ideas would be greatly influenced by his leadership. As one of Grimond's biographers has pointed out,

> He always believed in the importance of both policy and political philosophy ... His thoughtful and original contributions to the political debate from the 1950s onwards proved increasingly attractive to an impressive collection of academics and intellectuals who would, even five years before, hardly have considered wasting their efforts on the Liberal Party.[11]

Grimond disagreed fundamentally with the socialist belief that 'the State knows what is right and will pursue it and the individual will not'.[12] Conservatism he saw as no philosophy at all, but merely acceptance of whatever state of affairs a Conservative Government might happen to inherit at a particular moment. 'Freedom is probably the concept most closely associated with political Liberalism,' Grimond wrote in 1963, in a declaration which sounds like pure classical liberalism.[13] But Grimond was well aware that there were many people in other parties, and in none, who shared these views, and he looked to a coming together of such people.

The first general election after Grimond's arrival did not suggest that there was a quick public response to the new leadership. In 1959, the Liberals again stuck with six MPs. The capture of Torrington by Grimond's brother-in-law Mark Bonham Carter was cancelled out, though this loss was compensated by Jeremy Thorpe's capture of the adjacent constituency of North Devon.

Europe

After the 1959 General Election, a great change took place which some people regard as a break with classical liberalism. The European Economic Community (EEC), precursor of the European Union, was formed at the beginning of 1958. It was, at that stage, little more than a 'Common Market', by which name it was generally known. The member-states, France, West Germany, Italy and the three Benelux countries, occupied a block of territory corresponding closely with the empire of Charlemagne. They were pledged to remove trade barriers between themselves, and also to adopt similar trade policies towards outsiders. While EEC negotiations were proceeding, preliminary discussions were taking place to form another organisation, the European Free Trade Area (EFTA), composed of eight other European countries, of which Britain was the leading member. Like the EEC, EFTA aimed at removing trade barriers between member-states, but did not commit those countries to common policies towards non-members.

When the EEC first came into existence, no British political party showed much enthusiasm for Britain to join. Soon the official *Liberal News* carried a statement, with Grimond's authority, stating in the clearest terms that the UK ought to join the developing EFTA, but not the EEC, arguing that 'the more countries are committed to lowering tariffs while still free to fix the level of their tariffs against countries outside the Common Market, the more likely it is that tariffs all round will be low, so that trade will be increased'.[14]

Just what happened next behind the Liberal scenes is far from clear. The author suspects that the death of Philip Fothergill, an inveterate classical liberal and an important back-room boy of the Party, in January 1959 may have had something to do with it. On 14th July 1960, a cross-party group of MPs, including Grimond, Clement Davies, Jeremy Thorpe and Arthur Holt, issued a statement in favour of Britain beginning negotiations to join the EEC. Two months later, a resolution was carried at the Liberal Party Assembly, urging the government 'to start consultations with other members of the Commonwealth and of the European Free Trade Area with a view to the entry of the United Kingdom and other countries into the Common Market'. There was no implication that Britain should join if the terms were to prove too onerous – or too illiberal.

All three parties, and not least the Liberals, contained a wide range of opinions, from people convinced that Britain should join the EEC on almost any terms to people who opposed the whole idea. In 1961, the Conservative Government of Harold Macmillan, along with other EFTA countries, submitted an application for membership of the EEC. These negotiations continued until January 1963, when the British application was rejected at the instance of President de Gaulle of France.

There were various cross-currents among the Liberals, so that both classical and less-than-classical liberals found themselves split. Theoretically, the EEC was an economic unit, not a political one; but in practice the debate had two main aspects, political and economic. Politically, many pro-Marketeers saw the EEC as the first step towards a united Europe – or at least the unification of most countries west of the Soviet Union and its satellites. But if that happened, anti-Marketeers wondered, would it prove the first step towards a united world, or would it merely create another gigantic power-bloc? And the structure of the EEC was in no sense democratic, for most real power was vested in an unelected Commission. Was it desirable to sacrifice British sovereignty in favour of membership of such a body? In the economic field, there was a similar debate. Was the EEC a step towards the liberalisation of world trade, or the very opposite? Would Britain serve the interest of liberalisation better by joining the EEC and seeking to influence it from within, or by liberalising her own trading policies through international agreements or unilateral action? There were special implications for the Commonwealth, which in those days was a much more important institution than it is today. Various arrangements existed between the UK and Commonwealth countries by which both sides agreed to cut down trade barriers. Membership of the EEC appeared to mean that new barriers would be imposed which would hamper that trade. Would those countries be badly let down if Britain joined the EEC?

The Liberal Assembly of 1962 took place while the British application for membership of the EEC was under active consideration. A resolution was carried by a substantial majority in favour of British membership, without the qualifications made two years earlier. This was too much for some well-known Liberals. Oliver Smedley, a recent Vice-President, resigned his parliamentary candidature. Donald Bennett, a former MP, withdrew from the Party altogether. A considerable number of less prominent people dropped out. Others remained, determined to continue the fight. Perhaps they reflected that the issue of British membership would not be decided by what Liberals thought of the matter, and once it was resolved one way or the other, there would be many other matters on which a Liberal view should be expressed. To the best of the author's knowledge, no active Liberal at all took it as the occasion for joining either the Conservatives or Labour. 'Where else can we go?' asked Smedley rhetorically.[15]

In the course of the 1960s, the Liberal Party registered considerable progress. It was able to field over 300 candidates in the 1964 and 1966 General Elections, increasing its representation first to nine and then to twelve. Some candidates in the Liberal Party, as in both other parties, disagreed openly with their leaders' views on the EEC question, but whether either the official party lines or these heresies had much influence on voting behaviour is doubtful. Voters appear to have decided that the question was dormant, and perhaps dead.

Towards the end of 1966, Grimond decided to retire from the Liberal leadership: a personal decision, not in response to any pressure. The philosophical Jo Grimond was replaced early in the following year by the much more empirical and flamboyant Jeremy Thorpe. There was, however, no significant change in policy on the EEC or anything else.

In April 1969 de Gaulle retired from the French presidency and later in the same year Harold Wilson's Labour Government filed a new application for British membership. A general election in 1970 resulted in the return of a Conservative Government headed by Edward Heath, a particularly eager pro-Marketeer. It also resulted in a slump in the Liberal representation, which again reverted to six. Official Liberal support for entry to the EEC did not flag; at the Party Conference of September 1971 there was a call for considerable extension of EEC powers in both economic and non-economic fields. But there was still no unanimity in the Liberal Party, any more than there was unanimity in either of the other parties. A writer as late as 1981 noted the paradox that 'opinion polls consistently show the majority of Liberal voters wanted Britain to quit the Common Market even though the Liberal Party has been the most consistently pro-Europe party'.[16] In the crucial vote on the principle of EEC entry all parties broke ranks, one of the Liberals going into the lobbies against it. More remarkably still, Jo Grimond, who had long been an enthusiastic advocate of British entry, began to express doubts, although in the end he voted in favour'.[17] The Heath Government pursued the British EEC application with alacrity, and at the beginning of 1973 Britain joined the Community, along with two of the EFTA countries, Ireland and Denmark, both of which had economies very closely linked to Britain.

Imprudently, Heath called another general election early in 1974, in the middle of great industrial unrest. No party secured an overall majority. The Liberals won

fourteen seats, their best performance since the war, and miscellaneous Nationalists and Ulster Unionists scored 23. Labour eventually formed a government, and
was able to win a tiny overall majority at a second election later in the same year.

Labour had promised to renegotiate British membership of the EEC, and submit
the result to a referendum. It would be difficult to discern any significant difference
between the new terms and the old. A large majority of the media urged acceptance,
and the referendum resulted in a pro-Market majority. Control of the commanding
heights of Britain's international trade had now passed to the EEC. This limited the
potential scope of classical liberalism but it did not extinguish the idea.

After Grimond

Jeremy Thorpe's book suggests that his own adherence to the Liberal Party had
been influenced partly by perceived illiberalities in other parties and partly by a
combination of the ideas of the Liberal 'Yellow Book', *Britain's Industrial Future* of
1928 and the policies of Roosevelt's 'New Deal' in the United States,[18] rather than
by direct attraction to classical liberalism. A remarkable development during the
Thorpe period was what became known as 'Community Politics'. In practice, this
meant building up the local machine of the Party through focusing attention on
essentially local issues. Where a bus stop should be positioned, or when dustbins
should be emptied, or even where the catchment areas of schools should be
defined, was hardly a matter either of classical liberalism or its antithesis, but there
can be little doubt that this shift in tactics was of considerable importance in securing a lot of Liberal seats on local councils and helping constituency associations to
build up strength. It is likely that Community Politics was among the most important factors in enabling the Liberal Party to break permanently its old habit of
returning just six MPs.

Thorpe remained Liberal leader until 1976, when he withdrew in extraordinary
circumstances which had nothing to do with political ideology. His eventual
successor David Steel had been a strong supporter of British entry to the EEC long
before he became Party leader. In some respects, Steel's position had a strong basis
in classical liberalism. His biographer reflected that

> Basically, Steel is a curious and fairly rare political animal, a kind of throw-
> back to the sort of nineteenth century radicalism epitomised by Gladstone.
> This elevates the care and dignity of the individual into a high political
> objective to be protected from the power and intrusions of the state.[19]

His interest in matters directly affecting the individual and his personal liberty was
reflected in concern for closely monitoring police powers, and for holding back
vexatious restrictions on immigration. Steel's first major political action, as a fairly
new backbencher, had been to promote legislation which made abortion easier. He
had been president of the anti-apartheid movement which fought against racism in
South Africa. He had chaired the private charity Shelter which exists to promote
the housing of necessitous people.

How far Steel was behaving as a classical liberal in the next phase of his career is more dubious. The Labour Government which Harold Wilson formed in 1974 and James Callaghan inherited a couple of years later had never had much of a majority, and adverse by-elections eventually destroyed that majority altogether. It ran into various troubles which are not really attributable to its parliamentary weakness, notably rising unemployment and high inflation. In March 1977, the Conservative opposition, by this time headed by Margaret Thatcher and thirsting for blood, tabled a motion of no confidence in the government. There followed complex negotiations, the upshot of which was the so-called 'Lib-Lab Pact', engineered largely by Steel and Callaghan. The government would resile from over-contentious measures and engage in conversations with the Liberals, while the Liberals in their turn would give tentative support. Both sides were free to withdraw from the arrangements. The 'Pact' was viewed with considerable suspicion by both sides. It endured for about eighteen months and finally collapsed amid feelings of mutual relief. How far was the 'Pact' consistent with classical liberalism? At least the Labour Government was restrained from action which did serious violence to Liberal opinion, though it is difficult to see much positive achievement in a Liberal direction.

Labour remained in office for a few months more, but was eventually defeated on another 'No Confidence' motion in the spring of 1979. A general election followed swiftly and the Conservatives secured a substantial overall majority. The Liberals lost a little ground, and were down to eleven MPs; but they fared considerably better than many had feared.

Margaret Thatcher, who became Prime Minister, was a 'conviction politician'. In one respect there was a strong element of classical liberalism in her policies, for she was visibly anxious to remove economic restrictions for which there was not an overwhelming case. But Thatcher, like most politicians, had more than one item on her agenda, and in other respects the government was far from being 'liberal'. It made little effort to contain the rising unemployment trend which it had inherited from its predecessor: indeed, the figures rapidly became much worse. Some would even say that the government deliberately encouraged the process; and yet for a long time inflation remained rampant.

Evidence from by-elections and public opinion polls left little doubt that the Conservatives were rapidly losing ground in the first part of the Thatcher period, and the Liberals were proving the beneficiaries, for the Labour Party was also in deep trouble. At its 1980 Conference, Labour declared for unilateral nuclear disarmament and withdrawal from the EEC. Shortly afterwards, Michael Foot, generally seen as a figure of the 'left' (whatever that means!), was elected party leader in succession to Callaghan. Many voters would have found some of this attractive; but it was obvious to all that a profound struggle was taking place within Labour ranks, and voters are not usually disposed to support a disunited party.

Alliance and fusion

The most spectacular phase in Steel's career was his part in engineering first the alliance, and then the fusion, of the Liberal Party with the Social Democratic Party (SDP). With encouragement from David Steel, prominent dissatisfied members of the Labour Party formed first the Council for Social Democracy and then the new SDP. When the SDP was established in March 1981 it rapidly attracted a substantial number of Labour MPs, and even one Conservative, to its ranks. The leading figure in the SDP was Roy Jenkins, who had held the offices of Home Secretary and Chancellor of the Exchequer in Labour governments. There was a considerable streak of classical liberalism in Jenkins, particularly in non-economic fields, though noticeably less in some of his colleagues. He had backed Steel's abortion legislation. He used his influence for the abolition of hanging, the legalisation of homosexuality, the relaxation of Sunday Observance laws and of control of the theatre. By 1972, Jenkins had already begun, in his biographer's judgement, 'to move in the direction of accepting the need for a new progressive party that would transcend class'.[20]

Both the Liberals and the SDP began to deliver remarkably encouraging by-election results, and soon they started to move tentatively in the direction of a definite electoral alliance. Then, suddenly, everything changed with the Falklands War of 1982. Margaret Thatcher was able to cast herself as a charismatic national leader, and there was a big swing towards both her and her party. Thereafter Liberal–SDP negotiations proceeded apace and there was eventually agreement to the effect that each party would fight about half of the British constituencies, without opposition from the other, whenever a new general election should arise. When the election was eventually held in 1983, the resulting 'Alliance' arrangements were followed nearly everywhere, but the results were among the most anomalous ever recorded. The Alliance had scored 25.4% of the votes, yet it had only won 23 seats: 17 Liberals and six SDP. Labour, with 27.6%, won 209 seats, the Conservatives with 42.4% won 397. In many people's eyes, at least one traditional tenet of classical liberalism was vindicated by the result: that the will of the people ought to be expressed more adequately in the composition of the House of Commons.

The strange and difficult process by which the Liberal and Social Democratic Parties moved towards complete unification really lies outside the present story. Suffice to say that when the fusion eventually occurred in 1988, both of the original protagonists were largely out of the picture. Jenkins resigned from SDP leadership in 1983, being succeeded by the much less tractable and much less liberal David Owen. There was a sort of dual leadership by Steel and Owen in 1987, but this was by no means a success. Steel, who had been handling matters with remarkable skill in their early stages, made some serious errors of judgement soon afterwards, and by the time the merger was agreed he was effectively out of the running for leadership of the united party. Even the name of the party was in considerable doubt, but eventually the title 'Liberal Democrats', perhaps the least-worst in the circumstances, was accepted. As often happens when two bodies unite, there were significant numbers on both sides who resented the union. A small residual body which still calls itself the Liberal Party exists to this day. The 'continuing' Social Democrats collapsed quickly, thanks largely to the personality of Owen. The SDP, like the Peelite Tories of the 1840s, the Liberal Unionists of the 1880s and the Liberal Nationals of the 1930s, was a breakaway party comparable with the mule, said to be 'without pride in ancestry or hope of posterity' – and was only saved from a miserable fate by first alliance and later complete union with an established political party.

The Ashdown period

The first leader of the new Party was Paddy Ashdown. His background was remarkable, for an ex-commando to lead a party which always had a streak of pacifism. Yet with Ashdown as with Steel, his general sympathy with measures advancing personal liberty was never in doubt. The first general election manifesto of the new Party, in 1992, had a good deal of the spirit of classical liberalism:

> We aim to create a society in which all men and women can realise their full potential and shape their own successes ... We must change our political system to give the citizen more power and the government less; our economic system to confer power on consumers and to provide employees with a share in the wealth they create; our public services to guarantee choice and dignity to each of us; and our education system to equip us better for the modern world ... The free market is the best guarantee of responsiveness to choice and change ... we see the role of government as crucial in making the market work properly ... promoting competition, breaking up monopolies and spreading information.

This is one of the clearest official enunciations of classical liberalism since 1945; we can almost hear John Stuart Mill, the great nineteenth-century apostle of classical liberalism, cheering at most of these words, which were backed with a considerable battery of proposals.

The same spirit was continued in the 1997 General Election manifesto:

> Above all, Liberal Democracy is about liberty. That does not just mean freedom from oppressive government. It means providing all citizens with the opportunity to hold worthwhile lives for themselves and their families ...

By that date, there was even some implied criticism of the workings of the European Union (as the EEC had now become), and particularly the notorious Common Agricultural Policy. This time the electors took the Liberal Democrats much more seriously than they had taken any third party since 1929, increasing their representation from the 20 MPs returned in 1992 to 46 in 1997, all of them returned in triangular or polygonal contests. The credit for this appears to be due at least as much to the organisational skills of Chris Rennard, now Lord Rennard, as to any politician.

The run-up to the 1997 General Election involved some radical re-thinking about the roles of political parties. After the displacement of Thatcher in 1990, her last Chancellor of the Exchequer John Major succeeded to the premiership. To the considerable surprise of many observers, the new Conservative Prime Minister survived the General Election of 1992, still with an overall majority, though one much-reduced. As the 1990s advanced, both Liberal Democrats and Labour began to think very seriously about ways in which the long Conservative rule might be broken.

In 1994, Tony Blair became the unexpected leader of the Labour Party. He soon proceeded to dismantle most of the socialist elements of his party's policy which seemed to make it unelectable, including the notorious 'Clause IV' of Labour's Constitution, which had appeared to commit it to eventual all-out nationalisation. For many purposes the party's name was preceded by the adjective 'New', which implied that a fundamental change had taken place in its whole character.

When the 1997 General Election began to loom on the horizon, it seemed to many people that the Conservatives were likely to suffer defeat, but it was by no means clear that any other party would win an overall majority. Talks took place between Ashdown and Blair, and while neither man could commit his party, there began to appear a serious possibility that an accommodation might emerge by which Ashdown and some of his colleagues would acquire positions in a predominantly Labour government. Liberal Democrats and their predecessors had long aspired to 'equidistance' from the two opposing parties, but Ashdown soon made it clear that he preferred 'New Labour' to the Conservatives. Very close Lib-Lab relations might well have suited Blair and Ashdown alike. Blair would have acquired a perfect excuse for neglecting the wishes of his more socialist colleagues; Ashdown would have got his feet under the Cabinet table and might have been able to exert considerable influence on the government. No doubt many members of both parties would have viewed the upshot with horror, and what long-term effect it would have had is highly conjectural. In the event it did not happen. New Labour won a very convincing overall majority, and, whatever Blair might have wished, it soon became evident that the projected arrangements were not on.[21]

Blair and Ashdown were nevertheless able to establish a substantial measure of co-operation, and some of this involved significant moves in the direction of certain aspects of classical liberalism. Ashdown and some of his colleagues were invited to join a Cabinet Committee on constitutional affairs.[22] That did not give them executive authority, but it did seem to deliver some results. A commission was set up under Roy Jenkins (by then Lord Jenkins) on parliamentary representation. The eventual proposals, published in October 1998, were very different from the traditional Liberal policy of proportional representation, but they did seem to have the merit of promising fairer representation of parties at parliamentary elections. In the end the proposals ran into the sands. The Labour Party could hardly be expected to greet with enthusiasm a proposal which, however just, would greatly have reduced their current parliamentary representation.

The new co-operation may have played a large part in moves which led to the establishment of a Scottish Parliament and a Welsh Assembly in May 1999 – in both cases with a much closer representation of voters' wishes than prevailed at Westminster. It may also have had much to do with the nature of the European Assembly elections of the following month, where again a system was operated which ensured more accurate representation of opinion. In these respects, Lib-Lab co-operation had delivered some positive results in the direction of constitutional aspects of classical liberalism; but many people suspect that, if it had continued much longer, these beneficial results would have been vitiated by later developments not yet on the horizon.

Since 1999

Early in 1999, Paddy Ashdown announced his intention to stand down from leadership of the Liberal Democrats. The contest for succession was a prolonged one, and the result was announced in August, with Charles Kennedy emerging as victor. Kennedy had been elected SDP MP for a Highland constituency in 1983 at age 23, and later proved to be one of the SDP people most eager for fusion with the Liberals. As leader he showed perceptibly less enthusiasm for close relations with Labour than his predecessor had done, and the Liberal Democrats soon returned to 'equidistance'. As has been noted, Kennedy was sharply critical of both parties in his book of 2001. He went on to criticise with equal vigour the 'ideological extremists who gained sway under Thatcher' and the fury with which Labour had resisted the Alliance's disposition to raise the trade union political levy as a subject of debate. He expressed similar objection to Labour Home Secretary Jack Straw's 2000 proposal to restrict jury trial.[23]

In 2003, Blair's Government entered war against Iraq, despite the strong advice of many members of all parties, and in defiance of the greatest protest march ever seen in the United Kingdom. Liberal Democrats hated the regime of Saddam Hussein as much as anybody, but they had deep doubts about the merits of military intervention, and considered that in any event no such action should be taken without support of the United Nations. In the crucial division, all 52 Liberal Democrat MPs present voted against the war, along with 139 Labour, 15 Conservatives and 11 from other parties. Again there were strong echoes of classical liberalism.

In 2006, Kennedy resigned from the Liberal Democrat leadership for personal reasons. There is little reason for thinking that much has changed in the general orientation of the Party since then.

Reflections

While the broad 'classical' principle of a 'presumption of liberty' has continued to guide Liberal thinking for a very long time, the interpretation of what this means in terms of practical politics has changed considerably.

Economic liberty has been traditionally linked to free trade. Unfortunately, the term 'free trade' is widely used today in a highly pejorative way to mean, in effect, the power of strong commercial interests, actively backed by governments, to ride roughshod over the rest of mankind. That is completely different from the way in which the words were used in the past by supporters and opponents of free trade alike. Free trade always meant the right of people to buy and sell as they wished, without interference by governments.

That right was never understood in an absolute sense. Such qualifications as restrictions on the sale of dangerous or otherwise harmful goods; special provisions for contracts involving minors or other persons under disabilities; restrictions on fraud and deceit, have always been needed. But in comparatively recent times new factors have appeared which were largely unforeseen in 1945.

Some of these factors have turned on increased knowledge. In particular, much more is known about causes and prevention of ill health. To give but one example, before the 1950s there was little reason to consider that smoking was seriously deleterious to most people. Today it is universally known that smoking is the source of a great deal of ill health. This not only often causes suffering and prema-ture death to the smoker, but it also imposes burdens on others – including 'passive smokers', and the general public who are required to pay for health serv-ices. It was therefore generally accepted that new restrictions should be imposed on the sale and use of tobacco. With tobacco, and with other harmful 'recre-ational' substances, far more is also known about the effects of addiction, and it is realised that people are much less free agents in use of these substances than was formerly believed. The power of advertising, positive and negative, in influ-encing choice is also far better understood. So, paradoxically, restrictions on sales, advertising and use of objectionable substances may well increase rather than decrease the real freedom of the individual. If that is so, then such restrictions should be acceptable to classical liberals.

There are some economic fields in which the classical liberal should be more alert than he usually is today. There is much to be said for the view that the poor are much too poor, and the rich are much too rich, and that measures should be taken to redress that state of affairs. But at present everybody, from the richest to the poorest, is at the same moment receiving benefits which ultimately derive from taxation, and contributing in one way or another to those benefits. Everybody is living by taking in everybody else's washing. Classical liberals are not the only people to whom that state of affairs makes little sense.

Almost all existing forms of taxation are necessarily restrictions on freedom, but some are conspicuously more so than others. Indirect taxes like VAT or customs duties not only collect revenue but they also dictate consumption. If one commod-ity is taxed and another is not, this tilts people towards buying the second. In that respect direct taxes are less objectionable, but they too impose heavy burdens on the economy, and anybody who has had anything to do with the workings of (say) income tax will appreciate how arbitrary many of the rules are, and how govern-ment intentions can frequently be circumvented by use of a skilled accountant. By contrast, the traditional Liberal policy of Land Value Taxation, with its good 'classical' pedigree, continues to appeal to many classical liberals.

The manner in which taxation is levied is but one of the features of the modern system which calls for attention from the classical liberal. The volume of taxation has grown far beyond the measure of inflation. In 1934, a Liberal complained that, over the previous twenty years, taxation had increased from about one-tenth to about one-third of the total earnings of the nation.[24] The proportion has increased considerably since then, though it is becoming increasingly difficult to decide just which of the monies mulcted from the citizen by public authorities are properly designated taxation, and just where the line should be drawn between local and national revenue and spending. At the same time private businesses of all kinds are compelled to spend a great deal of money in acting as unpaid tax-gatherers, incurring what are euphemistically known as 'compliance costs'. We have come a very long way indeed from the celebrated plea of Gladstone that money should be allowed to 'fructify in the pockets of the people'.[25]

Quite as alarming as the vastly increased amount of public spending is the way in which that spending is managed. To a classical liberal, public money is a trust, which the responsible statesman should spend with at least as much care as he would spend his own. That point is receiving scant attention today, and it applies to all kinds of public spending. The Gladstonian idea of a Public Accounts Committee, designed to keep a close watch on how state money is spent, needs to be developed further, and effort should be made to encourage the administrator to avoid unnecessary spending, even for 'good' causes.

Yet the classical liberal should also reflect that all is not gloom, for there are many areas in which economic freedom has increased in recent times. A century ago, a worker in a 'feudal' village, and often his counterpart in an industrial town, had very little freedom even in an economic sense. It was frequently impractical for him to move to a different employer, still less to strike out in business on his own, however capable he might be. His wife was usually constrained to buy most of the household goods from a very narrow range of sources. So competition both in employment and in consumption was largely illusory – far more than it is today. The car, and now the internet, have changed things dramatically in the direction of more freedom. We may ponder whether all this owes far more to the engineer than to politicians of any brand.

Classical liberals have faced dilemmas which are partly economic and partly social. Long after 1945, job advertisements frequently offered different wages for males and females for the same post, or even excluded one sex altogether. Lodging houses often had notices reading 'No Coloureds' in the window. Today, such practices are illegal. Is this an advance or a retreat for classical liberalism? On one hand, the classical liberal hates any kind of discrimination based on 'status' – such as a person's sex or the colour of their skin. On the other hand, the classical liberal is reluctant to interfere with the power of the employer or the lodging-house owner to select the people with whom he wishes to deal, however foolish or even vicious his reasons for so acting. Today, the large majority of people who consider themselves classical liberals would probably approve of the modern laws, but the issue is not entirely one-sided.

Environmental issues continue to present new problems for the classical liberal. The importance of positive action by organs of government, national or local, in connection with public health problems was recognised far back in the nineteenth century. Strict rules of practice designed to control the spread of cholera or typhoid were generally accepted almost as soon as the way in which those diseases spread became understood. Whatever classical liberals think of the later career of Joseph Chamberlain, most would applaud his work in the 1870s, when he persuaded Birmingham Council to undertake a programme of slum clearance.

In more recent times, environmental problems have greatly increased. Since 1945, many species of animals and plants have become extinct as a result of human activity, and important environments, of which tropical forests are the most famous example, have been seriously eroded. There is every reason for thinking that both processes are taking place at an increasing rate, and that all kinds of undesirable and irreparable consequences are likely to result.

The population of the world at the time of writing is roughly three times what it was in 1945. Changes have been enormous, partly as a result of new inventions but largely as a result of spreading the use of old ones. In 1945, even in 1980, few people worried about global warming; fewer still linked it with human activity and the increased production of 'greenhouse gases'. Today global warming is not in serious doubt, and the general though not universal corpus of scientific opinion considers that it is largely due to human activity. It is also understood that global warming is likely to have enormous consequences, most of them detrimental to the interests of the mass of mankind, to say nothing of the natural environment.

Not only are there far more people than there were in 1945, but they are generating far more 'greenhouse gas' per person. In most of the northern hemisphere the number of car-miles per person has increased greatly, while domestic central heating has changed from a luxury of the affluent to a general expectation. It may be predicted with confidence that the demand for such things will soon increase even more rapidly in countries which at present rank as poor. More control of the adverse side-effects of these changes will be necessary, and the classical liberal should reflect that the loss of human freedom which will result if no effective action is taken will be a great deal more than the loss of human freedom if it is.

The principles of classical liberalism are not confined to economics, or to fields in which economics plays a substantial part, but extend to all kinds of activity where freedom is possible. In some aspects of personal behaviour, freedom has diminished since 1945, while in others it has increased. The so-called 'war on terrorism' (what is any war but terrorism on the maximum scale?) has provided an excuse for further executive powers of arrest and detention, sometimes of people who are suspected of actions which have nothing to do with terrorism in any ordinary sense of the word. We have already noted the classical liberal response of Charles Kennedy to the perennial demand of law-enforcers for more powers to control the citizen, and diminution in his legal right to liberty.

Yet there are also directions in which freedom has increased, which should delight the classical liberal. The law, and public opinion too, are much less disposed to prohibit 'unconventional' sexual activity than in the past, and individuals like David Steel and Roy Jenkins can claim considerable credit for that state of affairs. The old law of blasphemy is now a dead letter, and in most respects people are no longer required to be as cautious as they were sixty years ago in challenging traditional religious opinions and practices. People who do not wish to treat Sunday in a different way from other days are now under much less compulsion to do so.

Even in the direction of free expression, however, it is not all an advance towards freedom. In 2005, one read[26] that sixty thousand copies of a very far from Liberal periodical, an organ of the British National Party, had been seized by customs and police, apparently because in its coverage of terrorist bombings in London it complained that 'Britain gets bombed but it's Islam that gets the sympathy'. The BNP view is unfair and slanted, and a Muslim (or a classical liberal) has every reason to resent it; but it is even more objectionable to prohibit the expression of illiberal opinions by executive action. One recalls the remark attributed to Voltaire: 'I disapprove of what you say, but I will defend to the death your right to say it.'[27]

And so the classical liberal, with his perennial belief in liberty, continually records victories and defeats in many directions. Some of the advances are based on changes in public attitudes, some are based on actions of the legislature, some are rooted in technology. So, too, do some of the retreats have roots in one place, others elsewhere. The one thing that is certain is that his watchfulness will continue to be required for the foreseeable future. In the oft-misquoted words of John Philpot Curran, later defender of the Irish prisoners after the 1798 rising, 'the condition upon which God hath given liberty to man is eternal vigilance ...'[28]

Traditionally, the classical liberal has seen his political philosophy as the route to human advancement, and particularly to the removal of poverty and many other causes of human misery. Until quite recently, the main competing philosophy which made similar claims was socialism in its various forms. Today it appears that socialism has been generally discredited, and it becomes particularly important that classical liberals should perceive the many opportunities which lie ahead.

Notes

1 *The Liberal Way* (National Liberal Federation, London, 1934), p. 7.
2 House of Commons, 11th November 1947.
3 J. Grimond, *The Liberal Challenge* (Hollis and Carter, London, 1963), p. 30.
4 C. Kennedy, *The Future of Politics* (HarperCollins, London, 2001), p. xvii.
5 *The Times*, 28th August 1934. See also M. Watson, 'Learning the lessons of history: Liberalism in the 1930s', *Journal of Liberal History*, 55 (Summer 2007), pp. 13–15.
6 Liberal election manifestos are printed in I. Dale (ed.), *Liberal Party General Election Manifestos 1900–1997* (Routledge, London, 2000). All subsequent references to election manifestos are taken from this volume.
7 *The Times*, July 1945.
8 *The Times*, 22nd April 1946.

9   Bonham Carter to Murray, 20th December 1951, cited in M. Pottle (ed.), *Daring to Hope: The Diaries and Letters of Violet Bonham Carter 1946–1969* (Weidenfeld and Nicolson, London, 2000), p. 105.

10 D. Butler, *The British General Election of 1955* (Macmillan, London, 1955), p. 34.

11 M. McManus, *Jo Grimond: Towards the Sound of Gunfire* (Birlinn, Edinburgh, 2001), p. 400.

12 *News Chronicle*, 2nd August 1952.

13 Grimond, *The Liberal Challenge*, pp. 27–8.

14 *Liberal News*, 1st February, 1957.

15 R. Douglas, *Liberals: A History of the Liberal and Liberal Democrat Parties* (Continuum, London, 2005), p. 322.

16 P. Bartram, *David Steel: His Life and Politics* (W.H. Allen, London, 1981), p. 187.

17 P. Barberis, *Liberal Lion: Jo Grimond: A Political Life* (Tauris, London, 2005), p. 163.

18 J. Thorpe, *In My Own Time: Reminiscences of a Liberal Leader* (Politico's, London, 1999), pp. 83–4.

19 Bartram, *David Steel*, p. 187.

20 J. Campbell, *Roy Jenkins: A Biography* (Weidenfeld and Nicolson, London, 1983), p. 154.

21 P. Ashdown, *Ashdown Diaries* vol. 1 (Allen Lane, London, 2000) and vol. 2 (Allen Lane, London, 2001), *passim*; J. Rentoul, *Tony Blair, Prime Minister* (Little, Brown, London, 2001), especially pp. 488–99.

22 C. Cook, *A Short History of the Liberal Party, 1900–2001* (Palgrave, Basingstoke, 2002, 6th edition), p. 241 et seq.

23 Kennedy, *The Future of Politics*, p. 89.

24 *The Liberal Way*, pp. 105–6.

25 H.C.G. Matthew, *Gladstone: 1809–1898* (Oxford University Press, Oxford, 1997), p. 117.

26 *Keesing's Record of World Events*, 2005, 46838.

27 S.G. Tallentyre, *The Friends of Voltaire* (Smith Elder, London, 1906), p. 199.

28 Speech on the right of election of Lord Mayor of Dublin, 10th July 1790.

3   *Mark Garnett*

Centre

In July 1975, as a weak Labour Government grappled with an inflation-ravaged economy, *The Times* newspaper presented the case for a new administration that bore a closer resemblance to majority opinion in Britain. It would be a coalition government, rooted in the 'middle ground' which the Labour left and the Conservative right had deserted. *The Times* expected that such a coalition would detach moderates from both of the main parties, and would win unanimous support from the Liberals.[1]

The Treasurer of the West Midland Liberals immediately sent a furious letter to *The Times*, protesting that 'many Liberal Party activists, including myself, would have nothing to do with electing a so-called moderate government. We joined the Liberal Party as the most radical of the three [main parties] and the most idealistic of the three.' However, in its editorial *The Times* had merely expressed the prevalent public view of the Liberals, who were widely regarded as incurable centrists. Every member of the Party was assumed to be a limpet-like resident of the middle ground, regardless of the varying tides washing over them.

Yet the West Midlands stalwart was right. His point was reinforced a few months later, when a Liberal began a hunger strike in order to publicise the case for proportional representation.[2] Few Liberals of the mid-1970s retained their membership because they wanted a vehicle for safe, moderate policies which split the difference between the contrasting 'radicalism' of Labour and the Conservatives. As Alan Watkins had remarked back in 1966, 'it is doubtful whether [Jo] Grimond – or even anyone else who happened to be leading the Liberal Party – could have carried the majority of the Party activists with him in a centre party'.[3] Ivor Crewe and Tony King have written that 'being a Liberal meant being an outsider, pursuing lost causes, staying on principle in the political wilderness'.[4]

Such comments suggest that whatever the general public might have thought, identifying an ideological 'centre' within the Liberal Party in these years is not the elementary exercise that casual observers might expect. There is a further, related difficulty. In the two main parties, leaders tended to attract close supporters who were ready to compromise – sometimes on key issues of principle – when this seemed to be dictated by electoral considerations. However, the development of such a group was inhibited by the nature and circumstances of the post-war Liberal Party.[5] It was not an organisation which could attract many fellow-travellers or careerists; and once they had joined, members would not be socialised into a more pragmatic outlook by the imminent prospect of power. In the late 1960s this point was underlined by the growing media prominence of Young Liberals, like the anti-apartheid campaigner Peter Hain, and a series of defeats for the leadership on radical resolutions at Liberal Assemblies. On the one hand, the energy of idealistic Liberal activists was essential to the Party at and between elections. On the other, their antics threatened to confirm the impression that the Liberals were a protest movement rather than a serious political party. The absence of a strong institutional 'centre' within the Liberal Party forced the leadership to seek a compromise with the militants, who were thus encouraged to campaign even harder on behalf of their radical agenda.[6]

Rather than equating it with implacable moderation, it would be tempting to seek a Liberal 'centre' in the mid-1970s in relation to a belief in a single, specific ideology, in a way which was not true of the Conservatives or Labour who were deeply divided at the time. However, the situation was more complicated, chiefly because liberalism itself was capable of more than one interpretation in the British context. As a result, although the membership was not large the Liberal Party still contrived to be something of a 'broad church'. The division between 'classical' and 'new' liberals, dating back to the last years of the nineteenth century, could still be detected in the Party's debates. The twentieth-century experience of party members suggested that a Liberal 'centre' should be located on the 'new' liberal side of the debate, entailing an acceptance that a degree of state interference was necessary, in order to provide the poor with tolerable life-chances and security against ill-health, unemployment and old age. One important reason for the Liberal Party's survival was the memory of governmental action to combat poverty and misfortune, under the reforming administrations of Campbell-Bannerman and Asquith. The consolidation and extension of welfare measures after the Second World War could be marked down as an even greater Liberal achievement, since the main architects of the post-war 'consensus', Beveridge and Keynes, had invigorated Labour and 'converted' the Conservatives while retaining their own Liberal allegiance.[7] By contrast, classical liberal believers in the unrestrained free market had been gravitating towards the Conservative Party since the end of the nineteenth century, when the philosopher Herbert Spencer had accused Liberal leaders of betraying their original creed.

Yet the split between 'classical' and 'new' liberals was not entirely resolved within the Party even as late as the mid-1970s. The main legacy was an enduring suspicion of the central state, and a corresponding preference for local solutions. This was difficult to square with the spirit of the Party's 1969 constitution, which argued that 'the powers of the state will be used to establish social justice, to wage war against poverty, to spread wealth and power, to ensure that the country's resources are wisely and fully developed for the benefit of the whole community, and to create the positive conditions which will make a full and free life possible for all regardless of colour, creed or race'.[8] This prospectus is a tangible illustration of the dissonance between the moderate Liberal Party image and the radical reality; to be fulfilled, it would have entailed a considerable *increase* in the power of the central state, compared to the existing apparatus of 1969. Yet even senior Liberals were not required to confront the apparent contradiction, since they were not treated by the press or the public as realistic contenders for office. Thus as late as 1983, when Alan Beith made a fresh attempt to play down the image of Liberal moderation, he argued that 'a continuum based, for example, on acceptance of centralised power would show both the Labour and Conservatives at one end, protecting existing interests and arrangements, and Liberals at the other, fighting for change'. Yet Beith was happy to reprint the 'statist' Liberal constitution in the same volume.[9]

Other Liberals, notably Jo Grimond, were becoming more sensitive to the supposed threat from an over-mighty state. After relinquishing the leadership in 1967 Grimond stayed within the Party, even though his economic views were more akin to those of Conservative classical liberals like Enoch Powell.[10] This development caused no great surprise among Liberals, whose leaders lacked the institutional resources to impose a rigid orthodoxy on their members even if they had wanted to lay down an 'official' doctrine. After all, one point on which all good liberals agreed was the need to allow free debate between well-intentioned individuals, even if they reached different conclusions. For grass-roots members, declarations of principle could only be subjects for further discussion, even if they were enshrined within a constitution.

The emergence of a Liberal centre, 1974–81

Internal dissension meant that by the time of the June 1970 General Election the survival of the Liberal Party was in doubt, after a decade which had begun with high hopes and a spectacular by-election win at Orpington (March 1962). At the 1970 election the Liberals won just 7.5 per cent of the popular vote, returning only 6 MPs. But after this dispiriting result the fortunes of the Party improved – mainly because its two main rivals were losing support thanks to social change and a succession of policy failures, but also because Grimond's successor Jeremy Thorpe used the national media to transcend the divisions within the ranks and furnished the Party with the emollient image which so irritated the radical activists. Despite the efforts of Hain *et al.*, voters of all persuasions were increasingly ready to back the Liberals as the safe option when they lost faith in their first preferences. Of the nine seats which changed hands between the General Elections of June 1970 and February 1974, five were won by Liberals, including such contrasting figures as Alan Beith (Berwick) and Cyril Smith (Rochdale).[11]

Given the nature of the Party, it is difficult to identify a specific individual who exemplified the Liberal 'centre' in the mid-1970s. Instead, one might construct a kind of 'ideal type', representing a middle way between the various views on offer. He or she would believe in economic state intervention for the reasons advanced by T.H. Green and L.T. Hobhouse and reaffirmed in the Party's constitution – i.e., that the state could interfere if and only if its activities resulted in an expansion of liberty for the citizen-body. Such a person would tolerate relatively high levels of taxation, provided that the proceeds generated real benefits instead of being frittered away on centralised bureaucracy or creating a 'dependency culture'; without really thinking how this could be achieved without increasing the power of the state, the moderate Liberal would accept the case for income redistribution through the tax system in order to enhance equality of opportunity. The mixed economy was also approved, so long as the state only controlled public utilities which were 'natural monopolies', open to abuse if they were owned by profit-seekers. Industrial harmony should be pursued through profit-sharing and worker participation. Most Liberals were in favour of more efficient production, but they were not complacent about the impact of industry on the environment. A centrist of the mid-1970s would endorse modest measures such as incentives to increase recycling and the reclamation of derelict land, and even this attitude would be far in advance of the other main parties at the time.

Our moderate Liberal would instinctively oppose any legislation which threatened to impair intellectual freedom. Therefore, for example, the state should not censor any published material unless it could be shown to cause real harm to others. While some Liberals might agonise over the application of this principle in sensitive spheres like sex or race relations, the moderate would tend to argue (for example) that mature adults should be allowed free access to pornography, so long as no-one was harmed in its production, and that anyone who attempted to stir up racial hatred through the printed word should be prosecuted. Even a 'centrist' Liberal, in short, would be more in tune with the permissive society than the average Tory or Labour member – and would be keen to extend freedom even further, on the assumption that adult citizens were far more rational than either of the main parties were prepared to allow. This position ensured that a centrist Liberal would support plans to modernise the creaking British constitution, although he or she would reject the radical Liberal aspiration of abolishing the monarchy. Something like the European Convention on Human Rights should be incorporated into British law as an essential safeguard for the liberty of individual citizens.

Although Liberals had been bitterly divided over Britain's imperial connections before the First World War, by 1975 they were wholly supportive of the idea of national self-determination – which meant that Peter Hain's stance against the unsavoury legacy of the empire placed him within the mainstream of Liberal opinion. In line with the drive towards modernisation, virtually every prominent Liberal favoured UK membership of the EEC at the time of the 1975 referendum on the subject. Whatever the preferred extent of state interference in the domestic economy, all Liberals held that international trade should be as free as possible, and in this context the removal of barriers between major European nations was an important step towards a harmonious and peaceful future. Furthermore, for the 'average' Liberal the idea of eventual federal union in Europe held none of the irrational terror which was so easily engendered in Labour or Conservative ranks. It was hardly surprising that the 1975 referendum campaign increased respect for the Liberals amongst pro-Europeans like Roy Jenkins.

The characteristic Liberal attitude towards Europe underlined the mistake of assuming that the Party always sought the middle ground of British public opinion; their genuine enthusiasm, then and later, was very different from the grudging acceptance, forthright rejection, or hopeless confusion of most Britons on this subject. Ironically, though, the referendum was an unusual instance of the Liberal Party throwing itself wholeheartedly into a campaign which was highly congenial to real 'centrists', like Jenkins and Heath. In turn, it was not surprising that this reinforced public misconceptions about the Liberals; *The Times* was not alone in basing its suppositions about the Party's likely response to a coalition government on its attitude during the referendum campaign.

Grass-roots activists might like to deny it, but the coalition issue was undoubtedly tempting senior Liberals to make the Party more like its popular caricature. After the inconclusive General Election of February 1974, Jeremy Thorpe had taken part in discussions about a possible coalition government. The invitation from Heath would almost certainly have been extended whatever the Liberal share of the vote; after such a close contest, the Liberal tally of 14 precious seats was reason enough. But the Liberals had secured almost 20% of the vote – their best performance since 1929. Under a more proportional system of representation – a reform which any Liberal 'centrist' would be bound to support – a Conservative–Liberal coalition would have been the logical outcome in February 1974. Instead, to the discredit of the existing first-part-the-post system, Labour ended up taking power with just 37% of the vote, while between them the Liberals and the Conservatives represented more than 57% of the electorate.

The Liberal advance was halted at the ensuing election of October 1974, and the Party was seriously damaged by Thorpe's enforced departure from the leadership in May 1976. But the talks between Heath and Thorpe marked the emergence of a new ethos within a significant element of the Party. No longer was it nonsensical to talk of at least a meaningful share in power. This meant that the Party was faced with a choice – continuing as a coalition of somewhat unruly individualists, or accepting an element of discipline which would make the Liberals look like worthy members of a governing coalition whenever the opportunity might arise.

The Chief Whip, David Steel, was the overwhelming choice as Thorpe's successor, after a ballot of the whole Party membership. It was the first time that a British party had used this method of selection, and the poll established a dubious precedent. Ostensibly, the procedure meant that the leader was more responsible to ordinary members, and could more easily be called to account for unpopular decisions. In practice – as Labour and the Conservatives were to find when they adopted the same method – Steel's victory meant that if he so chose he could claim a popular mandate for decisions which the rank-and-file would not necessarily have approved in advance. And Steel was not truly representative of his idiosyncratic membership, despite his personal contributions in the field of social reform during the 1960s. As Alistair Michie and Simon Hoggart put it at the time, by the mid-1970s he was 'more a politician of the possible, a fixer rather than a campaigner'.[12] His victory owed almost everything to his relative youth, good looks, and fluent platform delivery: political principle was not a major factor. Significantly, in his first Assembly speech as Liberal leader, he told his audience that 'we are in being as a political party to form a government so as to introduce the policies for which we stand'. However, the rest of the speech acknowledged that compromise would be necessary in any future power-sharing arrangement, which begged the question of whether the Liberals might find themselves in office but lacking in influence.[13]

Back in February 1974, Steel had been aggrieved when Thorpe failed to consult his MPs before embarking on talks with Heath.[14] Yet Steel was equally determined to negotiate with a free hand when he agreed in March 1977 to shore up Jim Callaghan's faltering Labour Government. The resulting 'Lib-Lab Pact' bought valuable time for Labour, without leaving the Liberal Party with any corresponding credit. If anything, the deal produced negative returns, since it reinforced existing Labour suspicions that the Liberals were inappropriate coalition partners. The Chancellor, Denis Healey, who was forced to undertake token consultations with the Liberal MP John Pardoe, found their meetings particularly unhelpful. To make matters worse, although Pardoe had been unsuccessful when he challenged Steel for the leadership in 1976, he was more representative of grass-roots Liberalism. As Michie and Hoggart put it, 'Pardoe is an ideas man, forever dreaming up new schemes for solving the country's more intractable problems. Taxation too high? Then halve it, says Pardoe. Ulster proving insoluble? Abandon it, he says. Like the White Queen in *Through the Looking Glass*, he can believe six impossible things before breakfast.'[15] In any party which was seriously seeking power within the existing rules of British politics, Pardoe would not have gained admittance to the inner circle of decision-makers. But, Steel's efforts notwithstanding, most Liberals still despised the existing rules; thus Pardoe, rather than the Party leader, reflected the outlook of the majority.

Memories of the Lib-Lab Pact damaged the Liberals at the 1979 General Election; the Party's vote fell by more than a million compared to the October 1974 contest, which itself had marked a significant decline from February. Yet Steel stuck to his strategy of downplaying Liberal radicalism and presenting his Party as an unthreatening 'centrist' alternative to Labour and the Conservatives. The 1979 manifesto was still the most innovative offering among the three main parties, including the familiar root-and-branch proposals on the constitution as well as a package of tax cuts which outbid even the Tories. Yet all this was couched in the language of social and political conciliation.[16] After 1979 it seemed even more sensible to appeal to the 'middle ground', since both main parties were pursuing radical agendas of their own despite the persistent popularity of consensus politics. Steel could also realistically anticipate the realignment of political forces which his predecessors had promoted in vain. At the Liberal Party Conference of September 1981 he greeted the formation of the Social Democratic Party (SDP) by urging his audience to go back to their constituencies and prepare for government.

The Alliance and after

Steel's enthusiastic response to the breakaway of Labour moderates was based on the assumption that the overwhelming majority of his fellow Liberals shared his own belief that a share of power was better than the role of an ideological pressure group – 'an academic think-tank', as he put it dismissively in 1976.[17] Yet this was a gamble, for two reasons. First, the dismal experience of recent years had suggested to many Liberals that Westminster politics was now a game suitable only for opportunists. The Lib-Lab Pact showed that Liberals were not very good at it, and to master the rules was likely to require too many unsavoury compromises. Second, the development which had excited Steel could actually be seen as a snub to the Liberals. Rather than joining an established party with a long history of progressive achievement, Labour's social democrats had set up their own separate organisation. It was hardly surprising that Liberal loyalists like Cyril Smith wanted the SDP to be 'strangled at birth'.[18]

For most of the post-war period, the Liberal Party consisted of people who kept the Party alive because they thought that this was the only way to preserve their distinctive principles. Steel, by contrast, thought that the pursuit of power was the only way to preserve the Party. His understandable preference was to associate with people like himself, carrying light ideological baggage and always looking to strike a compromise which would advance the interests of the Party as an institution rather than a vehicle for ideas. To Steel – as to Roy Jenkins of the SDP – the two parties were natural allies in the middle ground which Labour and the Conservatives had vacated. However, this overlooked important differences of ideology and ethos. British social democracy shared common features with new liberalism; crucially, both traditions espoused equality of opportunity and social justice, seeing the state as a necessary agent of beneficial change. Yet, as we have seen, the Liberal Party still contained people for whom the central state was always an object of suspicion, while even new liberals constantly fretted about threats to individual freedom. The senior social democrats were used to the exercise of power, and had far fewer misgivings about the state. They preferred a more centralised party structure – after all, Jenkins and the other members of the 'Gang of Four' had deserted Labour at least in part because its grass-roots activists had begun to exercise too much power. While Jenkins himself found the contrasting Liberal ethos rather congenial, his colleague David Owen emphatically did not; and from the outset it was always likely that when Jenkins stepped down from the SDP leadership Owen would succeed him. The major policy differences between Owen and the Liberals also reflected a contrasting style of politics; Owen, in particular, had no doubt that Britain should retain its 'independent' nuclear deterrent, whereas a succession of Liberal Assemblies bore testimony to the Party's serious misgivings about weapons which greatly enhanced the internal disciplinary powers of the state, as well as endangering the future of humanity and perpetuating the existing enmity between nations.

The creation of the Alliance completed the process whereby the old Liberal approach to politics was gradually superseded. This had started with the February 1974 election result, but as one disillusioned Liberal reflected with hindsight, 'the association with the Gang of Four was the end of innocence'.[19] Ironically, the 1980 Liberal Party conference had featured a discussion of ideology, which resulted in a pamphlet written by a prominent councillor and party activist, Michael Meadowcroft. The intention of this publication was to show that liberalism could still form the basis of a highly distinctive policy programme – distinctive, not least, from anything the SDP was likely to offer. Meadowcroft went on to write an analysis of the SDP as a potential partner for the Liberals. He concluded by expressing a fear that the long-promised 'realignment of the Left' would end up as an opportunistic bolstering of the centre, and that the SDP would merely give the public a chance to shirk the hard decisions which faced the country as it recovered from the initial shock of Thatcherite dogma.[20]

Meadowcroft himself could be seen as a beneficiary of the Alliance, winning the parliamentary seat of Leeds West in 1983. However, he remained highly sceptical about the value of a merger with the SDP. In September 1987 – after losing his seat – he was appointed as a member of an eight-strong Liberal team ahead of negotiations for the merger, but withdrew along with three of his colleagues before the end of the talks. Although he supported Alan Beith's unsuccessful campaign to become the first leader of the merged party in the election of July 1988, he subsequently left to set up a new party which kept alive the old Liberal name. In short, someone whose ideas and outlook made him seem an ideological 'centrist' within the Liberal Party of the early 1980s had found it impossible to accept the changes of the subsequent decade.

It might be argued that Meadowcroft was a maverick, with unusually strong ideas of what it meant to be a Liberal and an idiosyncratic predisposition to stick to his guns regardless of changing circumstances. Yet in a sense it was those qualities which made him a typical member of the pre-Alliance Liberal Party, and hindsight has hardly detracted from the cogency of his position. Even in the polarised politics of the early 1980s, it was possible to depict both main parties as dysfunctional representatives of the broad liberal tradition, whose defects had arisen at least in part because of their untiring quest for cheap popularity. Margaret Thatcher, after all, owed her economic inspiration to nineteenth-century classical liberals; and although the right-wing press tried to depict Michael Foot as a totalitarian, his lineage and his writings suggested that at worst he was a good liberal fallen among trade unionists.[21] Meadowcroft and others like him dreamed of a day when the public would come to recognise that their best hope of preserving liberty lay with a party which was consistent in its liberalism, resisting all temptations to compromise. But if, after so many decades of heroic obscurity, the Liberals were to dissolve their old identity in a merger with the arch-compromisers of British politics, they would lose even the remote chance of taking their pristine ideas into government. They would become a slightly more acceptable version of the two parties which already dominated the picture – hardly a prospect to fire the imagination of the idealists who had saved the Liberals from extinction.

From Ashdown to Campbell, 1988–2007

On the face of it, Meadowcroft should not have been dismayed by Paddy Ashdown's facile victory over Alan Beith in the 1988 leadership election. The new leader, after all, was a living refutation of the idea that Liberals were too soggy and open-minded to take tough decisions. Commentators also thought that there was little ideological difference between Ashdown and Beith. Launching his campaign, Ashdown echoed the 1969 constitution by declaring that the Liberals should be a 'party of the left, taking the side of ordinary people against unacceptable privilege and the abuse of power'. He also promised to seek an overall election victory for the merged party, rather than hoping to join one or other of its rivals in a coalition. Ashdown did, though, seem rather less concerned than Beith about the traditions of the Liberal Party, and as a result was judged to be far more acceptable to SDP members. The new constitution of the merged party duly glossed over the ideological differences between liberalism and social democracy.[22]

However, for all his personal dynamism and initial intentions Ashdown did find himself increasingly preoccupied by the prospect of sharing power in a hung parliament, and splits within his Party over principles and tactics emphasised the fragility of the emerging Liberal Democrat 'centre'. True to his belief that the Liberal Democrats should position themselves on the left, he always preferred Labour as a coalition partner; but formally he had to respect the official policy of 'equidistance', which supposedly left the Party uncommitted in advance of any negotiations. This attitude might have made tactical sense – and obviously appealed to Party members who thought that the Conservatives and Labour were equally contemptible as *institutions*, even if they felt closer to Labour ideologically – but it did nothing to convince the electorate that the Liberal Democrats based their decisions on clear, distinctive principles. 'Equidistance' also proved infectious at constituency level: depending on the tactical necessity in each seat, local Liberal Democrat activists apparently felt free to outflank Labour on the left, or the Conservatives on the right. As a result, they were often accused of dirty tactics whenever they fought a closely contested by-election. The allegation was laughable enough in itself, since it merely reflected the anger of the bigger parties whenever they were beaten at their own game. But it was a significant comedown from the initial days of 'pavement politics', when Liberal candidates had tried to bring their distinctive principles to bear on local issues. It was not unduly cynical to associate the new Liberal Democrat 'centre' with the chameleon, adopting appropriate colours depending on its immediate environment, for its own advantage. One jaundiced former policy advisor thought that proposals during the Ashdown years tended to be 'so diluted as to be anodyne' because the Party now evinced 'a desperate desire to placate rather than to lead the voters'.[23] It was beginning to behave like a centrist organisation, whose leaders found it increasingly difficult to accommodate constituency members even if they privately agreed with their radical views.

Ashdown stood down as Liberal Democrat leader in August 1999. His decision surprised many observers, but it would have made sense even if Ashdown had been a less energetic character, with no desire to make a difference to the world. He had played for high stakes, hoping for a coalition with 'New' Labour and the implementation of electoral reform, leading ultimately to the formation of a single 'progressive' party with strong liberal leanings. A cursory glance at the parliamentary arithmetic after the 1997 election would have assured Ashdown that this was unlikely to happen for several thankless years. Although the Liberal Democrats had won 46 seats – a tally which, at last, gave them the look of a credible participant in government – Labour's position was now so strong that it was unlikely to need a coalition partner after the next election unless its performance in government proved to be so bad that no rational party would want to save its skin. Even then, instead of being a suitor for Liberal Democrat support, Labour was more likely to approach the smaller organisation as a predator rather than a partner, absorbing its members in a way which would further erode the old militant spirit. As it was, after the 1997 election Ashdown was strung along for a while by Tony Blair, who promised repeatedly that he believed in the 'project' of realignment but failed to throw his full weight behind Roy Jenkins' proposal for modest changes in the electoral system. This experience demonstrated that the Liberals and their successors had been living on an illusion since David Steel became leader; sharing power with either of the main parties would, after all, demand too many sacrifices of principle. It was therefore better for Ashdown to follow the example of Tony Benn, and leave the House of Commons in order to put his principles into practice on a wider stage.

When Charles Kennedy won the contest to succeed Ashdown, it seemed as if the initial bickerings surrounding the merger had faded away, and there was now a marriage of true minds between the Liberals and the SDP. Kennedy had briefly been a Labour supporter before becoming an SDP MP in the same year as Ashdown (1983) at the age of 23. He was generally popular among grass-roots members, regardless of their original allegiance. In the 2001 General Election his Party raised its parliamentary representation to 52; four years later it won an additional 10 seats. As leader, Kennedy had seen no reason to depart from the key policies of the Ashdown years, advocating increases in income tax to pay for higher spending on public services. In 2005, the Party argued for a new 50% rate of income tax, to be levied on those who earned more than £100,000 per year. This marked a return to the very different context of 1979, when Liberals had recommended a *cut* to the same 50% level on the grounds that this was the right way to square social justice with individual incentives. A previous commitment to a penny increase in the basic rate of tax had been dropped, but in the 2005 manifesto Kennedy expressed his pride at leading 'the most socially progressive party in British politics'.[24]

However, this boast owed more to Labour's lurch to the right under Blair than to a renewed burst of radicalism from Kennedy's Party. Under Paddy Ashdown, the Liberal Democrats had seen no reason to change tack in response to Labour's return to the 'middle ground' of British politics. While the Conservatives remained in power, a left-of-centre stance made tactical sense, as well as chiming in with the principles of most members. But after 2001 the success of New Labour encouraged some ambitious Liberal Democrats to undertake a rethink in the quest for distinctive ideological terrain. The *Orange Book*, published in 2004, was the main product of this endeavour. It implied that several key figures within the Party wanted to imitate Labour's rightward shift; and unlike Blair, it was possible for them to argue that they were being true to the traditions of their Party, rather than merely making a cynical bid to attract the voters of 'Middle England'. The attempt of the authors to 'reclaim' liberal principles included a much more positive assessment of classical liberal economics. Indeed, at times the volume sounded like an attempt to restore these ideas to their rightful home, after decades of misuse by the Conservatives.

Charles Kennedy's response to the *Orange Book* was conspicuously unenthusiastic, and for two very good reasons. First, it showed that some members of the parliamentary party were at odds with the clear majority of constituency activists, who regarded classical liberalism as reactionary rather than progressive. While Liberal Democrats certainly favoured the free market over a centrally-controlled economy, like Keynes they hoped for more egalitarian outcomes.[25] Second, the book threatened to promote a renewal of the debate which Kennedy's election as leader had apparently closed – whether the Liberal Democrats should be a vehicle for liberal ideology, in its various forms, or an eclectic organisation capable of accommodating representatives of other traditions. In this context, Kennedy's own background suddenly became a source of contention rather than a symbol of healing between the merged parties. Whether or not this was deliberately fostered, there was a distinct impression after the appearance of the *Orange Book* that the ideological future of the Party should be determined after a debate confined to committed liberals, excluding former Social Democrats like Kennedy. The question of the Liberal Party's attitude to the state had been resumed; but whereas the old Liberals had claimed to be distinctive and non-centrist because unlike their rivals they were suspicious of the state, the supposedly radical contributors to the *Orange Book* were trying to join the post-Thatcherite consensus of outright antipathy towards bureaucracy and high taxes on the rich.

The liberal ideologues saw their opportunity after the 2005 election, arguing that the Party ought to have polled better given its popular stance on the Iraq War. But this was merely a pretext for action against the leadership. At the post-election Liberal Assembly, delegates had defeated a proto-Thatcherite motion on the privatisation of the Royal Mail. Kennedy had supported the motion, and thus shared in the indignity of defeat; but his right-wing critics had grounds for complaining that his advocacy had been lukewarm. *The Times* was predictably disappointed that the Liberal Democrats had not swung to the right in New Labour style, complaining in an editorial that the Party should adopt 'a more professional and realistic approach to politics'.[26] For Rupert Murdoch's *Times*, this meant a concerted drive to remove any vestige of radicalism – or, rather, of anti-Thatcherism.

A lurch of this kind was inconceivable under Kennedy, and ambitious Liberal Democrats had no difficulty in taking such talk as a hint that the leader should be ditched. Compared to the problems which beset Jeremy Thorpe after 1976, Kennedy's difficulties with drink were barely worth serious consideration. At first, indeed, the key figures within the Party – the newly-formed institutional 'centre' – seemed to be rallying around him. By January 2006, however, the whispering campaign against Kennedy had overcome this residual loyalty. By that time it looked as though debate within the Liberal Democrats had come full circle. The merger of 1988 can be seen as a defeat for the ideological 'purists' who formerly gave the Liberal Party its closest approximation to a 'centre', bringing to a close a process which can be traced back to the mid-1970s. After that, the centre had taken on a clearer definition, and gradually came to resemble the traditional arrangement within the other main parties – that is, the people of the centre were those who were prepared to compromise for the sake of party or personal advantage. The originator of this process was David Steel, champion of the pact with Labour and the alliance with the SDP. Although Paddy Ashdown and Charles Kennedy were principled politicians, both took over the leadership in circumstances which prompted them, against their instincts, to focus on the potential for pacts and mergers and to fear public manifestations within their ranks from ideological enthusiasts of any kind.

Ironically, at the time of writing the relative success of Liberal Democrat strategy under Ashdown and Kennedy has presented the liberal ideologues with their opportunity to strike back and redefine the Party's 'centre' on their own terms. When the Liberals and their successors were languishing with twenty seats or (far) fewer, their claim to be the true custodians of liberalism looked like a token of eccentricity; indeed, the affable, disorganised image of the Party's Assemblies added to the impression that its radical ideas could not be taken very seriously unless and until they were adopted by either of its rivals. But once both Labour and the Conservatives had moved to the right, the nature of the Liberal Democrat dilemma was transformed. Even the Party's pragmatic centrists were suddenly vulnerable to the charge of leftist radicalism, compared to the policies on offer elsewhere.

In the early days of the Alliance, Liberals had been enthused by the idea of replacing Labour as the main party of the left. But they had felt at the time that a truly progressive party, shorn of embarrassing links to the trade unions, could win power. By 2005 this hope had faded. To ambitious Liberal Democrats, it could seem that their tally of 62 MPs was about the limit of their realistic ambitions on the left, especially in view of the advantage offered by the Party's stance on the Iraq War. There was an ever-increasing desire to re-acquaint the public with the tougher side of liberalism, even in policy areas like criminal justice where liberals were generally held to be hopelessly woolly. If the Party was to carry credibility in the new political environment social discipline had to begin at home. In any case, the tough liberals of the *Orange Book* tendency seemed less willing to tolerate evidence of dissent within an enhanced parliamentary cohort which was bound to come under greater media scrutiny. Coincidentally, the 'centralising' trend has also been enhanced by the Party's exposure to power-sharing in Scotland.

The election of Sir Menzies Campbell as Kennedy's replacement represented the consummation of the attempt by ideological liberals to reconfigure the recently forged Liberal Democrat centre in a rightwards direction. Campbell's focus on foreign affairs would allow the liberal ideologues to make the running on domestic policy; in any case his views on domestic matters placed him on the right of the Party. Above all, he was old enough to allow the 'Young Turks' to expect that one of their number would take his place shortly after the next election. Afterwards they would inherit the tendency towards greater internal discipline which had been developing within the Party since the time of the merger. As it turned out, Campbell's tenure proved even more fleeting, and in October 2007 he was coaxed into volunteering his resignation. The main reason for his departure was his supposed lack of media appeal, largely due to his age (66). There was a strong impression that the new 'centre', represented in particular by Campbell's Deputy (and temporary replacement) Vince Cable, would try to use this opportunity to shift the Party further to the right; and the eventual victor in the leadership election, the suspiciously telegenic Nick Clegg, was closely identified with this tendency.

On the face of it there was a reasonable tactical case for a rightward tack, since the Liberal Democrats seemed better placed to gain seats from the Conservatives in the south than to make inroads into Labour's northern heartlands. Yet it was fairly clear that the new 'centre' would have wanted to take this course regardless of electoral considerations. This was reflected in a change of ethos within the Party that pre-dated Charles Kennedy's departure. In earlier times, the dominance of ideological liberalism had been reflected in the Party's relatively democratic practices, which allowed grass-roots members ample scope to influence debates, if not to shape the final policy decisions. By 2005 the top-down ethos of the SDP had gradually infected the Party's policy-making process, and its impact had been reinforced by the media's more general concentration on the role of party leaders – a development which had helped electorally since the days of Jeremy Thorpe, at the cost of gradually making the Party less distinctive. It had become 'bad form' for activists to argue forcefully against the views of the Liberal Democrat leadership. Thus, for example, the Party's pledge of a substantial increase in taxes on the rich to pay for better public services did not long survive the 2005 General Election. A progressive element supposedly remained in the new income tax policy, thanks to changes in the basic rate and personal allowances. But however they were presented these measures would also benefit the rich, just like Margaret Thatcher's cuts in the basic rate after 1979. Plans to increase taxes on air travel would barely affect wealthy pleasure-seekers; their main impact would fall on the frequent flyers who were forced to use aeroplanes for business purposes, and the poor who had exploited low fares as their only chance to broaden their horizons through overseas travel. In a way the proposal to replace a significant proportion of income tax revenue with 'green' charges was a reflection of the traditional naivety of Liberal Democrat policy-making. But now it was more difficult to argue that impractical measures were being prompted by a philanthropic impulse. At the 2007 Assembly the displaced Charles Kennedy spoke about the need for a 'war against poverty'. Although this message was welcomed by the rank-and-file, it jarred against the new centre's anxiety to allay the fears of affluent voters.

This is not to say that Liberal Democrat activists did not want to see a sharper focus on the environment, and to use this approach as a means of keeping an element of redistribution in tax policy. The environment was the subject on which the average member had probably changed the most from the mid-1970s; a 'centrist' at that time would certainly have been concerned about the threat to the planet, but three decades later almost every Liberal Democrat recognised the need for drastic remedial action. Yet increased radicalism in this sphere has coincided with a marked decline in the old Liberal *militancy* and in bold, plain speaking. Changes in the policy-making process have meant that the revival of the ideological liberals has gained official recognition through comparatively illiberal methods.

At one time, the Liberal Party tended to be disregarded by political scientists because it seemed to be an exception to Roberto Michel's 'Iron Law of Oligarchy' – or maybe an exception which helped to prove the rule, since the Liberals were not important enough in the great scheme of things to make central control worth the effort. But once the Party had passed the totemic figure of 50 MPs, the 'Iron Law' began to operate with a vengeance. Ironically, though, the Party was being made to swing to the right just at the time when it had the chance of prospering still further on the left, thanks to the historic aberration of New Labour and the ambivalent attitude of many Conservatives to the 'modernising' strategy of David Cameron. The evidence strongly suggests that the Party's new institutional centre is significantly less progressive than the average Liberal Democrat member, producing a potentially dangerous dissonance in the ranks which could not entirely be quelled by Nick Clegg's early pledge of higher taxes on the rich matched by relief for the low paid. Coincdentally – or not – the Party had also become embroiled in funding scandals, suggesting that its top officials have been prepared to play the same games as its bigger, bad rivals.

For any third party these changes in ideology and ethos represent a dangerous gamble. Possibly the Liberal Democrat membership, like its New Labour counterparts since 1994, is desperate enough for a taste of power to accept the need to join the post-Thatcherite consensus if there really is no other way to achieve their objectives. But the turnout in the 2007 leadership election – a fall of more than 10,000 compared to the electorate which chose Menzies Campbell – suggests a high level of discontent, if not of defection from the ranks. The objective for the old Liberal Party was political and social change, rather than the exercise of power for itself. Bringing the Party closer to its rivals threatens to make it redundant even as a potential recipient of protest votes. If the wider public develops the idea that the Liberal Democrats are merely a greener version of the two main parties their attraction as a means of protest might also begin to fade, increasing the popularity of the Greens, who in many respects resemble the old, anarchical Liberals.

Notes

1   *The Times* editorial, 8ᵗʰ July 1975.
2   *The Times*, 11ᵗʰ July, 24ᵗʰ October 1975.

3 A. Watkins, *The Liberal Dilemma* (Macgibbon and Kee, London, 1966), p. 29.

4 I. Crewe and A. King, *SDP: The Birth, Life and Death of the Social Democratic Party* (Oxford University Press, Oxford, 1995), p. 171.

5 A. Cyr, *Liberal Party Politics in Britain* (John Calder, London, 1977), p. 277.

6 Ibid., pp. 195–6.

7 Though Beveridge did not actually join the Party until 1944.

8 Quoted in A. Beith, *The Case for the Liberal Party and the Alliance* (Longman, Harlow, 1983), pp. 140–1.

9 Ibid., pp. 4–5.

10 On the classical liberal strand in Liberal economic thinking, see A. Gamble, 'Liberals and the economy', in V. Bogdanor (ed.), *Liberal Party Politics* (Oxford University Press, Oxford, 1983), pp. 191–216; for an interesting insight into Grimond's economic liberalism see 'Interview with Jo Grimond', in E. Bolkestein (ed.), *Modern Liberalism: Conversations with Liberal Politicians* (Elsevier Science Publishers, New York, 1982), pp. 71–108.

11 Another, at Lincoln in March 1973, saw the triumph of the Labour defector Dick Taverne in a contest which foreshadowed the rise of the SDP.

12 A. Michie and S. Hoggart, *The Pact: The Inside Story of the Lib-Lab Government, 1977–8* (Quartet, London, 1978), p. 66.

13 Quoted in Beith, *The Case for the Liberal Party and the Alliance*, p. 146.

14 D. Dutton, *A History of the Liberal Party in the Twentieth Century* (Palgrave, Basingstoke, 2004), p. 222.

15 Michie and Hoggart, *The Pact*, p. 47.

16 *The Real Fight is for Britain*, Liberal Party manifesto, 1979.

17 Quoted in Beith, *The Case for the Liberal Party and the Alliance*, p. 147.

18 Crewe and King, *SDP*, p. 170.

19 David Benedictus in D. Brack (ed.), *Why I am a Liberal Democrat* (Liberal Democrat Publications, Dorchester, 1996), p. 24.

20 M. Meadowcroft, *Liberal Values for a New Decade* (North West Community Newspapers, Manchester, 1981, 2nd edition); *Social Democracy, Barrier or Bridge?* (Liberator Publications, London, 1981).

21 His father Isaac Foot (1880–1960) could almost have been portrayed as a member of the Liberal 'centre' of his time.

22 *The Times*, 2nd and 6th June 1988; T. Jones, 'Liberal Democrat thought', in D. McIver (ed.), *Liberal Democrat Politics* (Harvester Wheatsheaf, Hemel Hempstead, 1996), pp. 76–78.

23 Benedictus in Brack (ed.), *Why I am a Liberal Democrat*.

24 Liberal Democrat press conference, 14th April 2005.

25 See P. Whiteley, P. Seyd and A. Billinghurst, *Third Force Politics: Liberal Democrats at the Grassroots* (Oxford University Press, Oxford, 2006), pp. 48–67.

26 *The Times*, 19th September 2005.

Social liberalism

For much of the post-1945 period, the term 'social liberalism' was almost unused within Liberal politics. Liberals were Liberals without prefix. They pursued policies based on tackling abuses of power in order to advance individual freedom, whether such abuses were by the state, businesses or individuals. No prefix to liberalism was necessary. It was only when Margaret Thatcher was described as a liberal of the nineteenth-century type, that anybody felt the need to qualify or nuance their liberalism.

Consequently, by the late 1980s, it was common to hear comments within the Liberal Democrats to the effect that Thatcher may be a nineteenth-century liberal, but that 'we' were 'social liberals' in the tradition of those New Liberals who had exposed the flawed and limited nature of Gladstonian Liberalism on socio-economic issues. Crucial to that conception of social liberalism, both in the 1980s and eighty to ninety years before, was a belief that inequality was a barrier to freedom, and that the state had a duty to reduce inequality in order to advance freedom. This was a radical distinction from Thatcherism's brand of nineteenth-century liberalism. With this 'social liberalism' widely accepted inside the Party, there was little discussion of the nature of liberalism within the Liberal Democrats in the 1990s. Indeed, Party members accepted the development of pro-market policies on a wide range of economic matters under Paddy Ashdown's leadership, without seeing them as incompatible with social liberalism.

A significant change came with the publication of *The Orange Book: Reclaiming Liberalism* in 2004. This argued that there was a clear distinction between economic and social liberalism, and that the Party had been overly influenced by a concern with the latter. Such over-influence meant, it was argued, that the Party was interventionist in too many areas that should be matters of personal choice. The *Orange Book* was deeply anti-state in its tone, criticising the Liberal Democrats for advocating 'nanny-state liberalism' on a range of issues, and arguing that the Party must examine 'to what extent we can utilise choice, competition, consumer power and the private sector' in areas such as benefits and public services.[2]

From this emerged a debate within the Party over the balance between social liberalism and economic liberalism. The media fuelled the debate by presenting it as one of social liberals *against* economic liberals, as if Liberal Democrats were one or the other, and that the two were mutually exclusive. This is a massive oversimplification. Any Liberal Democrat who believes that inequality is a barrier to freedom – a 'social liberal' in media eyes – accepts that markets are better than the state at allowing individuals to make choices over matters where individual choice is the key, such as the purchase of a car or a holiday. So-called social liberals would accept that markets are crucial – for example, through the effects green taxation – in making the economy more sustainable. Moreover, on their key concern of equality, social liberals see a role for economic growth in creating wealth and opportunity.

As for so-called economic liberals, look at material in the *Orange Book* from David Laws, often characterised by the media and some Liberal Democrats as a high-priest of economic liberalism. One finds there a clear recognition of the effects on freedom of 'poverty, poor housing, poor schooling and second-rate public services'.[3] Within the Liberal Democrats, in internal discussions on manifesto and other policy statements, he has personally been a strong advocate of state spending on early years education, on the basis that this is the best place to tackle those inequalities which have the greatest impact on the life chances of children from the poorest families. These are not the views of a nineteenth-century Liberal. The distinction between social and economic liberalism looks even more simplistic when one considers that all those characterised as being in one camp or the other are strongly influenced by a commitment to both political and personal liberalism. There is no obvious divide within the Party between those labelled as social and economic liberals over matters such as constitutional reform or the role of the state on civil liberties.

So in many ways, there is a case for banishing the terms 'social liberal' and 'economic liberal'. However, they do have a purpose: they act as a label for a crucial debate within the Party: the extent to which the state should wage war on economic inequality in order to advance freedom. For that reason, 'social liberal' has been incorporated into the title of a volume of essays exploring these issues and others.[4] Two key questions are at issue within the Liberal Democrats today: how much inequality can be tolerated, and how far should the state tackle it? In this debate, the social liberals are those who are most egalitarian and most 'statist', although they share the broad Liberal belief in the dangers of the state, a matter on which their views contrast with those of social democrats.[5] They believe that economic inequality is a major barrier to freedom and that state action is the best way to tackle it: through redistributive (and potentially higher) taxation, allowing either higher levels of benefits or tax cuts (the latter being the Party's favoured option at time of writing) for the poorest, and greater investment in public services. On the latter policy area, they tend not to favour introducing greater private sector involvement into health and education, believing that the state is more able than markets to act progressively. But to tackle problems of centralisation in public services they favour devolution and democratic local accountability (as do some economic liberals).

Therefore, one can use the term 'social liberal' to describe those within the Liberals and Liberal Democrats who have been, or are, on the egalitarian and statist side of arguments. It is used as such as a form of shorthand in this chapter. Such a social liberal tradition is a long one within the two parties and this chapter starts with an analysis of the work of New Liberals such as L.T. Hobhouse and J.A. Hobson, although as we shall see, there were differences between them. Their principles have influenced liberalism throughout the twentieth century, and into the twenty-first, with remarkably little change. That enduring influence means that to understand social liberalism's impact on post-1945 Liberals, there has to be sustained attention to the first half of the twentieth century. The first section then examines the impact of two key figures in the development of social liberal thought, Keynes and Beveridge, before considering two more recent thinkers, John Rawls and Conrad Russell, while also drawing in other relevant figures. The second section examines Liberal and Liberal Democrat policies since 1945. In so doing, it touches on the influence of social liberals on the overall direction of the parties, and considers how the Party might develop in the future. Throughout, it is argued that while the social liberal commitment to tackling inequality has been central to Liberal and Liberal Democrat philosophy, the parties' policies have been drawn from a range of sources. Crucially, attitudes to the state are explored. Here it is shown that social liberals have been clear that the state is not the only tool in the weapon against inequality. However, this argument has been largely rhetorical in that the main social liberal initiatives have focused on state action. Social liberals have been theoretically committed to, for example, a range of providers in public services, but have not been wildly enthusiastic about such an approach, and have not developed new initiatives in this area. Where the two parties have taken that line, they have been influenced by other strands within liberalism, and by the political context of the time.

Thinkers and principles

New Liberals did not emerge from a vacuum in the late nineteenth century. They were informed by previous liberal thinkers and in claiming liberal thinkers for social liberalism it would be possible to draw on the work of many. John Stuart Mill could be claimed for social liberalism, but since all political liberals claim Mill, it would not explain much about social liberalism's distinctiveness. A more useful focus for nineteenth-century origins is T.H. (Thomas Hill) Green (1836–1882). When *The Reformer* – a Liberal Democrat magazine influenced heavily by the social liberal and social democratic traditions – began a series of articles on 'thinkers and influencers' in the late 1990s, one of the first pieces was on Green, written by Geoffrey Thomas, a leading Green scholar.[6] Green wrote about the effect of socio-economic inequalities which made freedom limited to many: he wrote of the 'untaught and underfed-denizen of a London yard with gin-shops on the right hand and on the left'.[7] In other words, he recognised the extent to which socio-economic factors could have a profound impact on how free individuals could really be. Yet Green's attitude to the state is more problematic, and as Michael Freeden says, Green's view of the policies to which a concern with inequality should lead were rather limited, focusing on traditional liberal concerns such as temperance and access to land.[8]

A more radical and constructivist approach to the state was at the heart of 'New' Liberalism, dominant within which stands L.T. (Leonard Trelawny) Hobhouse (1864–1929). He published *The Labour Movement*, his first book, in 1893. In this, he developed some of his early ideas on the merits of collectivism and these were influential on the policies of the radical Liberal Government elected in 1906. However, it was not until 1911 that he published what remains the definitive statement of social liberalism entitled, simply, *Liberalism*. The work blends philosophical issues with the concerns of Edwardian politics, and some of the text therefore engages with subjects that are no longer of concern to social liberals. But at its core was a conception of the state that remains at the centre of contemporary social liberalism. Hobhouse saw the state as a tool with which people should work to secure social reform, and he was crucially concerned with socio-economic limits to freedom. Two sections sum up his approach. The first relates to the shared ground between the pursuit of freedom – the cause of all liberals – and the pursuit of greater equality. Hobhouse argued that:

> the struggle for liberty is also, when pushed through, a struggle for equality. Freedom to choose and follow an occupation, if it is to become fully effective, means equality with others in the opportunities for following such occupation. This is, in fact, one among the various considerations which leads Liberalism to support a national system of free education, and will lead it further on the same lines.[9]

Hobhouse was right in his prediction for this approach led social liberals to advance the cause of public services throughout the twentieth century. In an abbreviated form as 'the struggle for liberty is the struggle for equality', Hobhouse's approach has even informed recent Liberal Democrat policy statements, and Charles Kennedy as leader cited it regularly, along with Hobhouse's most famous quotation, 'liberty without equality is a name of noble sound and squalid result'.[10]

In Hobhouse's struggle for both liberty and equality, the state was a weapon. He did not believe it was the only source of collective action and described it as 'one form of association among others'. But he had little to say about the other forms of association, and was clear that it was on attitudes to the state that New Liberals 'stand furthest from the older Liberalism'. He argued that:

> the 'positive' conception of the State which we have now reached not only involves no conflict with the true principle of personal liberty, but is necessary to its effective realization[11]

Although Hobhouse believed that the concerns of classical liberalism should inevitably lead to endorsement of the state, his own overt statement of distance between 'new' and 'old' liberalism showed how far Liberals had travelled from the days of Gladstone to those of Asquith and Lloyd George. This conception of the state has underpinned key developments in Liberal thought since 1911: the contemporary work of the Asquith Government; Beveridge's proposal of social insurance; and Liberal Democrat enthusiasm for public services, especially education.

Even though Hobhouse is the starting point for twentieth-century social liberalism, the influence of one other New Liberal, J.A. (John Atkinson) Hobson (1858–1940) needs to be highlighted. Hobson was strongly influenced by hostility to the British Empire, which troubled Hobhouse less, and his arguments were heavily rooted in the belief that the Empire sustained domestic poverty by providing the UK with easy access to markets across the world, rather than selling goods in the home market. This, he believed, enabled the poorest to be kept poor because the market did not depend on their purchasing power to sustain industry. Indeed, they were production fodder for industrialists. From this concern, in four works written over seven years, he developed the idea of 'underconsumption', a belief that the economy could only thrive if large numbers of people were able to consume industry's products. He believed that the solution was greater equality and argued for progressive taxation to develop welfare schemes and tackle poverty. Hobson's approach was more 'advanced' than Hobhouse in his advocacy of state action and redistribution partly because of this,[12] and both ideas were not only influential on the Liberals in power after 1906, but have remained influential among post-1945 Liberals. Hobson formally joined the Labour Party after the First World War (with some discomfort over its trade unionism and zealous socialism),[13] while Hobhouse advised both the Labour and Liberal parties in the 1920s. Yet perhaps because Hobhouse did not actually join the Labour Party, he is today the Liberal Democrats' favourite New Liberal thinker.

From the basis of New Liberalism, social liberalism developed through the thinking of both Keynes and Beveridge from the 1920s to the 1940s, and the implementation of many of their ideas by successive UK governments after 1945. Arguably both men are the most cited – or at least referred to – Liberal thinkers by contemporary Liberal Democrats. Their ideas are seen as problematic in the contemporary world: aspects of Keynesianism are widely held to have failed by the 1970s, and many of the assumptions of Beveridge, and his failure to allow more flexible contributions, are out of step with modern lifestyles and gender roles. Yet both have left an important legacy for social liberalism: social liberal support for intervention in the economy and provision of welfare is heavily informed by the thinking of Keynes and Beveridge.

The contributions of John Maynard Keynes (1883–1946) to economics and social liberalism come from the same source: *The Theory of Employment, Interest and Money* (1936).[14] This argued that governments could and should use budget deficits as part of a wider strategy of managing the economy to tackle unemployment. It was a more theoretically solid version of the general approach taken in the 1928 Liberal 'Yellow Book' formally entitled *Britain's Industrial Future*. The inquiry which produced this was chaired by Walter Layton, rather than Keynes, who was merely a member. Yet these plans to tackle unemployment are remembered as part of Keynesianism rather than a non-existent Laytonism.

It is this attitude which has informed social liberalism: markets can fail, with damaging social consequences, and government can and should take action to avoid such problems. To some extent, that is an oversimplification of Keynes, but whether or not it is an accurate summary Liberals have drawn from him: social liberals have clung on to aspects of Keynesianism despite its apparent failure in the 1970s. For example, as we shall see later, the Liberal Democrats advocated investment in public works to kickstart the economy as recently as in their 1992 manifesto. This continued endorsement of the Keynesian approach can be more readily understood if one accepts assessments of Keynes which have suggested that he was misunderstood in the 1960s and 1970s and that his theories were meant to be applied to economies in a state of depression, rather than those prone to inflation. A notable advocate of this is Gordon Brown,[15] and other aspects of Keynesianism have wider circulation, such as his attitude to economic uncertainty. That helps to explain why Liberal Democrats cling to Keynes.

William Beveridge (1879–1963) is perhaps even more revered than Keynes by Liberal Democrats. There is a narrative which runs along the lines of the Liberals establishing the welfare state after the election victory of 1906, with radical enhancements made following the Beveridge Report of 1942,[16] which though implemented by a Labour Government, makes Beveridge the founder of the modern welfare state. That overlooks the extent to which the National Health Service was really only imagined in outline by Beveridge, with planning carried out by officials who learned from the wartime Emergency Medical Service, and then implemented by Labour – driven by Nye Bevan. But it is a tempting approach which informs Liberal Democrat values statements today.[17]

However, we should not see social liberals as supporting without criticism the collectivism of the post-war years. Indeed, the Liberal Democrats have been openly critical of the extent to which 'the collectivist way in which [the ideas of Keynes and Beveridge] were implemented did not reflect the wishes of Beveridge or of Liberal Democrats today'.[18] This is because it is all too easily forgotten that Beveridge proposed a mixed system of benefits: the aim was for all to pay into a system of National Insurance which would, on the basis of contributions, pay the most generous benefits possible to those in need. Those who were not able to pay into the insurance scheme would receive National Assistance from a safety-net scheme. Such benefits would be at a lower rate than those paid to previous insurance contributors. Thus one of the core thinkers of social liberalism argued not for a 'one size fits all' system, but for benefits structured in such a way as to encourage some individual responsibility. Such support for individual initiative is a core difference between social liberalism and socialism. However, there was still a relatively limited amount of flexibility in the system, with flat-rate benefits and flat-rate contributions, allowing little incentivisation to save more as would become necessary in the long term. We should also remember that Beveridge was arguing for a *state-run* system, not for one in which private companies compete for business, and this belief in an overall state framework for benefits is equally central to social liberalism.

Fundamentally, the Beveridge approach was underpinned by a concern for fairness, a concept which is also at the heart of the philosophy of the most eminent post-war Liberal thinker, albeit an American who is surprisingly unknown by Liberal Democrats: John Rawls (1921–2002). Rawls is not a thinker whom Liberal Democrats instinctively cite in speeches or articles. Indeed, probably very few have actually read his work, in the same way that Conservatives would rarely be experts on Michael Oakeshott – although admittedly they have had the excuse of conservatism apparently eschewing ideology. Yet Rawls' work stands as the most thorough adaptation of social liberalism to modern times. His two main works are *A Theory of Justice* (1972) and *Political Liberalism* (1993). Rawls' theory is of 'justice as fairness'. His concept of fairness was defined by two principles. First, the 'equal liberties' principle is that 'each person is to have an equal right to the most extensive basic liberty compatible with a similar liberty for others'. This involved, for example, freedom of speech, association or worship. Second (and for Rawls it does have a lower priority than equal liberties) is the 'difference' principle. This posits that 'social and economic inequalities are to be arranged so that they are both (a) reasonably expected to be to everyone's advantage, and (b) attached to positions and offices open to all'.[19] In other words, Rawls, like Hobhouse, recognised the limits on freedom imposed by inequality. Rawls reworked his overall approach in *Political Liberalism* nearly twenty years later to respond to social changes which meant that one of his key concepts – a well-ordered society – was challenged by the growing diversity of western societies. His answer to this was to say that society need not be united in its moral beliefs so long as its members shared a concept of political justice. This approach has much to say to the world as it grapples with issues around cultural diversity, but it remains the case that Rawls' difference principle puts him firmly in the social liberal camp.

In addition to Rawls, there have been other post-war thinkers who have informed social liberalism, but social liberals have had to pick and choose from their work rather than embracing them wholeheartedly. One of those was the Liberal Party leader, Jo Grimond. Grimond's inspiring leadership helped to drag the Liberal Party from the electoral darkness of the 1950s to the sunrise of Liberal revival. He did that partly through sheer charisma on the campaign trail, but he also encouraged new ideas in the Party. Yet like any such intellectual ferment, the Liberal Party of Grimond's days drew on many sources, and the work he produced himself is difficult to place firmly in the social liberal tradition. For example, while he was clear on the need for a strong state role in social services, he also advocated the expansion of payments by patients for NHS treatment,[20] and his most expansive work was on the need for political reforms.[21] Moreover, his involvement with the Party's 'Unservile State Group', reflected a fear of the state on the basis that it could discourage individual initiative. This fear went beyond widespread liberal concerns about the potential for state power to be abused, and makes it difficult for social liberals to claim Grimond as belonging distinctively to them rather than to the wider Party.

Another politician on whom social liberals can draw is Tony Crosland, whose book *The Future of Socialism* (1956) was not about socialism at all, but represents the most important post-1945 statement of social democracy in a UK context. Crosland's thinking on both public services and the need to tackle inequality is closely in line with what social liberals before and since have thought. However, as this author has argued elsewhere, Crosland, like all social democrats, has nothing to say about the dangers of abuses of state power and that makes him uneasy reading for many liberals.[22]

Social liberals have to be equally choosy about Isaiah Berlin (1909–97). One aspect of his earlier (1958) writings is profoundly at odds with social liberalism: his view that 'liberty is liberty, not equality or fairness or justice or culture, or human happiness or a quiet conscience'. He gave 'negative' liberty (the freedom *from*) priority over 'positive' liberty (the freedom *to*) describing the latter as 'at times, no better than a specious disguise for brutal tyranny'. However, he later (in 1969) qualified this by saying that 'the sense of freedom, in which I use this term, entails … the absence of obstacles to possible choices and activities … Such freedom ultimately depends … on how many doors are open, how open they are'.[23] The latter position is far more comfortable reading for social liberals. Moreover, social liberals have found within Berlin's work some ideas of interest, most notably his emphasis on the importance of accepting and cherishing a plurality of values in society. In social liberal eyes, this does at least help to mitigate some of the dangers of his views on positive liberty, and Berlin's relevance to Liberal Democrats has been discussed by Tim Razzall.[24]

One might also point to Berlin's biographer, Michael Ignatieff (1947–), as a modern thinker whose work has (or should have) relevance to social liberals. His book *The Needs of Strangers* (1984), written in the political context of Thatcher's efforts to roll back the frontiers of the state, is a powerful and eloquent defence of the need for the state to distribute social goods, while also warning of the dangers of the state walling individuals off from each other. In many ways it is a contemporary echo of Hobhouse and Green in its argument that 'freedom is empty as long as we are trapped in physical necessity'.[25] It also makes a persuasive case for needing a new political language which can reconcile different human needs for freedom and solidarity.

Yet like Rawls and Berlin, Ignatieff has not been inside the Liberals or the Liberal Democrats, even though he did give the first major lecture to the Centre for Reform, a think tank aligned with the Liberal Democrats.[26] For that reason, his impact has been relatively small compared to the most well-known thinker inside the Party over the past few decades: Conrad Russell (1937–2004). Russell was not a political philosopher by profession, though he was one of the world's most eminent historians of seventeenth-century Britain and was a great thinker in his own field. However, he did write a summary of the Party's philosophy in his *An Intelligent Person's Guide to Liberalism* (1999). Even more importantly, his contribution to social liberal thought came not through writing about it but by being engaged in party politics as a Liberal Democrat peer. In this role he pushed the social liberal case in internal Party meetings, informed by his own wide reading of political philosophy and his skill at relating issues of the day back to first principles. One of the most powerful strands of his thinking was around the idea of government action to help the poorest. As he said in his *Guide*, the view that liberty is the absence of restraint,

> leads to Thatcherism, not to Liberalism. It leads to an identification of liberty with minimum government action, and that is something in which Liberals have never believed. That is the liberty of the powerful: it is not the liberty of a party which, at all stages of its existence, has been dedicated to defending the powerless against privilege.[27]

There was perhaps only one word missing from Conrad Russell's account: 'social'. Somewhere it could have been in that paragraph before either liberalism or Liberal. His non-use of it shows how far many Liberal Democrats do not feel the need to distinguish between, for example, social and economic liberalism. However, he still belongs in any account of social liberalism as defined here because of his strong commitment to tackling inequality.

Policies

In determining the impact of a specific strand of thought within a political party, it is vital to consider the importance of political context. In manifestos, parties talk partly about the issues which concern them, but they also address those issues which they believe are most resonant with the public. In doing both, they use language which is in tune with the times, and if the party is an opposition party, that language is often focused primarily on the perceived weaknesses of the party in government. Thus the policies advocated by a party at any given moment have as much to do with events and issues outside the party as they do with the success or failure of a faction within a party. For the present day situation, the impact of this on manifestos is clear. In 1997 and 2001, the Liberal Democrats highlighted the need for greater investment in public services. By 2005, they were talking more of the need for decentralisation. This did not mean that the Party had suddenly changed, rather that the political context had changed. In 2005, the Liberal Democrats still believed in investing in public services. But that approach had a lower political saliency in 2005 after significant investment by Labour, than it did in when services were still suffering from previous years of underinvestment.

The impact of political circumstances on which policies are pursued can often be most evident when comparing different European Liberal parties. A snapshot of British and Swedish Liberals in 2001 shows the Britons arguing for higher investment in education and less central planning, while the Swedes wanted to cut spending and introduce more central controls. Yet these very different policies were primarily responses to different political circumstances – underinvestment and centralisation in the UK and the reverse in Sweden – and Liberals in the two countries were working towards similar goals.[28]

This means that any analysis of Liberal and Liberal Democrat manifestos over a long period of time must recognise the impact of political context (which some might describe as political 'fashion') and not assume that the presence or absence of any specific policy indicates a rise or fall of social liberal influence. Despite that caveat, several trends can be discerned which point to a strong social liberal influence throughout the post-1945 period, but they also point to concerns for personal liberalism, constitutional reform and, increasingly, environmental issues, which are shared by all liberals. This section considers manifestos in three separate sections: the solely Liberal manifestos of 1945–79, the joint Liberal–SDP Alliance manifestos of 1983 and 1987, and the post-merger Liberal Democrat platforms.

The first clearly observable social liberal strand within the 1945–79 manifestos is support for redistribution. In 1945, this meant support for the Beveridge programme of social security, perhaps unsurprisingly given Beveridge's personal Liberal credentials. The 1945 manifesto associated the Party with the Beveridge Report, effectively claiming the report as its own in saying of the fear of poverty that 'with the Beveridge schemes for Social Security and Full Employment, the Liberal Party leads a frontal attack on this Fear'.[29] The Beveridge system remained largely unquestioned by Liberals until the 1964 manifesto when the Party said it needed to be brought 'up to date'. This included measures to allow pensioners to work and earn money without losing out on their pension, and it involved replacing insurance stamps with a social security tax with employers paying two-thirds of the cost and employees one-third. This was a significant revision of Beveridge, though in keeping with the basic principle of a contributory system. However, to some extent the Party moved further away from a state-run scheme with its advocacy of greater use of occupational schemes to supplement pensions.[30] In its February 1974 manifesto, the Party broke with the Beveridge system. But it did so in a more radically redistributive direction. Instead of the existing tax and benefits system it advocated a 'credit income tax scheme' with everyone paid a personal credit which would later be talked of as a 'citizens' income'.[31] By 1979 the policy had been given capital letters as the Credit Income Tax and was the centrepiece of the Party's efforts to deal with tax complications and low incomes in one swoop, with the aim of drawing in benefits claimants, pensioners and student grant-holders.[32]

The second area of policy in which the social liberal trend can be seen is the call for greater democracy at work which drew on the egalitarian emphasis of social liberalism. The idea of industrial partnership had Liberal roots as far back as the 1928 *Yellow Book* but it only found its way into post-war Liberal manifestos in 1964 (although there were earlier references to employee share ownership in 1959). In 1964, the argument was that employees should be represented on boards of directors, and by 1966, the proposal had developed into all companies being required to have consultative Works Councils, and a steadily developing framework for involving workers in decision-making and the sharing of profits was a theme of Liberal manifestos until 1979.[33]

Social liberal influences can also be seen in two other areas. One is the attitude

to decentralisation, a core social liberal concern since the days of T.H. Green. This
has not meant reducing the size of the state, but relocating it to a more local level.
Devolution for Scotland and Wales were Party commitments before 1945, and
from the 1964 manifesto, devolution was also applied to England with support
(albeit in rather vague terms) for regionalism, and this approach remained crucial
for the Party in future years.[34] In addition to decentralisation, the Party's commitment to education in post-1945 manifestos was also influenced by social liberalism
which had always emphasised education as a key battleground in the struggle for
creating greater equality of opportunity. In 1945, the Liberal Party proposed
raising the school leaving age and increasing nursery places; in 1950, reducing
primary school class sizes was a central issue; 1959's manifesto proposed expanding
universities; and similar ideas were reworked throughout the 1960s and 1970s.[35]

However, even though education was a concern for social liberals, other types of
liberals also emphasised its importance and we should not necessarily see Liberal
post-war education policy as being solely inspired by social liberalism. Moreover,
what is striking about manifestos from 1945 to 1979 is how far they major on
constitutional reform – which is a policy area influenced by all types of liberalism
within the Liberal Party – and include a strong commitment to civil liberties. It was
perhaps the unifying nature, in internal party terms, of this approach to politics
which placed it at the heart of the Liberal agenda. One should be careful, therefore,
of overstating social liberal influence on the 1945–79 Liberal manifestos.

Exactly the same can be said of the two Liberal–SDP Alliance manifestos of
1983 and 1987, which were heavily influenced by the context of the SDP's departure from Labour and the wider political context of the day. One would expect that
the SDP would have brought from the Labour Party a greater concern with equality than that held by some Liberals, and that this might have made social democrats
natural allies with social liberals. Thus the 1983 manifesto, *Working Together for
Britain* was built around the idea of industrial partnership in a firm social liberal
tradition, and there were similar arguments in the 1987 manifesto.[36] However, this
emphasis can also be seen to have flowed from political positioning: in the context
of 1983, and to a lesser extent 1987, the Alliance was firmly a 'centre' party. It was
against the aggressively free market approach of the Conservatives and equally
opposed to the nationalisation and trade union influence favoured by the Labour
Party. Thus the emphasis on industrial partnership gave the Party a distinctive position in the centre ground, but that owed as much to political context and the
nature of the SDP's birth as to a strong belief in social liberalism. Meanwhile, the
two Alliance manifestos were heavily influenced by an emphasis on constitutional
reform and the issues over which the Labour split had occurred such as multilateral nuclear disarmament and membership of NATO and the EEC. Again, the
political context, and the way in which the Party could best exploit the opportunities provided by it, were crucial in giving these issues saliency as well as the fact
that few Liberals could object to a high profile for constitutional reform.

In 1992, in the first Liberal Democrat manifesto, the agenda began to shift in a
more overtly social liberal direction with a new emphasis on Keynesian measures

to kick-start the economy at a time of recession. In particular, the Party argued for an emergency programme of investment in infrastructure and public works to boost employment. It also included a policy that was the most well-known policy for the party over three general elections: increasing investment in education, funded by increasing the basic rate of tax by 1p in the pound. These two policies seem to point to the Party turning in a more egalitarian and social liberal direction in the early 1990s, and they certainly suggest a continued influence for social liberalism. However, they also relate to the political context of the recession of the early 1990s and long-term underinvestment in public services by the Conservatives, both of which made these issues especially politically salient. Moreover, other traditional liberal concerns on constitutional reform were still included in the 1992 manifesto, and some of the rhetoric around business was markedly free market and pro-competition in its tone.[37] This balance between social liberalism and economic liberalism would remain in the 1997 manifesto.[38]

However, from 1999, when Charles Kennedy took over as the Liberal Democrat leader, the Party did turn in a more self-consciously social liberal direction. One clear sign of this was the Party's development of a distinctively social liberal interpretation of 'freedom' in its 2000 pre-manifesto, *Freedom in a Liberal Society*. Freedom was promoted as the core value which characterised the Party and was defined in three ways: the classical liberal concern with liberty; the core belief of New Liberalism a century before that social injustice was a barrier to freedom; and the growing view that pollution and environmental change should be seen as limits to freedom, prompting the Party to put policies for 'green action' in every section of the pre-manifesto. The social justice dimension to freedom was particularly important and the Party borrowed heavily from social liberal themes set out by Hobhouse ninety years before.

The Party continued to develop the core value of 'freedom' in the 2002 values document *It's About Freedom*. This was commissioned before the 2001 General Election and represented the first full reassessment of the Party's principles since 1988 when it published *Our Different Vision*. The document's summary began with a classical liberal definition of freedom: 'we start from the autonomy and worth of the individual. Any interference with the freedom of the individual to live as he or she chooses requires to be justified, if it can be, by reference to a system of values drawn from that primary recognition of individual freedom.' However, it also stressed that individual freedom is 'limited or non-existent if he or she is prevented by economic deprivation, lack of education, disadvantage or discrimination from exercising choices about how to live or from participating in the democratic process'.[39] The document also approvingly quoted Hobhouse on equality.[40]

Over 2001–2 the Party also refined its policies on tax and decentralisation. On the former, the shift in policy might indicate a move away from social liberalism, yet here as on previous occasions, political context dictated the direction of policy. From 1997, but particularly after the 2001 election, in the context of steadily rising investment in public services which exceeded the additional funding put forward by the Liberal Democrats, many in the parliamentary party asked if more funding for public services remained the right policy. Was it credible to continue to argue, however much Labour increased budgets, that even more spending funded by higher taxes was the answer to problems in the public services? Of course, there were other arguments that could have been made for higher taxation: for example, the need to tackle economic inequality, or the differential environmental impact of different social and economic groups. However, in the 2001–3 period, it was remarkable that these arguments were not live ones within the Party, which instead framed debates on taxation primarily within the question of whether or not more money was needed for public services. Had social liberals within the Party made a wider case for the redistributive benefits of taxation – as they have done more recently – they might have been less on the defensive in the evolving policy agenda. As it was, the debate rumbled on for some time focused on taxation, and it was not until the Party's response to the budget in 2003 that the 1p addition was finally dropped. Despite this, the Party retained the policy of scrapping tuition fees, calculating that this could now be funded by the 50p rate, which, due to the country's rising affluence, would bring in larger revenues than in previous years.

Further major shifts in the Party's tax policy have taken place since the 2005 General Election. At the 2006 Party Conference a new package was endorsed. This did not include any proposals for putting up income tax: the 50p rate was dropped. Instead, a cut of up to 2% was proposed for the basic income tax rate, while the threshold of the 40p rate was raised to £50,000 per year. This was to be funded by changes to capital gains tax (meaning that the wealthiest would pay more than previously) and tax relief on pensions contributions, plus new green taxes, particularly on the most polluting cars and on airline flights.[41] The Party had proposed green taxation measures before, but the scale of them, and their centrality to the entire Liberal Democrat programme, greatly elevated their importance. Meanwhile, although the Liberal Democrats have talked the language of redistribution throughout the time in which they have emphasised social justice, the 2006 proposals were actually more redistributive than the Party's previous plans since they involved capital gains tax increases for the wealthiest alongside cuts in income tax for the bulk of tax payers. So even though some see the dropping of the 50p rate policy as symbolising a reduction of the Party's commitment to reducing inequality, the alternative adopted will actually do more to redistribute wealth than the symbolic policy. That argument was central to the leadership's success in dropping any increases to income tax for top earners at the Party's September 2006 conference.

At the same time as making changes to tax policy, the Liberal Democrats have placed a renewed emphasis on decentralisation in public services. One must stress 'renewed' because the Party has not suddenly become decentralist in the last decade. However, it has fleshed out some previously vague ideas on how decentralised public services would be run. Crucial to this was the Public Services Working Group, led by Chris Huhne in 2001–2. The group's report in the summer of 2002 contained several major proposals, some of which have subsequently been altered. However, the overall thrust of greater democratic local accountability, and new powers for local authorities to take major financial decisions, set the tone for the Party's future public services policy. Meanwhile, the group proposed far fewer central targets in public services, with the aim of freeing up professionals in schools and hospitals. It also showed that the Party was willing to experiment with the way in which services were delivered 'by encouraging the growth of mutual/voluntary providers as an attractive further option for public service provision as Public Benefit Organisations'.[42] Despite the rhetorical commitment of social liberals to such diversity of provision, they had never done anything to promote this within the Party and the new policy should be seen as coming from other strands of thought, especially economic liberalism with its emphasis on the value of competition.

Conclusion

What do the recent changes in Party policy mean for the place of social liberalism – in so far as it represents a commitment to greater equality and greater use of the state to secure that – within the Liberal Democrats now and in the future? In terms of the central aim of reducing inequality in order to advance freedom, the Party now has a more redistributive tax policy than it has had in recent decades. Arguably, in dropping the proposal to increase the top rate of income tax (even if it was an important piece of political symbolism), and accepting a new tax package, the Party moved more in a social liberal direction by advancing greater redistribution. Moreover, in arguing for decentralisation of public services, the Party is firmly in line with the localist element of social liberalism: this approach seeks not to *reduce* the role of state and encourage individual provision, but instead to *relocate* the state at a level where it can be made more accountable to communities. However, in proposing a diversity of providers in public services, the Party's approach to public services can be seen as being at odds with an aspect of social liberalism: support for the state as a key provider of healthcare and education.

In the Party's increasing emphasis on environmental policies, one can also detect social liberal influences in advocacy of state intervention in markets which fail to deliver environmental goods. This can be seen as a simple adaptation of the social liberal advocacy of intervention to secure greater equality. However, it is also the case that environmentalism has grown within the Party in its own right, independent of social liberalism. Like constitutional reform, and personal liberalism, environmental policies have a life of their own within the Liberal Democrats.

A more open question is how far the Party will continue to adopt a social liberal approach to the state. Under Paddy Ashdown, it became a vogue in the Party to respond to centralism by talking of the need for 'a government which steers more, and rows less', a phrase which originated with American New Right thinkers David Osborne and Ted Gaebler, but which reached a wider British audience in the joint statement by Tony Blair and Gerhard Schroeder in June 1999.[43] That could be seen as an implicit attack on 'big government' and the state. Yet under Charles Kennedy, Liberal Democrats preferred to describe the location rather than the size of government as the problem, wanting a decentralised rather than a centralised state, but state action nonetheless. The Party was reinventing and refocusing the state for social liberal ends rather than destroying it.

The choice for the Party now is how far it will continue to react to Labour's centralism by devolving power to democratic local government – the local state – or whether it will adopt more consumer-based individualist approaches. In the *Orange Book*, there was very little explicit consideration of the state. Yet implicit in its proposal for an insurance-based health system,[44] was a view that the state should be drastically reduced as a provider, and even a commissioner, of public services. Instead, individuals would become consumers in a marketplace of services, making choices about how much they want to spend on insuring themselves, and buying their services from a range of providers. Although the state would have a role in ensuring that there was a safety net for the poorest, its role would greatly diminish. Such approach is diametrically opposed to current Liberal Democrat policy which emphasises a crucial role for democratic decentralised government. Even if current policy accepts that the state should be able to commission services from a range of different providers,[45] government at a local level, rather than individuals, makes the choices. Moreover, from a social liberal perspective, social insurance schemes might well exacerbate those inequalities which social liberals already wish to reduce. The most recent contributions to these debates come from two sources which may suggest that the impetus for new ideas is coming more from the social liberal camp within the Party. The first, produced by the Institute for Public Policy Research, contains contributions from both those who have been labelled as 'economic Liberals' and those who are more comfortable with a 'social Liberal' badge. However, it makes a strong case for Liberal Democrats needing to focus more on 'agency' (or socio-economic constraints on freedom) in the future, and emphasises the importance of the state. Meanwhile, an edited volume of essays takes an overtly social liberal approach to policy, arguing for a reinvention of the state along localised lines.[46] However, even if we are now in a time when social liberals are driving the debate forwards, it is not clear what the Party will adopt as its policy. In particular, the fate of such ideas on the state within the Liberal Democrats has crucial implications for whether the Party is likely to go in a more or less social liberal direction – pursuing greater equality through state action – in the future.

Notes

1 I am very grateful to my colleague at Goldsmiths, Ed Randall, for reading an early draft and providing a wide range of insightful and challenging comments. He will (still) not agree with everything contained in this chapter, but it is all the better for his engagement with it.

2 D. Laws, 'Reclaiming Liberalism: a Liberal agenda for the Liberal Democrats', in p. Marshall and D. Laws (eds), *The Orange Book: Reclaiming Liberalism* (Profile, London, 2004), pp. 24 and 36.

3 Ibid., p. 36.
4 D. Brack, R.S. Grayson and D. Howarth (eds), *Reinventing the State: Social Liberalism in the 21ˢᵗ Century* (Politico's, London, 2007).
5 R.S. Grayson, 'Social democracy or social liberalism? Ideological sources of Liberal Democrat policy', *Political Quarterly*, 78:1 (2007), pp. 32–9.
6 G. Thomas, 'Thomas Hill Green', *The Reformer*, 5, 4 (Summer 1998), pp. 15–17. See also Thomas's study, *The Moral Philosophy of T.H. Green* (Clarendon, Oxford, 1987).
7 T.H. Green, *Lectures on the Principles of Political Obligation* (first published 1883: Longmans, London, 1941 edition), p. 8.
8 M. Freeden, *The New Liberalism: An Ideology of Social Reform* (Clarendon, Oxford, 1978), p. 58.
9 L.T. Hobhouse, *Liberalism* (first published 1911: Galaxy Press, New York, 1964 edition), p. 21.
10 Ibid., p. 48. For use by Liberal Democrats, see Liberal Democrats, *It's About Freedom* (Liberal Democrats, London, 2002), p. 11 and C. Kennedy, *The Future of Politics* (HarperCollins, London, 2001), p. 82.
11 Hobhouse, *Liberalism*, p. 71.
12 Freeden, *The New Liberalism*, pp. 70–1.
13 J.A. Hobson, *Confessions of an Economic Heretic* (Allen and Unwin, London, 1938), p. 126.
14 R. Skidelsky, *John Maynard Keynes: Volume Two, The Economist as Saviour 1920–1937* (Macmillan, London, 1992), pp. 537–623.
15 See The Royal Economic Society's 2000 Annual Conference Report at www.res.org.uk/society/mediabriefings/conferences/conf2000.asp (accessed 16ᵗʰ February 2008).
16 J. Harris, *William Beveridge: A Biography* (Clarendon, Oxford, 1997), pp. 365–412.
17 Liberal Democrats, *It's About Freedom*, p. 11.
18 Ibid., p. 11.
19 J. Rawls, *A Theory of Justice* (Clarendon, Oxford, 1972), p. 60.
20 J. Grimond, *The Liberal Future* (Faber and Faber, London, 1959), pp. 101 and 107.
21 J. Grimond, *The Liberal Challenge* (Hollis and Carter, London, 1963).
22 Grayson, 'Social democracy or social liberalism?' pp. 34–6.
23 I. Berlin, *Four Essays on Liberty* (Oxford University Press, Oxford, 1969), pp. 131 and xxxix.
24 For a review of M. Ignatieff's *Isaiah Berlin: A Life* (Chatto and Windus, London, 1999), which places Isaiah Berlin in a Liberal Democrat context, see T. Razzall, 'A fox or a hedgehog?', *The Reformer*, 6, 4 (1999), pp. 16–17.
25 M. Ignatieff, *The Needs of Strangers* (Chatto and Windus, London, 1984), p. 136.
26 Centre for Reform, *Identity and Politics: A Discussion with Michael Ignatieff and Sean Neeson* (Centre for Reform, London, 1998).
27 C. Russell, *An Intelligent Person's Guide to Liberalism* (Duckworth, London, 1999), p. 66.
28 Grayson, 'Social democracy or social liberalism?', pp. 38–9; N. Clegg and R. Grayson, *Learning from Europe: Lessons in Education* (Centre for European Reform, London, 2002).
29 I. Dale (ed.), *Liberal Party General Election Manifestos 1900–1997* (Routledge, London, 2000), p. 63.
30 Ibid., p. 113.
31 Ibid., pp. 159–60.

32 Ibid., p. 195.
33 Ibid., pp. 101, 109 and 193.
34 Ibid., p. 111.
35 Ibid., pp. 65, 76 and 100.
36 Ibid., pp. 207–12 and 249–52.
37 Ibid., pp. 287, 289 and 299.
38 Ibid., pp. 324 and 331.
39 Liberal Democrats, *Freedom in a Liberal Society* (Liberal Democrats, London, 2002) pp. 7–8.
40 Hobhouse, *Liberalism*, p. 48.
41 Liberal Democrats, *Fairer, Simpler, Greener: Policies for Tax Reform* (2006).
42 Liberal Democrats, *Quality, Innovation, Choice* (2002), p. 10.
43 Liberal Democrats, *Moving Ahead* (1998), p. 10; D. Osborne and T. Gaebler, *Reinventing Government: How the Entrepreneurial Spirit is Transforming the Public Sector* (Addison-Wesley, Reading MA, 1992); www.socialdemocrats.org/blairandschroeder6-8–99.html (accessed 16th February 2008).
44 D. Laws, 'UK health services: a Liberal agenda for reform and renewal', in Marshall and Laws (eds), *Orange Book*, pp. 191–210.
45 Liberal Democrats, *Quality, Innovation, Choice*, p. 10.
46 J. Margo (ed.), *Beyond Liberty: Is the Future of Liberalism Progressive?* (IPPR, London, 2007); Brack, Grayson and Howarth (eds), *Reinventing the State.*

Part II

Themes and issues

Constitutional reform

For the Liberal Democrats, constitutional reform has remained at the core of the Party's ethos as the embodiment of a genuinely third force in national politics. The issue is integrally connected to its identity and strategy as a radical alternative to both Labour and Conservative parties.

Michael Foley, *The Politics of the British Constitution*[1]

Foley's assessment of the significance of Liberal Democrat constitutional policy at the start of the Blair premiership had been true of Liberals for the whole of the post-war period, and remains true today. Continuous demands for reform of parliament, the courts and British elections have been something of a badge of honour for the third party since the Second World War, but their motives for wearing it, and the consistency of Liberal policy in historical context, have been questioned by some observers. Mapping out Liberal policy over the last century, Bogdanor wrote recently that 'there is no specifically Liberal approach to the constitution. The Liberal approach has differed according to whether the Liberals have been a party of government or a party of opposition without a realistic hope of power.'[2] The questions addressed here, therefore, are not only of what the policy of constitutional reform has included, but also why and to what effect it was adopted.

Liberal commitment to constitutional reform is reflected in the Party's struggles over reform of the Lords before the First World War and the extension of the franchise in the nineteenth century. Earlier still, the tradition of liberal thought represented by Mill and Bentham, Charles James Fox and John Locke advocated constitutional government, separation of powers and wider participation.

Since 1945, the depth of the commitment and the nature of reform have sometimes been variable. That fluctuation is, according to critics, a signal of the circumstantial, even cynical nature of the policy's origins; for the Liberal Democrats themselves it is, to the extent that they acknowledge it, a reflection of the limited scope for manoeuvre the Party has enjoyed for the last fifty years. The following explores what is and has been Liberal policy, its determinants and its impact. The examination of policy will take in issues of electoral, parliamentary and judicial reform; it is, of course, also worth comparing and contrasting the patterns of policy in these areas and those of devolution and European integration dealt with elsewhere in this book, which also have a constitutional dimension.

Electoral reform

Liberal policy in this area is evident from manifestos, Assembly resolutions and other Party publications calling for the introduction of proportional representation, preferably using the Single Transferable Vote. By the 1950s, electoral reform was advocated by leading Liberals from all wings of the Party including Muir,[3] Samuel,[4] Harris,[5] Lakeman and Lambert,[6] Grimond,[7] Fulford,[8] Bonham Carter[9] and even T.L. Horabin who stressed the way in which inter-war Conservative dominance had been made possible by first-past-the-post.[10] All but two of these writers gave particular endorsement to STV, as did Wallace in a later review of Liberal policy.[11]

Liberals had a history of supporting the widest possible representation in parliament, drawing on a tradition including Fox, Bentham and Russell. From its first conception by Thomas Hare in 1854, STV was favoured by leading Liberals such as J.S. Mill, and others promoted proportional alternatives such as the Limited Vote, advocated by Russell in 1867. Half of the MPs who founded the Electoral Reform Society in 1884 were Liberals, and supporters included other Liberals such as *Guardian* Editor C.P. Scott. For Liberals, PR offered the combined advantages of encouraging participation, consensus-building and the best guarantee of representing minorities – of religious faiths, geographical communities, or of the propertied – against the overbearing majority or plurality.

Adopted in the 1920s, this policy was confirmed in a wartime report[12] and at the Speaker's Conference of 1944, Megan Lloyd George and Lord Rea introduced and supported resolutions calling for the use of proportional representation or the Alternative Vote. Liberal MPs proposed PR during the passage of the 1945 and 1948 Representation of the People Acts.[13] PR was a regular commitment in Liberal manifestos, which referred either to STV's preferential character (1945), its proportionality (1955, 1959, 1966 and October 1974), its specific name (1950, 1970, 1979 and 1983) or its use in Ireland (February 1974). In 1982 details of a proposed electoral system were set out in an Alliance Report[14] and in 1987 the 'Great Reform Charter' was the centrepiece of the Party's campaign. The place of electoral reform in the official programme is undisputed.

This consistency of policy is perhaps unsurprising; but the intensity of the Liberals' commitment to this policy is striking. In almost every decade since the Second World War it has prevented Liberals from taking a share in national power; it is the *sine qua non* of Liberal co-operation.

Following attempts at creating an electoral pact with the Liberals from 1945 onwards, Churchill offered to establish an enquiry into electoral reform in his reply to the King's speech in 1950, and offered a Cabinet post to Clement Davies in October 1951. Though Davies declined, as Prime Minister Churchill received a

Liberal deputation on reform in February 1953 and Violet Bonham Carter assured the Liberal Assembly the following April that the Prime Minister was in favour of PR; but in 1954 he declined any enquiry.[15] Despite this, Liberals including Bonham Carter and Jeremy Thorpe took part in a deputation to Home Secretary and former colleague Gwilym Lloyd George in February 1955 to demand a Royal Commission on Voting. Lloyd George was 'very laconic' according to Thorpe, and offered no support for the proposal.[16] Only isolated voices on the right showed an interest in electoral reform after this.[17]

Bonham Carter's embittered rebuke to Lloyd George which followed conveys the frustration of one who had favoured co-operation with the Tories that the Liberals' central aspiration had been so dismissively disposed of:

> When Winston made his speech in the House of Commons asking for an enquiry into our electoral system my hand was immensely strengthened. There were of course a few cynics who said he was 'leading us down the garden path' but the great majority of Liberals were full of gratitude and simple faith and I know that large numbers voted Conservative in the many seats where the was no Liberal candidate in <u>1951</u> on this one issue. I encouraged them to hope and to believe – assuring them that he meant business. It is now 1955 – and nothing has happened and nothing looks like happening. You can imagine there is widespread disillusionment.[18]

The same importance of PR is confirmed by Clement Davies's correspondence entreating Attlee to consider electoral reform as the basis of a Lib-Lab agreement during 1950–51.[19] On all sides and to all comers, electoral reform was at the top of the Liberal wish list.

The next time parliamentary arithmetic gave the Liberals hope of wringing concessions from the main parties on electoral reform was during the first Wilson Administration of 1964–66. Again it was the Liberal insistence upon PR which became the sticking point in the attempt to develop a relationship with Labour. Aware that this would be part of any deal, Wilson allowed supporters to raise the possibility of reform publicly, and asked Transport House to research the likely effect of using AV.[20] The outcome was pessimistic enough for Labour to drive Wilson to hold another election rather than introduce reform. Though some opinion in the Labour Party did turn towards the introduction of PR after heavy defeats in the local elections in the south of England in 1967–68, the prospect of reform had again receded. The last public supporters of reform had disappeared from the Labour benches by 1974.[21]

It was at this point, however, that circumstances caused the main parties to address Liberal demands for electoral reform again. The inconclusive result of the February 1974 election forced Edward Heath to concede to Jeremy Thorpe the promise of a Speaker's Conference on the Electoral System. Though this was insufficient to forge a coalition agreement, the promise was retained in the October Conservative manifesto. Three years later electoral reform was again on the agenda as one of only three specific legislative demands made by the Liberals at the start of the Lib-Lab Pact in March 1977 following consultations throughout the Party.[22] The electorally and organisationally weak position of the Liberals meant that they felt able to demand PR only for elections to the European Assembly and the proposed devolved institutions in Scotland and Wales; and even on these issues they were eventually outmanoeuvred by the use of free votes in the Commons, which went heavily against reform.

The defeat of PR did not end the Pact immediately, but it meant that the Liberals had only negative reasons for continuing it. A meeting of the MPs voted 4–6 against ending the Pact, but in some cases out of loyalty to Steel, and only after he had pretended to them that Callaghan was going to see the Queen. Steel waited a month and a half to hold a special Assembly to decide the future of the Pact – called for by the Party Council if PR failed – so as to let tempers cool, and effectively placed his leadership on the line. Though the Assembly voted in favour of continuation, Michie and Hoggart concluded that this was only because Liberals recognised their survival could be at stake, and even PR for European elections had to take second place: 'however important it might be to the Party – and it was important to an almost lunatic extent – it meant little or nothing to voters'.[23]

Away from even the periphery of power in the 1980s, Liberals continued to campaign for electoral reform, for example by supporting the Electoral Reform Society's cross-party million-strong petition calling for PR after the particularly disproportional 1983 election outcome.[24] So obvious was support for electoral reform as a condition for the formation of the Alliance with the SDP that even those former Labour ministers who formed the new Party and had not previously expressed enthusiasm for PR made no attempt to raise the issue: on a walk following discussions amongst Liberal and SDP leaders in April 1981, Shirley Williams asked Liberal Party President Richard Holme rhetorically and mischievously, 'Does this mean I'll have to support proportional representation?'[25] As 1997 approached, the convergence of New Labour and the Liberal Democrats on constitutional matters brought hope that a change of government would bring a chance to implement the long-held policy of reform.

Neil Kinnock had flirted with the possibility of electoral reform during the 1992 General Election campaign, but it was John Smith who made the commitment to a referendum on the question, a promise which was strengthened with the relationship between Blair and Ashdown. Within two months of the arrival of the new Labour leader, Ashdown was stressing that PR was 'the one issue on which Blair has to be moved'; in later discussions he insisted to Robin Cook that any co-operation required 'a reasonable prospect of PR for Westminster' as well as a guarantee of it at European and devolved levels, and assured David Steel that he had made PR a basic requirement of the relationship. He specified STV as his preferred system to Blair and told him that his reluctance on the issue was 'the only thing that stands in the way' of a full realignment of the party system.[26]

Commitments to proportional elections to the Scottish Parliament, the Welsh Assembly and for European elections appeared in the Labour manifesto and were fulfilled within two years of the 1997 election. The Mayors of London and other towns and cities were elected from 2000 onwards using the preferential Supplementary Vote system. The Independent Commission on Voting established to identify an alternative system by which the Commons might be elected following a referendum, also promised in the Labour manifesto, was chaired by leader of the Liberal Democrat peers Roy Jenkins. Although the system proposed by Jenkins in October 1998 was not STV but AV plus, the Liberal Democrat leader welcomed the prospect of a referendum, and gave his support to Jenkins's recommendation, albeit on the negative basis of 'the opportunity to break out of the prison of first-past-the-post'.[27]

Of course, there was no referendum. Opinion in the Labour Party turned sharply away from reform, and the cool reaction of Blair and Home Secretary Jack Straw to Jenkins left Ashdown 'very angry and very depressed', knowing that the failure to win PR meant he would have to resign – initially, he thought, the following week. The indignation and hurt he expressed to Blair the following day confirms the non-negotiable status of PR in the Liberal policy profile, and its tone is reminiscent of Violet Bonham Carter's attack on Gwilym Lloyd George a third of a century earlier:

> We are all feeling very bruised. The form of words you used was not what we had originally agreed. And our input made no substantial difference to them. They were, if anything, even worse than the ones you and I discussed earlier in the week. The word 'persuasive' had been removed. And I was shocked that you were not even prepared to use the words you had used the day before at Prime Minister's Questions on the timing of the referendum. It would have cost you nothing but would have been of immense help to me. I spent most of last night wondering whether the whole thing was worth the candle.[28]

A statement in the 2001 Labour manifesto, agreed after Charles Kennedy pressurised the government in his speech to the Spring Liberal Democrat Conference, promised only another review of electoral systems following the devolved elections of 2003, but that review was never held.[29] The Scottish Liberal Democrats won their own compensation after the 2003 vote, however, by insisting upon a review of the electoral system for Scottish local authorities. This resulted in the introduction of a variant of STV for those elections, which was first used in 2007.

The perceived breach of promise over PR soured relations between the Liberal Democrats and New Labour before tax, tuition fees or Iraq emerged as issues, and has contributed significantly to the fate of both parties and their leaders since. The legacy of determination to hold out on the issue was reflected by Menzies Campbell in a recent statement on the prospects of working with any other party in government at national level: 'PR is fundamental to our analysis of what is wrong with the United Kingdom. It would be inconceivable for us to be in a full-blown coalition with a party that does not accept that.'[30]

Liberals are sometimes accused of selling themselves cheaply to other parties: in fact they more often price themselves out of the market by setting electoral reform as the tariff. It is indispensable and unanimously agreed as a policy, and almost always the starting-point of negotiations with others. When the Party is at its weakest – 1951 or 1977, for example – electoral reform may drop out of the manifesto or become one of several terms in negotiations. Normally, however, Liberals are prepared to go back into the political wilderness rather than be denied the promised land of PR. This might explain the mistaken impression that Liberals have 'no cause, theme, culture or strategy, beyond a yearning for the eternal coalition of proportional representation'.[31] It has been a necessary, if insufficient, condition of being a post-war Liberal.

This is explained by the convergence of interest and ideology. Whilst there is a centuries-long tradition of some Liberals favouring proportional representation, this is consolidated by the knowledge that such systems usually give Liberals greater representation than first-past-the-post, and that this policy can sometimes be a distinctive electoral asset. Hence critics have described the policy as being 'all about winning a slice of power for parties that have failed to convince the electorate of their case'[32] and even 'the surest sign of despair'.[33] The debate as to the motives of post-war Liberals in favouring electoral reform assumes that they are mutually exclusive, whereas the combination of both is inscrutable in its balance, but enhanced in its impact. That effect is more easily quantifiable: Liberal persistence on the issue of electoral reform has helped to sustain its profile to the point at which United Kingdom elections at all levels other than Westminster are conducted using electoral systems of varying degrees of proportionality. This is an achievement with which any post-war Liberal would have been pleased.

Parliamentary reform

Liberals have periodically proposed reforms of the Commons and its behaviour, usually focusing upon the limited opportunities for backbenchers and minor parties and the malign influence of the whips. Criticism of the power of the executive is a regular theme, addressed by Lord Samuel as early as 1947,[34] and particularly bluntly reasserted in the 2005 manifesto.[35] Remedies consistently advanced for this include the introduction of fixed-term parliaments and strengthening of Select Committees. Debate about structural change, however, has more regularly focused on the powers and composition of the House of Lords. On this, like the other parties, Liberals have had less difficulty in agreeing on the error of the status quo than in achieving unanimity about the best route of reform.

Liberals have a history of conflict with the Lords: since Victorian times their propaganda has promised to 'End it or Mend it', and their last government promised that the 1911 Parliament Act was the prelude to the substitution of the upper House by a more 'popular' chamber. Out of office, however, Liberals found themselves forced to respond to others' proposals. This was partly responsible for the inconsistencies and divisions amongst them which emerged; however, there is also evidence of a more fundamental uncertainty about the role of the democratic mandate which modern Liberal thought has not fully resolved.

Liberals after 1945 promoted reforms determined by broad principles rather than a strict policy: that the Lords was to be a complementary, not rival, chamber to the Commons, and that wholesale election and the legislative veto were therefore inappropriate; that no party should have an overall majority in it; that membership should be earned through contribution to public life and not hereditary in itself; and that, as working legislators, members should be paid, and could be removed if they proved unfit.[36]

During the passage of the 1949 Parliament Act reducing the Lords' delaying powers to one year, Liberal MPs initially objected that the hereditary principle was being left untouched, but Samuel, Liberal leader in the Lords, initiated an all-party informal discussion about the House's composition and powers. This eventually broke down. The Liberals blamed this on Conservative intransigence, and subsequently – if reluctantly – supported the Bill on its second reading. Ten years later another opportunity to showcase Liberal principles was lost, when the Life Peers Bill was supported by Liberals in the Lords, Rea describing it as 'a small advance to that reform which we … consider to be desirable' and Samuel concurring that the Bill 'is inadequate; it is illogical; but we are not likely to get anything better'.[37] Despite this, the measure was forthrightly opposed by Clement Davies, who told the Commons 'I see no virtue in it; I think it is a pretence', and Grimond described it as 'a shot in the dark'.[38] Although all Liberals referred to the key elements of the Leaders' Conference of 1947–48 and the subsequent White Paper[39] as the basis of Liberal policy, and thus the differences were tactical rather than matters of principle, the poor co-ordination between Liberals in the two chambers was the most obvious feature of the episode.

The next episode of attempted Lords reform gave a similar impression. Jeremy Thorpe and Lord Byers were members of the Inter-Party Conference preceding the Parliament (No. 2) Bill, which sat from November 1967 onwards. Byers is described by one historian of the period as one of the 'committed reformers' who included Crossman and Callaghan. However, when the White Paper was presented to parliament, proposing a further reduction in the legislative delaying powers of the Lords without changes in composition, all eight Liberal MPs present voted against; but of Liberal peers, thirteen voted 'content' and only three 'not content'. By the second reading of the Bill itself in February 1969, the MPs had divided three for, three against and one abstention.[40]

All parties were split over the Crossman reforms, and so the Bill failed. To a large degree the divisions between Liberals over all these post-war proposals were tactical: some Liberals objected to the divorcing of the issues of composition and powers, whereas others were prepared to accept only part of what Liberals wanted. There were also problems of poor co-ordination between the Liberals in the two Houses: regular joint meetings of the peers and MPs were not held until the 1960s, an omission about which complaints were made to Davies and Samuel; as Party leader, Grimond met his opposite number in the Lords formally no more than once every eighteen months, and one Liberal Lord told Janet Morgan in the 1970s that 'Liberal MPs tend to regard us as being very wayward. Jo Grimond was very anti-peer.'[41] Yet after organisation has been improved, and composition of the Lords has become the central issue of legislation, Liberals have still been unable to unite fully.

Optimism was high amongst Liberal Democrats that the proposals agreed by Robin Cook and Robert Maclennan prior to the 1997 Labour victory would herald the final transformation of the Lords into an elected, or mainly elected, body. The following ten years have shown that as with electoral reform, these hopes were only partially fulfilled, and – unlike electoral reform – Liberals have been at least somewhat divided amongst themselves.

Liberal Democrats welcomed the initial announcement of the removal of hereditary peers and the establishment of the Wakeham Commission to set out how the transition to an elected chamber would proceed. Lord Thurso, grandson of former Party leader Archibald Sinclair, said after hearing the 1998 Queen's Speech that 'I feel very elated that something I have believed in and worked for politically for quite a long time is actually going to come to pass, which is the reform of this House';[42] on the publication of the White Paper for the 1999 House of Lords Bill and the announcement of the Wakeham Commission, spokesman in the Commons Robert Maclennan declared himself 'delighted there is now the prospect of proposals for proper reform before the next election'.[43]

There was already an element of strategic pushing of the government in such talk. As Lord Richard and Cook lost influence in Labour, the prospects of a democratic replacement for the Lords were already receding. Ashdown had already spoken angrily to Blair about the timing of the White Paper, early sight of which had been denied to Liberal Democrats, saying 'I don't want something so clearly inimical to what we signed up to in Cook/Maclennan published on the day I go.'[44] When the government conceded the preservation of 92 hereditary peers to the Conservatives, Liberal Democrat Lords abstained; and less than a year later the report of the Wakeham Commission, on which there were no Liberal Democrats, reported, further undermining hopes of achieving a predominantly elected second chamber. Maclennan dismissed it as 'probably the least persuasive royal commission report to have been issued in my political lifetime. It is neither informed by democratic principle nor a practical concern to strengthen Parliament's capability to oversee the work of central government.'[45]

In the next parliament, Liberal Democrats rejected Cook's proposals for a four-fifths-appointed House, and issued their own, consistent with the policy in the 2001 manifesto, of introducing an elected Senate with more legislative powers,[46] 80% elected by STV based upon Euro-constituencies for 12–year terms. However, the government's abortive attempt to resolve the issue in February 2003 exposed divisions. Seven different alternative compositions for the Lords were set before MPs and peers, and amongst the 48 Liberal Democrat MPs voting, no more than seven opposed any of the three predominantly-elected options; in the Lords, however, a third of Liberal Democrats, including former leader in the upper chamber Bill Rodgers, and former MPs Ronnie Fearn and Russell Johnston, voted for a fully-appointed House. 15 out of 49 opposed a fully-elected House, and 13 out of 53 a four-fifths-elected Lords. The Liberal Democrats' 2005 manifesto

sneered that 'reform of the House of Lords has been botched by Labour'[47] but it
was evident that a significant minority of their own supporters in the Lords had
refused to come into line.

This situation was repeated at the most recent debate on Lords reform. On 7th
March 2007, all 59 Liberal Democrat MPs present voted for the option of a fully-
elected second chamber. 'We took the view,' said Chief Whip Paul Burstow, 'that
given we'd had a consistent policy position for ninety – nearly a hundred – years,
it would be actually quite odd for us to not whip.'[48] A week later however, 15
Liberal Democrat peers – more than a quarter of those voting – were led by Lord
Steel against the Liberal Democrat whip and in support of a fully-appointed upper
house. Steel had already argued in print that circumstances had changed since the
days when the Liberals favoured an elected second chamber:

> The conditions in which Prime Minister Asquith made his commitment have
> changed in three important respects: the hereditary principle has all but gone;
> the primacy of the House of Commons is universally accepted; and it has now
> been agreed by all parties that none should have a majority in the Lords.[49]

The reaction of Party leader in the Lords Tom McNally to the rebellion was swift
and forthright: 'a veto on constitutional reform by the House of Lords is not
acceptable. It is now up to the House of Commons to assert its primacy. The
Liberal Democrats' 100–year-old commitment to an elected House of Lords
remains intact.'[50]

Liberals have remained committed to reform of the Lords for over a century, but
have been constrained in their practical steps towards this by being out of office,
and by weaknesses in their own organisation and strategic coherence. There is also
reflected in this story, however, a long-term ideological problem for Liberals
connected with the authority of democratic representation. Liberals are not democrats *per se*: they regard democracy as an instrument for the improvement and
protection of individuals; and it can only serve that purpose if properly checked.
Even the most advanced democrats of their time have feared that two elected
Houses could strengthen the hand of the oppressive majority, and therefore jeop-
ardise the Liberal society. That this explains in part Liberal uncertainties about the
composition of the Lords is confirmed in the resonance between Steel and a radical
Liberal parliamentarian of a century and a half earlier: 'If one House represents
popular feeling,' wrote Mill in 1861, 'the other should represent personal
merit, tested and guaranteed by actual public service, and fortified by practical
experience.'[51]

Judicial reform

Advocacy of a special role for the judiciary as the guarantors of civil rights – the
chief purpose of government – is a distinctive feature of liberal thought from Locke
to Madison, Montesquieu to Rawls. The legislature, wrote Locke, 'cannot assume
to its self a power to rule by extempory arbitrary decrees, but is bound to dispense

justice, and decide the rights of the subject, by promulgated standing laws and known authorised judges'.[52] In particular, the separation of the judiciary as defenders of individual and minority rights from the distortive and punitive influences of a parliament increasingly dominated by an overbearing government and popular opinion have characterised liberal policy towards the judiciary. The reasons for this, and the impact of the policy, however, have been mixed.

The Liberals' commitment to civil liberties gave rise after the war to a number of specific promises: concern focused on the increasing use of tribunals to determine rights, particularly in social security cases, and the Liberals demanded a right of access to courts in all appeals. The growing remoteness and power of ministers and officials through delegated legislation and under the Supplies and Services Act 1945 was also condemned, and the Liberals promised more detailed parliamentary powers over Statutory Orders and regulations. The issue of burgeoning executive power highlighted by the Crichel Down case in 1954 was exploited in the 1955 Liberal General Election campaign. The 1950 manifesto pledged that a Liberal Government would make its domestic and colonial administration conform to the UN Declaration of Human Rights, and went on to say that all ministerial orders would be subject to challenge in court, that no one would be tried except in a court of law, and that inspectors' powers to enter private property under the SSA would be reduced.[53]

During the first decade of the post-war era, Liberals focused upon protecting liberties in such a way as to draw the support of Conservative sympathisers. The Liberties of the Subject Bill presented by Lord Reading in 1947 proposed limitations on the use of ministerial powers through delegated legislation, the entrenchment of defendants' rights in tribunals and the assertion of individual workers' rights against trade unions and particularly the closed shop. The Bill eventually failed, but it generated some publicity and morale. In fact on its second reading it was carried by 37 votes to 19 with the support of Conservative peers (including two frontbenchers), as it was again in 1950 when introduced by Samuel. On that occasion, 66 peers joined to support the Bill against 24 who followed the Labour Government whips opposing it.

In 1947, 1950 and 1958, Liberal peers introduced the Preservation of the Rights of the Subject Bills to entrench various individual rights against executive power, which were resisted on each occasion by Labour or Conservative Governments. In November 1952, Clement Davies called for a Select Committee to consider the question of delegated legislation, and was subsequently made chairman of an inquiry on the matter established by the Churchill Government.

Once in office, however, Conservative enthusiasm cooled. Samuel felt obliged to acquiesce in a diluting amendment from Salisbury to his Liberties of the Subject resolution of 1952; by 1956, Grantchester's Coercive Action (Relief) Bill focusing upon the provisions of the Liberties Bill dealing with unions and trading associations was opposed by both main parties. Lord Rea made a further attempt to bring in a Liberties of the Subject Bill, gaining a first reading for it with a sense of historical irony on 4 July 1957.

Related issues included the curtailment of workers' rights by trade unions, on which a Royal Commission and a new charter of rights were proposed; continued press freedom during print and paper shortages or industrial disputes; parliamentary control over broadcasters through the 14–day rule, against which Liberal MPs protested vocally throughout 1955; the abolition of the death penalty;[54] and the elimination of the 'colour bar' both in the UK and abroad. John Arlott and Violet Bonham Carter had both expressed themselves sufficiently controversially about South Africa during broadcasts of *Any Questions?* in the late 1940s that BBC officials raised the matter with their Director-General.[55] Perhaps most distinctive of all was the Party's commitment to the equal pay and treatment of women in government employment, made the subject of a discrete section in the manifestos of 1945 and 1950.

Later, policy on the courts was used to reflect the greater willingness of the Liberals to challenge the Conservative Government and find common ground with Labour. 1956 saw Liberals support Sydney Silverman's Death Penalty Abolition Bill. In March 1960, Lord Swaythling aimed to rationalise and update financial penalties for petty offences. In December 1962, Liberal and Labour peers joined forces to move a successful amendment to the Children and Young Persons Bill, raising the age of criminal responsibility to 12.

Over a ten-year period, these bills established the Liberal peers with a reputation for expertise and interest in human rights legislation which has continued to, and borne fruit in, recent years. Philip Norton acknowledged that 'on certain issues, Liberals have been in the van of a growing and influential movement favouring change … A Bill of Rights has been … such [an] issue, especially so in the House of Lords'.[56] They also built bridges with the other parties at a time when their generosity was important to the Liberals' fortunes.

In the 1960s and 1970s, Liberal MPs supported the introduction by the Wilson Government of the Ombudsman to enforce citizens' rights against government maladministration, and Race Relations laws using the courts to combat prejudice; they also opposed attempts by the same government to remove citizens' rights from immigrants with British passports. Thorpe took particular pride that his MPs had 'led the fight against racialism' in the early part of his leadership.[57]

From 1978 onwards, Liberals pressed for the introduction of a Freedom of Information Bill. The first was brought forward that year after Clement Freud won top place in the ballot to introduce a Private Member's Bill. This attracted considerable support, but was opposed by the Labour Cabinet, and fell when the 1979 election was called. The cause was taken up more successfully nine years later by Archy Kirkwood, whose Access to Personal Files Act gave the public the right to see their manually-held social work and housing records; access to school records, originally in the Bill, was brought in under existing legislation by agreement with the government. In 1988, Kirkwood piloted through the Access to Medical Reports Act, but his Freedom of Information Bill of 1991 was talked out.

This policy area provided fruitful ground for co-operation between the Liberals and the SDP, illustrated by the two parties' reactions to the near-coincidental cases of Sarah Tisdall and Clive Ponting, civil servants prosecuted for disclosing classi-fied information regarding defence. Both cases were used by the Alliance to highlight the need for a 'public interest' defence in such cases; Ponting, a member of the SDP, was feted at the Party's 1984 Conference; Tisdall was made an honorary Vice-President of the Young Liberals.

As with electoral and parliamentary reform, the first Blair administration repre-sented a moment of opportunity for Liberal aspirations to strengthen the role of the judiciary in reigning in the executive. Liberal Democrats supported the intro-duction of the Human Rights Act in 1998, consistent with their own demands of the previous four decades, and sought to embolden the Labour leadership's approach to the issue of freedom of information. The eclipse of David Clarke as the minister responsible saw a dilution of the terms of the Freedom of Information Act and Labour's programme again ran short of Liberal ideals. 'At some political cost,' said Lord Goodhart, 'the Liberal Democrats accepted compromises to the Freedom of Information Bill to ensure speedy passage and implementation of the legislation.' Once the Act was on the statute book, however, the Liberal Democrats fought a rearguard action to widen its impact despite the restrictions which had been imposed by the government. Just after the 2001 election, for example, Party spokesman Norman Baker won a High Court ruling overturning the blanket exemption of the security services from the provisions of the Act,[58] and in Novem-ber Goodhart brought forward a motion in the Lords condemning the government's decision to delay the release of information to individuals until 2005: 'proof' he argued, 'that the Government has lost all the radical impulses it may have once had, and is now a comfortable and compliant prisoner of the Whitehall culture of secrecy'.[59]

The break with New Labour over civil liberties had also appeared in the area of crime, where the extension of police powers and increasing mandatory sentencing characterised government policy, leading the Liberal Democrats to accuse the first Blair Government of 'trying to sound as tough, or tougher, than the Conservatives, but [being] no more effective'. The manifesto went on: 'Labour too often proposes simplistic solutions. Many are impractical or irrelevant. Some actually undermine civil liberties.'[60]

This breach became a chasm with Labour's support for the 'War on Terror' of President Bush. Liberal Democrats were at the forefront of campaigns to win release for detainees in Guantanamo Bay, to investigate alleged 'rendition' flights from UK locations, and to resist in parliament new controls on public protest and, notably, the failed attempt in 2006 to grant the police a 90–day period of deten-tion of terrorist suspects without charge. 'Liberties, once lost,' intoned Shirley Williams in the 2005 manifesto, 'are rarely restored. The freedom of the individual lies at the heart of liberal democracy, and we Liberal Democrats are determined to defend it.'[61]

The belief that the central function of the state is to protect individual freedoms is liberalism's most undisputed tenet within the doctrine's ranks. Yet the ultimate instruments for securing this aim – a written constitution, a binding bill of rights and genuine separation of powers – remain remote dreams. Liberals have stuck to their principles on civil liberties, at times swimming against strong tides of public sentiment on issues of national security or race. They have, however, chosen the liberties to defend to suit the occasion, and win support from the government or opposition of the day; they have played their hand no further than they thought it wise in order to achieve concessions. It remains one of the contradictions of the British constitution that a free citizen's rights are protected only by the state which can threaten those same rights, and by the voices that resist it. Liberals have added to those voices.

Conclusion

Liberals had been united for a long time about most of the policies described above. Simon Hughes reiterated in a recent account of current Party leadership thinking the need for proportional representation to elect the Commons and most of the second chamber, and his concern that 'the independence of the judiciary must be constitutionally defended'; he also proposed the extension of electoral registration and polling times, the introduction of a citizenship ceremony for all 16-year-olds, and – a long historical echo – the disestablishment of the Church of England.[62]

Such unity is unsurprising, because constitutional reform was at the point of confluence between liberal ideology and interest. The essence of liberalism is concerned with what Locke referred to as 'the true original, extent and end of government' – the nature of the state and its relationship with the citizen. The Party's heritage of reform and its own constitution reflect its belief in the dispersal of power. Its under-representation under first-past-the-post, and the remoteness of the prospect of executive power, only gave Liberals additional incentive to promote the break-up of the unitary constitution.

There was also a presentational benefit in these measures. They contrasted with the conservatism of the main parties, being found by the Liberals' own research to be their only distinctive policy at the 1951 General Election.[63] The more fundamental implications of reform were likewise distinctive: of multi-party politics and sub-UK national identity, of individual rights rather than collective bureaucracy, and even of a sort of modernity and openness which could form a useful bridge between the great Liberals of the past and the need for a contemporary appeal.

Where digression occurred, it was for two reasons: either ideology offered an imperfect guide – as with the reform of the Lords – or circumstances dictated that tactical adaptations were necessary. During the 1950s, for example, if Liberals sang in close harmony from the constitutional reform hymn-sheet, they sang quietly and even infrequently. Lords reform appeared in only one manifesto before 1964; civil liberties were not mentioned in two; and in one case even proportional representation was neglected. Between 1951 and 1956, parliamentary and electoral reform were raised only five times in total by Liberal MPs.

Likewise neither the Assembly nor Liberal candidates showed great eagerness to publicise their constitutional policies. Amongst candidates' addresses before 1964, demands for constitutional reform only constituted three of the forty items to rank in the ten most popular (devolution, mentioned by 53% of candidates in 1950, and civil liberties, mentioned by 77% in 1955 and 59% in 1959). Electoral reform did not register any references in 1950 or 1959, and was never raised by as many as a quarter of Liberal candidates at any election in the 1950s.

Constitutional affairs had a low profile amongst Assembly agenda ballot topics, providing one or two of the top ten choices at only two Assemblies: resolutions on administrative tribunals in 1957, and in 1960 on local government and the introduction of an Ombudsman. It was left to the Executive to submit a resolution on electoral reform in 1958.[64]

One explanation for the low profile of constitutional issues is that they were not thought important by enough voters to be worth pursuing. Indeed, there were objective reasons for this relative indifference to the failings of the British constitution, since they were less manifest than they subsequently became. The electoral system generally allowed power to alternate between parties which were supported by only marginally less than half those voting; growing executive power and the decline in parliamentary control over legislation were less controversial than they subsequently became. Liberal leaders, accused by their own successors of being 'a brains' trust standing on the sidelines of politics'[65] found at 'the fireside of Oxford studies',[66] avoided close association with solutions to apparently theoretical problems.

At the same time the attitude of the main parties, who for most of the period under consideration were opposed to constitutional changes which would limit their power, made agitation futile. When Churchill contemplated electoral reform in 1950, it was his own party which would not entertain the idea; in 1951, though Labour lost power despite winning more votes than the Conservatives, David Butler remarked that the Party 'made remarkably little complaint'.[67] Liberals saw crying in the wilderness as a poor use of their time, and chose to invest their efforts elsewhere.

Lastly, though all parts of the Party agreed upon the policy of constitutional reform, it was for none the first priority. Local parties emphasised their candidate or local issues to guarantee a core vote; Assembly delegates were most interested in debating contentious issues; MPs' first interest was the retention of their seats, and therefore the promotion of their dominant interests such as agriculture or textiles. Even Grimond, whose interventions accounted for half of the Party's total, talked far more about herring, historic buildings and Highland crofters than about federalism or PR.

The impact of Liberal policy has been underestimated. The implementation of Liberal policies does not prove that the Liberals caused it, and indeed the Party's leaders continue to distance themselves from the measures that have been taken, stressing their inadequate character, leaving Britain in a 'constitutional limbo'.[68] Menzies Campbell has called for a constitutional convention, and argues that 'while the government has delivered devolution, the list of necessary constitutional reforms still to be implemented is longer still – fair votes for Westminster, an elected House of Lords, real devolution of power from Whitehall and Westminster to local government, and action to modernise government and ensure it is properly held to account'.[69] Nonetheless, Liberals were for much of the post-war period the lone champions of these policies, and kept them on the agenda.

For three generations at least, Liberals have had clear policies on constitutional reform; for two generations they have publicised them well; and during this generation many have been implemented, though they are reluctant to recognise it. Bogdanor's observation that the Liberals' opposition status drives their policy is arguable; but ironically, it might be responsible for their caution about acknowledging their own success.

Notes

1 M. Foley, *The Politics of the British Constitution* (Manchester University Press, Manchester, 1999) p. 135.

2 V. Bogdanor, 'The Liberal Party and the Constitution', *Journal of Liberal History* 54, Spring 2007.

3 R. Muir, *Future for Democracy* (Nicholson and Watson, London, 1939), pp. 119–26.

4 H.L. Samuel, *Memoirs* (Cresset Press, London, 1945), pp. 129 and 199

5 P. Harris, *Forty Years In and Out of Parliament* (Andrew Melrose, London, 1946), p. 196.

6 E. Lakeman and J. D. Lambert, *Voting in Democracies: A Study of Majority and Proportional Systems* (Faber and Faber, London, 1955).

7 Grimond in G. Watson (ed.), *The Unservile State: Essays in Liberty and Welfare* (Allen and Unwin, London, 1957), pp. 50–1; J. Grimond, *The Liberal Future* (Faber and Faber, London, 1959), p. 40; J. Grimond, *The Liberal Challenge* (Hollis and Carter, London, 1963), pp. 113–14.

8 R. Fulford, *The Liberal Case* (Penguin, Harmondsworth, 1959), pp. 10–38.

9 M. Bonham Carter in G. Watson (ed.), *Radical Alternative* (Eyre & Spottiswoode, London, 1962), p. 37.

10 T.L. Horabin, *Politics Made Plain* (Penguin, Harmondsworth, 1944), p. 22.

11 W. Wallace, *Why Vote Liberal Democrat?* (Penguin, Harmondswoth, 1992), pp. 41–2.

12 *A People's Parliament and How to Get It* (LPO, London, 1944).

13 The attempt to allow local councils to adopt PR was defeated in 1945 by 208 votes to 17.

14 *Electoral Reform: First Report of the Joint Liberal/SDP Commission on Constitutional Reform* (Poland St. Publications, London, July 1982).

15 House of Commons, 27th July 1954.

16 J. Thorpe, interview 26th October 1999. In fact, Home Office records show that Lloyd George was too laconic even for his Cabinet colleagues (HO 328/8): he saw a deputation from the all-party Committee for a Royal Commission on 21st February 1955. He was not encouraging, and made no reply in writing to the paper they submitted. After a letter of complaint from the Committee on 1st November, and some chasing by Eden, Lloyd George argued that no Commission was necessary, and Cabinet agreed. Lloyd George had to be prompted again to write and inform the Committee.

17 See, for example, an editorial in *The Economist*, 8th March 1958; and Randolph Churchill's appeal for a deal with the Liberals in the *London Evening Standard* the

following April. The same year, the Liberal Party Executive put a motion, proposed by J.F.S. Ross, confirming support for PR, on the Torquay Assembly agenda.

18 Violet Bonham Carter to Gwilym Lloyd George, 1st March 1955, Home Office papers.

19 Davies received replies from Attlee confirming the government's refusal to set up an enquiry into electoral reform on 14th and 23rd March, and finally a letter telling Davies there was no point in any further correspondence on the subject, and inviting Davies to publish the exchanges if he wished, on 16th July 1950. Clement Davies MS J/4/9.

20 M. Cole, 'Prospects for PR', *Politics Review* Vol. 2, No. 2, November 1992.

21 Dingle Foot (defeated 1970), E.L. Mallalieu (retired 1974). See S.E. Finer, *Adversary Politics and Electoral Reform 1975* (Anthony Wigram, London, 1975), pp. 50–1.

22 David Steel's letter to the Prime Minister, in D. Steel, *A House Divided* (Weidenfeld and Nicolson, London, 1980), p. 37.

23 A. Michie and S. Hoggart, *The Pact: The Inside Story of the Lib-Lab Government, 1977–8* (Quartet, London, 1978), p. 155.

24 *The Social Democrat*, 8th July 1983.

25 D. Steel, *Against Goliath: David Steel's Story* (Weidenfeld and Nicolson, London, 1989), p. 224.

26 P. Ashdown, *The Ashdown Diaries, Volume 1* (Penguin, Harmondsworth, 2000), pp. 278, 312, 344, 353 and 358.

27 BBC News, 29th October 1998.

28 Ashdown to Blair, Friday 30th October 1998: Ashdown, *The Ashdown Diaries, Volume 1*, pp. 318–19.

29 G. Hurst, *Charles Kennedy: A Tragic Flaw* (Politico's, London, 2006), p. 129.

30 Interview, *New Statesman*, 16th July 2007, p. 15.

31 S. Jenkins, 'The strange dearth of Liberal England', *The Times*, 17th May 2002.

32 Brian Mawhinney MP, House of Commons, 7th February 1996.

33 'No Gunfire', Editorial, *The Spectator*, 20th December 1963.

34 *The Times*, 9th September 1947.

35 'Stop the abuse of power', *The Real Alternative*, Liberal Democrat Manifesto 2005, p. 18.

36 Ibid., pp. 188–9.

37 *Hansard*, 5th series, 206, cols 627 and 670

38 *Hansard*, 5th series, 582, cols 430, 585 and 324.

39 HMSO, Cmd. 7380.

40 J. Morgan, *The House of Lords and the Labour Government, 1964–70* (Clarendon, Oxford, 1975), pp. 176ff., 206–7, and 210ff.

41 Ibid., p. 128.

42 *The House of Lords*, BBC TV, 1999.

43 *The Guardian*, 21st January 1999

44 Ashdown to Blair, 12th January 1999: P. Ashdown, *The Ashdown Diaries, Volume 2* (Allen Lane, London, 2002), p. 384. Ashdown was about to announce his resignation following the failure of the Jenkins Report.

45 'Dismay at Lords plan', *The Guardian*, 21st January 2000.

46 *Freedom, Justice, Honesty*, Liberal Democrat Manifesto 2001, p. 14.

47 *The Real Alternative*, Liberal Democrat Manifesto 2005, p. 18.

48 P. Burstow, interview, 23rd April 2007.

49 Lord Steel, 'Don't destroy the Lords', *The Guardian*, 5th February 2007.

50 Lord McNally, Liberal Democrat Party website, 15th March 2007.

51 J.S. Mill, 'Considerations on representative government', 1861, in R. Wollheim (ed.), *Three Essays* (Oxford University Press, 1975), p. 339.

52 J. Locke, 'Second treatise on government', 1689, in p. Laslett (ed.), *Two Treatises on Government* (Mentor, New York, 1963), p. 404.

53 *No Easy Way: Britain's Problems and the Liberal Answers* (LPO, London, 1950).

54 This, unlike in the main parties, was a measure for which the Liberal Party Council and *Liberal News* editorial statements had explicitly called, and on which Liberal peers worked together with Cross-Benchers such as Lord Birkett, a leading jurist and former Liberal MP.

55 J. Arlott, *Basingstoke Boy* (Fontana, London, 1992), pp. 176–7.

56 P. Norton, 'The Liberal Party in parliament', in V. Bogdanor (ed.), *Liberal Party Politics* (Oxford University Press, Oxford, 1983), p. 170.

57 J. Thorpe, 'Foreword', in R. Douglas, *History of the Liberal Party, 1895–1970* (Sidgwick and Jackson, London, 1971), p. xvi.

58 1st October 2001. See: www.libdems.org.uk/news/story.html?id=1935&navPage=news .html (accessed 1st July 2008).

59 14th November 2001. See: www.libdems.org.uk/news/story.html?id=2144&navPage=news .html (accessed 1st July 2008). Goodhart's Lords motion was introduced on 28th November.

60 *Freedom, Justice, Honesty*, p. 6.

61 *The Real Alternative*, p. 18.

62 J. Astle, D. Laws, P. Marshall and A. Murray (eds), *Britain After Blair: A Liberal Agenda* (Profile, London, 2006).

63 See D.E. Butler, *The British General Election of 1951* (Macmillan, London, 1952), p. 96. LPO issued a questionnaire to 445 constituencies where no Liberal candidate stood, and received replies from other parties' candidates in 160 of these. Of the eight questions asked, half were principally concerned with constitutional issues: electoral reform; devolution; the Liberties of the Subject Bill; and parliamentary control of public boards. Only on the first two did most Conservative and Labour candidates reject the Liberal position, and in Butler's words 'critics observed that none of these questions touched substantially on the country's main problems'.

64 See 'Topics for Torquay', *Liberal News*, 12th June 1958, p. 1.

65 J. Grimond, *Liberal News*, 27th September 1957.

66 David Steel in I. Bradley, *The Strange Rebirth of Liberal Britain* (Chatto and Windus, London, 1985), p. xi.

67 D.E. Butler, *The Electoral System in Britain Since 1918* (Oxford University Press, Oxford, 1963), p. 209.

68 Astle, *et al.*, *Britain After Blair*, p. 271.

69 M. Campbell, 'Introduction' in Astle *et al.*, p. 3; House of Commons, 3rd July 2007.

Decentralisation

Introduction

> Your measure should not only be a great Local Government Bill, but a great
> decentralisation Bill; that should be the principle of our local expenditure,
> and should replace the principle of administration from the centre which has
> of late been forcing itself into our system.[1]

So wrote Liberal Prime Minister William Gladstone to Sir John Dodson (President
of the Local Government Board) upon the latter's introduction of the Local
Government Bill of 1881. Gladstone's remarks set the cornerstone for Liberal
policy from then until the present day. Decentralisation, then, is an area of political thought which has produced lots of debate about the methods by which it
should be implemented but not the actual fundamentals of doing so. In essence
therefore we should be aware that Liberals have constantly seen decentralisation as
a core value and for them it has meant three differing areas. These are: 1) decentralisation (devolution) of central government (Westminster's and Whitehall's)
political power (commonly referred to as federalism); 2) decentralisation within
local government management and political structures (which combines with the
notion of 'community politics'); and 3) decentralisation within the delivery of
government services such as health. Each one of these areas could easily encompass
an entire book on its own. This chapter therefore can only provide a potted history
of the Liberals and decentralisation and in this respect it will examine just the first
and second types of decentralisation with the third being discussed in the next
chapter.

Federalism as a means of decentralisation

The Liberal Democrats see British government as being over-centralised with too
much power lying in the hands of Westminster. This they would decentralise, to
lower levels of government, but with defined levels of power within a written
constitution and appropriate legal structure (federalism). The concept of a federal

Britain as envisaged by the Liberals and others would involve two relatively autonomous levels of government. Both Westminster (federal) and regional (state or English regions) government would possess a range of powers which the other could not easily encroach upon.[2] For many in the Liberal Democrats, federalism isn't the 'bread and butter' issue of everyday politics. It has, however, become a core value with which no leader since 1945, nor major player in the Liberal Party, has ever disagreed with whilst in the Party.

Pre-Second World War, the Liberals had been the most pro-federal of all of the mainstream political parties. In their 1945 Liberal manifesto, they reconfirmed their long-held support for 'Home Rule' which was now clearly defined as 'devolution'. Although the manifesto specifically stated that each nation should have its own parliament, it did recommend that they should 'assume greater responsibility for their own affairs', in part to redress the 'drift of population of those countries to congested cities in England'.[3] By 1950, there was a firm commitment to a Welsh and Scottish Parliament.[4] This continued in all subsequent manifestos and was joined from time to time by other devolutionary demands, such as the 1959 manifesto demanding the immediate inclusion of a Welsh Secretary in the Cabinet so that Wales would have the same status as Scotland.[5]

The 1964 election manifesto stressed both devolving further powers to Northern Ireland (over tax) and decentralising powers such as education, health and regional planning to regional government in England as well.[6] During the period of Harold Wilson's Labour Government (1964–70), the Liberals continued to develop their federalist policies. In 1965, at the Scarborough Liberal Assembly, they produced policy motions for devolution across the UK. It was the first time that a truly federal agenda had been debated at conference. This policy was put into something more concrete in April 1968, when the Liberal Party's Regional Government Committee produced their report on federalism entitled: *Power to the Provinces*.[7] The report envisaged not only a Scottish and Welsh Parliament but also 12 provinces for England. The largest would be 'Greater London' and the smallest the 'West Country'. The provincial assemblies that ran these provinces would be elected triennially. These would be able to largely run their own education, housing, ombudsman systems, social security, docks, trunk roads (not motorways) and green belts (but not national parks). Perhaps most importantly they would be able to 'raise their own taxes and spend them according to the will of the people'. The Westminster Parliament would be reduced in size and look after defence, law and order, power, excise, railways, foreign affairs, non-provincial taxation and other clearly federal issues. The existence of these assemblies and national parliaments would be enshrined in a Bill of Rights which would establish a written constitution. *The Times* described the Liberal policy as having the Marxist notions of the 'weathering away of the state'.[8] The 1968 Edinburgh Assembly made no mention of Marxist doctrine but did back 'Power to the Provinces' and its federalist ideals.[9]

The Eastbourne Assembly in 1970 went on to pass a resolution supporting a federal system with local and regional matters decentralised as far as possible. This remained the policy of the Party that was endorsed at subsequent Liberal

Assemblies. Between 1937 and 1988 decentralisation of government had come up as a motion and had been passed at twenty-six Liberal Assemblies, making it one of the most frequent policies to be debated. Those Liberal Assemblies which debated decentralisation can be seen in Table 6.1.

Table 6.1 Liberal Party Assemblies and decentralisation policy motions 1937–88

Assembly	Year	Federalism	Scottish Parliament	Welsh Parliament	English devolution	Decentralised local government
Buxton	1937		X	X		
Scarborough	1939		X	X		
London	1942		X	X		
London	1945		X			
Hastings	1949		X	X		
Hastings	1952		X	X		
Ilfracombe	1953					X
Torquay	1958			X		
Edinburgh	1961		X			
Llandudno	1962			X		
Brighton	1963					X
Scarborough	1965	X	X	X	X	
Edinburgh	1968	X	X	X	X	
Brighton	1969				X	x
Eastbourne	1970	X	X	X	X	X
Southport	1973	X	X	X	X	X
Brighton	1974	X	X	X	X	
Llandudno	1976	X	X	X	X	X
Brighton	1977		X	X		
Southport	1978		X	X		
Bournemouth	1982		X			
Harrogate	1983				X	
Dundee	1985					X

The 1974 Labour Government under Harold Wilson was committed to exploring devolution but only for Scotland and Wales. This was not sufficient for the Liberals. At their 1976 September Llandudno Assembly, they debated and endorsed their own policy document, *A Programme for Action*, which called upon the Party:

1. To support in Parliament the principle of immediate devolution to Scotland and Wales, as a first though inadequate step towards a federal Britain;
2. To press in parliament and in the country for the extension of devolution to England;
3. To use all opportunities to encourage people in communities to take and use power to control their own lives and environment.

Devolution and decentralisation were seen as being the central planks for the Lib-Lab Pact. A further Party meeting in March 1977 chaired by Frank Byers and also attended by Jo Grimond, on the decentralisation of power, reaffirmed the Party's demand for a federal solution. This would involve decentralisation of power to Scotland, Wales, Northern Ireland and regions of England. They expected a steady progress towards English devolution including a White Paper on this subject at an early stage.[10]

The Liberals also supported devolution in Northern Ireland and were generally in agreement with the political consensus on the issue at the time. The Liberal Party in Northern Ireland had been in terminal decline whilst the non-sectarian Alliance Party eventually took its place in the early 1980s. The SDP–Liberal Alliance in the 1980s continued to support the concept of federalism with an injection of some political muscle to support it. Their 1983 joint manifesto, *Working Together for Britain* gave a list of policies aimed at the decentralisation of the British state into a federal structure. Both David Steel and Roy Jenkins pushed these issues on the election platforms of that year. When the two parties merged in 1988, decentralisation (if not the actual word 'federalism') continued to be endorsed in all general election manifestos by both Paddy Ashdown and Charles Kennedy, and at numerous Liberal Democrat conferences.

In the 1990s, the Party's key policies over education, crime and health had pushed constitutional reform to the back. In addition, as part of the process of realignment that been occurring within the Liberal Democrats since the Lib-Lab Pact in the 1970s, the Party had abandoned equidistance and consequently in October 1996 a joint Labour–Liberal Democrat working group examined Britain's constitutional future. It was led by Robert Maclennan for the Liberal Democrats and Robin Cook for Labour. The results, when published on 5th March 1997, were officially known as the Joint Consultative Committee on Constitutional Reform but became better known as the Cook-Maclennan Pact. It committed the Party to supporting Labour's plans for devolution if they were to win the next general election.

Although the Cook-Maclennan Pact eventually led to the setting up of a system of regional government in England and gave devolution to Scotland and Wales, it was at the very bottom end of the Liberal Democrats' expectations of federalism. In the late 1990s, the Liberal Democrats, therefore, continued to develop the concept of federalism, which enjoyed particular support from Malcolm Bruce, Ed Davey, Robert Maclennan, Dick Newby, Tony Vickers, Margaret Shape (Baroness) and Liberal Democrat Director of Policy, Richard Grayson. In 1999, a number of these drew together their collective thoughts on how Britain could operate federalism by drawing on international examples in their report *Funding Federalism*. They indicated that it was quite possible to undertake, although due to the political situation of the time, the dominance of New Labour, it was unlikely to occur.[11] The Party supported all devolutionary attempts that sought to develop federalism in Northern Ireland, Scotland, Wales and the Greater London Assembly.

In July 2000 the Liberal Democrat Working Party chaired by Bob Maclennan

MP (Constitutional Affairs Spokesperson), entitled 'Reforming Governance in the UK', endorsed a federal system of government for the United Kingdom. As well as many changes to the Westminster Government, the report proposed referenda on regional assemblies in England, on the basis of a minimum set of core powers, with the possibility of further devolution of powers and boundary changes to allow smaller regions, after a subsequent referendum.[12] The later point was needed, in part, to satisfy the Party's grass-roots in the West Country, who would have been happy to see county-based regions based on Cornwall and Devon occur. Much of 'Reforming Governance' found its way into both the general election manifestos of 2001 and 2005 and also further internal working groups which examined federalism. The first was a group chaired by Alan Beith MP in 2002 that very much endorsed the 'Reforming Governance: agenda.[13] Some five years later, in 2007, the same policy document formed the basis of a further Better Governance Working Group led by Lord Tyler, which reconfirmed the decentralised agenda.[14] Then, under its 2007 Policy Paper 79, devised by a group led by Andrew Stunnell MP, the Party continued to support regional government in England but also advocated city regions. These would be like those of some of the German Länder, and in the UK, the Greater London Authority was seen as a future model for decentralised regional government in England.[15] This was similar, in many ways, to reinstating the metropolitan counties abolished by the Thatcher Government in the 1980s. The Party's policy was continuing to evolve.

The Welsh Liberals and the campaign for a Welsh Parliament

The Liberal Democrats already operate their own internal federal system for their Party structure. There are three state parties (England, Scotland and Wales) which are also broken down into regional parties in England. This means that each one has played its own distinct part in shaping federalism and centralisation within its respective geographical area. This was strongly the case in Wales, where in the late nineteenth and early twentieth centuries the Liberal Party in Wales had failed to deliver Home Rule. It concentrated instead on the issue of the disestablishment of the Church in Wales and the Irish problem. Lloyd George was initially supportive of Home Rule for Wales as part of a 'Home Rule all round package' in solution to the Irish problem. His bad experience in South Wales Liberal politics, while supporting the liberal political movement *Cymru Fydd* (Wales to be), however, meant that he no longer trusted the South to govern the North and his enthusiasm for Home Rule therefore ended.[16]

Although Lloyd George had rejected Home Rule a number of Welsh Liberal MPs always supported the notion and in the immediate post-war era, Welsh Liberals were drawn into the Parliament for Wales Campaign headed by Megan Lloyd George, with the support of Liberal leader Clement Davies. After giving in a petition of some quarter of a million signatures demanding a Welsh Parliament to former Welsh Liberal MP, Gwilym Lloyd George (now the Conservative Minister for Wales) in 1956 the Campaign came to an abrupt end that same year. The

Liberal Party of Wales' manifestos continued to support devolution for Wales as did most Party activists but they were now being overshadowed on devolution by the rise of the Welsh nationalists, Plaid Cymru.

The first practical move on the road to devolution occurred just over seven months after the Welsh State Party had been founded. On St David's Day, 1st March 1967, Emlyn Hooson introduced The Government of Wales Bill 1967 into the House of Commons. It had been drafted by both himself and Martin Thomas. The Labour Government, however, refused to grant facilities for a Private Member's Bill, and therefore the Bill was killed off. It was Welsh and Scottish nationalist pressures rather than those of Welsh Liberals that led Harold Wilson's Labour Government in 1968 to announce that a Royal Commission on the Constitution would be undertaken. The Commission was initially chaired by Geoffrey Crowther, a former editor of *The Economist*, but following his death Lord Kilbrandon, a Scottish lawyer, chaired the Commission until it published its report in 1973.[17] In Wales, Alun Talfan Davies, the former chair of the Welsh Liberal Party and candidate for Carmarthen and Denbigh, was selected as one of the eleven commissioners. Davies, a top barrister and later a judge, did his best to ensure that the Welsh Liberal vision of a legislative parliament came out of the Commission.

There was much debate in both the Party and Wales about what requests should go into the Commission and what could come out. It eventually reported back in October 1973. Although the majority of Commissioners (six) including Talfan Davies favoured legislative devolution for Wales, almost half, and more importantly, most of the Wales Labour Party, favoured executive devolution only for Wales.[18] Scotland and Wales would both get assemblies and not parliaments. It was executive, not legislative, devolution therefore that would eventually be put to a referendum. The 1974 Brighton Liberal Assembly welcomed the Kilbrandon report but regretted that it did not call for devolution across the UK on equal principles and this remained what the Liberals were committed to, based on election by STV.

The first attempt at getting an assembly into existence failed when the Scotland and Wales Bill 1976 was defeated. The Liberals, in part due to their commitment to devolution, then supported Callaghan's Labour Government in the Lib-Lab Pact and two separate Acts were now passed for Scotland and Wales in July 1978. The senior Welsh Liberals backed the 'Yes' campaign in the referendum set for 1st March 1979 – St David's Day. Welsh Liberal MPs Geraint Howells and Emlyn Hooson and future MPs and Lords Alex Carlile and Richard Livsey as well as future Lords Roger Roberts and Martin Thomas all actively supported the 'Yes' campaign. The 'No' campaign, however, backed by the Conservatives and a number of Welsh Labour MPs, triumphed and won the eventual vote by nearly 5–1. Needless to say, the 1979 Welsh Liberal Party manifesto did not mention having a future Welsh Parliament.[19]

It was only four years before the aim of a Welsh Parliament was back in a Welsh Liberal manifesto. This was because the Alliance between the SDP and Welsh Liberals in 1982 led to a reinstatement to the commitment to both a federal solution to Britain's government and a Welsh Parliament.[20] Whilst the Welsh Parliament remained in Alliance and then Liberal Democrat manifestos for the next decade it would be 1996 before the Party updated its proposals, when Russell Deacon, the Party's Welsh Director of Policy, wrote *A Senedd for Wales: Beyond a Talking Shop*.[21] The policy document advocated a tax-raising and law-making parliament (senedd) of around 100 members. It also introduced the concept of a quasi-bicameral Welsh Parliament through the introduction of a Local Government Senate which would represent Welsh local government.[22]

In March 1997, the Welsh leader Alex Carlile announced that he had signed a joint declaration with Shadow Welsh Secretary Ron Davies to give his Party's support to a 'Yes' vote in any Welsh Assembly referendum on Labour's proposals. There was to be no constitutional convention in Wales. When Labour won the 1997 General Election Mike German and Russell Deacon were the Welsh Liberal Democrats on the 'Yes for Wales' steering committee in Cardiff. Newly re-elected MP Richard Livsey, always a strong devolutionist, was the Westminster lead. Labour's Welsh Assembly was far from the Liberals' own goal, but the element of proportional representation was enough to persuade the key activists to back the campaign. The victory of the 'Yes' side was by just 0.3% of the vote. When the elections were held to the Welsh Assembly in 1999, it was Mike German who became the Party's leader in the Welsh Assembly. Within a year German would become deputy First Minister in the Lab-Lib Pact that ran the Assembly between 2000 and 2003. It was during this period that the Welsh Liberal Democrats were able to persuade their coalition partners to hold a commission to review the powers and role of the Welsh Assembly. The cross-party Commission was led by Lord Richard, a senior Welsh Labour peer. The Welsh Liberal representative on the Commission was Peter Price, a former Conservative MEP, but now an active Welsh Liberal Democrat.

The Commission when it reported in 2004 backed almost exactly the Welsh Liberal Democrat policy for a law-making Welsh Parliament, with some 80 members elected by STV. Labour, however, rejected the Commission's proposals but did allow a limited form of primary legislative powers to be introduced. The Welsh Liberal Democrats, now out of the coalition and back on the opposition benches, despaired at Labour's rejection and sought unsuccessfully to reverse it at Westminster when the new Government of Wales Act 2006 went through. Their next chance to do so would have to wait until the post-May 2007 Welsh Assembly elections when the Labour Party went into the Red–Green Coalition with Plaid Cymru and set the date of 2011 for a further referendum on primary legislative powers for the Welsh Assembly.

Scottish Parliament

Like the Welsh Liberals, those in Scotland had an equally long history of pro-Home Rule policies from the late nineteenth century onwards. In the immediate post-war period, 1945, however, the Party had lost all of its seats in Scotland. For a five-year period there were no Scottish Liberal MPs to support the notion of Scottish devolution at Westminster or anywhere else. When, in 1950, Jo Grimond was elected for Orkney and Shetland, he became for the next 14 years the sole Scottish Liberal MP. Almost as soon as he was in parliament, he tabled an amendment to the Queen's Speech calling for a Scottish Parliament; a move that was inevitably defeated but still provided evidence of the Scottish Liberal desire for Home Rule. It would be another 14 years before Grimond brought the Liberal revival to Scotland, and progress on devolution was therefore slow.

In September 1964, a Scottish Liberal Party Panel, commissioned in November 1962, under the chairmanship of Michael Stafforth, made its findings public. The Panel stated that a parliament was needed due to series of problems with the existing constitutional settlement. The main one was that there was too little Westminster legislative and scrutiny time available for Scottish matters. It was also evident that in Scotland the current structures and legal system already existed for establishing a parliament.[23] This set the scene for that October's general election when three new Scottish Liberal MPs were elected in addition to Grimond, including George Mackie (Caithness and Sutherland) and Russell Johnston (Inverness). Then within a few months David Steel was elected in the Roxburghshire, Selkirkshire and Peebleshire by-election of 24th March 1965. The Scots had now replaced the Welsh as the backbone of the British Liberal Party. Over the coming decades, Grimond and Steel would be instrumental in the development of the Scottish Liberal Party. Johnston would also play a role of being one of the central drivers behind the Scottish Home Rule movement, both within and outside of the Party.

On St Andrew's Day 1966, Johnston introduced the Scottish Self-Government Bill, advocating a law-making parliament with power to raise taxes in Scotland. The Bill was defeated, but the Scottish Liberals continued to develop the intellectual argument for Home Rule. In their *Vanguard* series of publications in November 1968, Williams Riddell, then Liberal leader of Greenock Town, outlined the type of Scottish Parliament the Party envisaged.[24] A few months later, David Steel wrote *Towards Scottish Home Rule by Council* in which he argued that 'Westminster does not examine Scotland enough and all the mechanisms it has such as the Grand Committee need to meet more often'. This could only be changed by a Scottish Parliament.[25]

In early 1970, the Scottish Liberal Party produced *Scottish Self Government*, a policy document resulting from a 25-person committee including Russell Johnston and David Steel. The document proposed setting up a 142-member parliament within a federal UK. This was then endorsed by the Scottish Party's August conference. In its evidence to the Crowther Commission that same year the Scottish Liberal Party proposed 'federalism' with the UK government continuing to tax-raise in the short term.[26]

On 30th July 1970 Johnston, now Chair of the Scottish Liberals, met with William Wolfe, Chair of the Scottish National Party (SNP), to see if they could agree a joint policy on devolution. The Scottish Liberals' policy of federalism and the SNP's of independence proved to be incompatible. From now on, the Liberals would only make common course with those who wished to see a devolved Scottish Parliament within the United Kingdom.[27]

The Kilbrandon Commission reported back during the Heath Government in October 1973. The Scottish Liberals mainly regretted the fact that they had not taken the opportunity to introduce a federal solution to government in the United Kingdom.[28] The Conservatives in Scotland initially supported devolution but it was left to Harold Wilson's Labour Government to try to introduce it. With a small parliamentary majority and a large number of anti-devolutionist MPs, the Labour Party was only able to bring the proposal for a Scottish Assembly through Westminster with the help of the Liberals and SNP. The Scotland Act 1978 was passed with a much weaker version of devolution than that advocated by the Scottish Liberals. In addition to this, an anti-devolution Labour MP, George Cunningham, had succeeded in getting an amendment to the Act passed: a repeal motion would be laid before the House if fewer than 40% of those Scots entitled to vote had said 'Yes'. Cunningham had done this in part to ensure that a poor turnout in the referendum did not mean that devolution was granted on a minority vote. The referendum held on 1st March 1979 produced a highly unsatisfactory result for Scotland since, while a majority voted for devolution, a turnout of 62.9 per cent meant that the 'Yes' vote did not reach the 40% threshold.[29]

When the 1st March referendum failed to deliver a Scottish Parliament, the Scottish Liberal Executive informed its members that the Party intended to stay a Home Rule party, despite English Liberal MPs John Pardoe and David Penhaligon declaring Home Rule a dead duck.[30] The Executive would support the Scotland Act and any future 'Yes for Scotland' campaign would have to avoid the 'anti-devolutionary Labour Stalinists that had wrecked this one'.[31] The Scottish Liberal MPs duly voted against the repeal of the Scotland Act in 1979. The following year they joined the Campaign for a Scottish Assembly (Parliament after 1994), a cross-party grouping of mainly SNP, Labour and Liberal members.

On 30th March 1988, the Scottish Constitutional Convention was formed. Made up of Labour, Scottish Liberals and representatives of Scottish civil society, it would spend the next eight years coming to agreement on the type of Scottish Parliament that the consensus in Scotland wanted. David Steel was appointed as co-chair of the Convention; Scottish Liberal leader Malcolm Bruce actively supported it. When Bruce stepped down as Scottish Party leader in 1993, he was replaced by arch pro-devolutionist James Wallace. Wallace, through the Constitutional Convention and later on as Deputy First Minister, would be at the heart of shaping Scottish Liberal Democrat policy on devolution for the next decade.[32] Wallace was the main Liberal Democrat negotiator in the convention with Labour's George Robertson. They agreed on the proportional electoral system and struck a non-binding agreement on gender balance.

On 30th November 1995 (St Andrew's Day), *Scotland's Parliament, Scotland's Right* was published, becoming official Scottish Liberal Democrat Party policy. After the Labour victory in the 1997 General Election, a referendum was duly held in which the Scottish Liberal Democrats backed the 'Yes-yes' campaign (support for devolved government with tax-raising powers). In the 1999 Scottish General Election, Jim Wallace went into the Scottish Parliament with a number of other MPs or former MPs, including Sir David Steel. Whilst Steel was to become the parliament's Presiding Officer (Speaker) Wallace was to join his Party with the Labour Party in a coalition for the next two parliamentary terms, serving as Deputy First Minister and Law Minister until June 2005 when Nicol Stephenson took over. He was the first Liberal minister to serve in Britain since fellow Scottish Liberal Sir Archibald Sinclair served in Churchill's wartime coalition government.

Despite the Party being in the Scottish coalition government, Scottish Liberal Democrat devolution policy continued to develop. To this effect, the largest ever review of Scottish devolution by the Scottish Liberal Democrats occurred between 2003 and 2006 under the chairmanship of Sir David Steel. The Steel Commission was charged with preparing the Liberal Democrats for a second Constitutional Convention planned for 2009, ten years after the parliament first came into being. The Commission, which started work in December 2003, comprised some 20 Commissioners including Chris Huhne MP, Malcolm Bruce MP and numerous Liberal MSPs and public figures connected to the Scottish Liberal Democrats. It began work in the summer of 2004, and produced an Interim Report which was endorsed by the Scottish Liberal Democrat conference in February 2005.

The final 135-page report was the most detailed study on Scottish devolution ever undertaken by the Scottish Liberal Democrats.[33] When the Commission reported back on 6th March 2006 in Edinburgh it concluded that due to the asymmetrical devolution occurring across the UK with the assemblies in Northern Ireland, London, Wales and Scotland it was now an ideal time to introduce a federal system of government across the UK. Federalism would be supported by the other Liberal federal notions of a written constitution and Supreme Court. Its main recommendations were related both to a review of the Scottish Parliament's powers and greater power of over taxation in Scotland.[34]

The report would then provide the forefront of Scottish Liberal Democrat policy at the 2007 Scottish Parliamentary elections after which the Party stepped out of the coalition government unable to support the new SNP-led government's aim of Scottish independence. The Scottish Liberal Democrats continue to strive like the rest of the Liberal Democrat Party for a federal Britain in which the Scottish Parliament is one component part.

Local government and decentralisation

In the 1950s and early 1960s, the Liberal Party under Jo Grimond laid the ideological foundations to the Party's later conversion to community politics. Grimond drew on the philosophies of Thomas Hill Green (1836–1882).[35] Green's political thought was drawn from Kant and Hegel rather than the Liberal traditionalists of J.S. Mill and Hebert Spencer. He believed that the individual's ability should be channelled through active citizenship within the community. It was the role of the state to foster these conditions.[36] Green's influence was seen on some of the new

Liberals such as L.T. Hobhouse whose major work, *Liberalism*, noted that 'liberalism was a philosophy that rooted the individual with a collective whole'.[37] It was Grimond who built upon these ideas of Green and Hobhouse and his advocating of these that inspired a number of future Young Liberals to join the Party. Green, Hobhouse and Grimond saw the need for a rebalancing of the role of the individual in society by providing individuals with both the choice and opportunity to take a 'more active part' in the running of their own lives. Decentralisation and community politics would help facilitate this process.[38] In the 1960s, these Liberal ideas were promoted by a number of Liberal councillors inspired by Grimond, most notably Wallace Lawler in Birmingham, Trevor Jones (Jones the Vote) in Liverpool and Michael Meadowcroft in Leeds. They were later joined by Bernard and Tony Greaves and Gordon Lishman.[39] It was they who developed community politics into a political art form.[40]

In 1962, the future leader of Liverpool City Council, Cyril Carr and his agent Alex Gerard produced the first *Focus* leaflet. It was based on the idea that a regular newsletter would show the electorate that the Liberals were campaigning all year round. The leaflet became both punchy and populist and was taken up by other Liberal councillors in Liverpool and pushed forward by one its greatest exponents, Trevor Jones.[41] In the same period, the 1963 Brighton Assembly[42] backed both the reform of local government and the devolution of maximum responsibility to elected regional authorities, with extensive administrative powers in part financed by local taxation. Then, in November 1965, the Oxford University Liberal Club held a conference on the Machinery of Government which brought together a number of experts. The result of the meeting was a published pamphlet in the New Directions series, 'The Machinery of Government'.[43] This endorsed the concept of federalism across the UK with unitary authorities and an enhanced role for parish councils.

The next policy statement in respect of local government decentralisation occurred with the *Power in the Provinces Report* in 1968. This stated that the structure of local government within each nation state should be a purely state matter, but the Liberal preference was for a single tier of local government above parish or neighbourhood level, 'in order to remove unnecessary and costly levels of government'.[44] Local government nationally was undergoing a period of review during the late 1960s. In 1969 a three-year Royal Commission on the Reform of Local Government in England under the chair of Lord Redcliffe-Maud examined the current varied system of local government in England. The Commission unanimously recommended a system of unitary authorities across England with the three largest metropolitan areas, including London, having a system of metropolitan and borough councils. The Liberals rejected the Redcliffe-Maud proposals on the grounds that 'they would destroy local democracy, create a sham form of regional government and further strengthen central bureaucracy'.[45] They reaffirmed their own commitment to 'Power to the Provinces' and urged all Liberals to 'publicise this policy as widely as possible'. The Conservatives returned to power in 1970 and soon scrapped Redcliffe-Maud's proposals.

Community politics arrives firmly on the agenda

In 1970, the Eastbourne Assembly passed a motion supporting a federal system with local and regional matters decentralised as far as possible. The motion had been brought by William Wallace, the candidate for Huddersfield West in the 1970 General Election.[46] The conference, however, was more notable for the advance of the Young Liberals and their views on community politics rather than for notions of federalism. Liberals had become infiltrated to a degree by a number of Young Liberal activists whose ideology was, at times, more closely related to Marx than Hobbes or Locke. At the Eastbourne Assembly on 25th September 1970, they successfully introduced 'community politics' onto the Party's policy.

The Young Liberals wished to take politics out of Westminster and onto the streets in community politics. At the forefront of this move was Young Liberal Chair, Tony Greaves. He saw the only way forward for gaining seats on parish and district councils as through community politics. Greaves would later become head of the Association of Liberal Councillors (ALC). He would then continue to push for decentralisation as part of community politics, almost as an article of faith, from the 1970s into the next millennium. Like Greaves, the Young Liberals' press officer, Peter Hain, saw community politics as taking politics beyond Westminster. But his future lay in a different party.[47] The Liberals were now committed to the future community pavement politics that they were already undertaking in places like Liverpool and Leeds and would develop across the whole UK in the coming decades. They had also in effect decentralised their own political campaigning, often to ward level.

'Power to the People'

In November 1971 the Liberal Party started work on its 'Power to the People' working party on the Machinery of Government. It set up a Standing Committee of the Liberal Party Organisation which reported back in September 1973. This report was then put to and passed by the Liberal Assembly in Southport and published in a revised version in March 1974. The next Liberal Party report on decentralisation, *Power and Responsibility for Local Government* came out in 1980. It pushed for the parish council to have both more powers and to be the underly-ing strength beneath decentralised local government.[48] In the same year the Association of Liberal Councillors produced a booklet entitled *The Theory and Practice of Community Politics* written by Bernard Greaves and Gordon Lishman. The booklet argued that community politics would not end in uncontrolled popu-larism but instead act as a barrier against tyranny.[49] The following year, in May 1981, the Liberal Mid-Term Programme, entitled 'Humanity, Community and Interdependence' further stressed the need for community politics: 'a group of people sharing a neighbourhood, taking action together to change their common situation – and in the process finding a greater sense of individual satisfaction'.[50] A new party, the Social Democrat Party, had now also arrived on the political scene and was soon closely allied with the Liberal Party. When the Liberals compared their policy on local government with that of the SDP it was seen to be without any substantial differences.[51] In June 1983 they therefore went into the general election together with the joint policy document 'Decentralising Government'.[52]

For almost two decades, decentralisation had been seen by academics, professionals and those politicians on the left and centre as a way of radically altering the way that local government operated and as a bulwark against the ever-advancing centralisation of Thatcherism. Copious volumes were written on the subject, mainly from the perspective of Labour authorities. It was the new revolutionary way of running local government, but the input was nearly all from Labour and not Liberal councils.[53] The main problem for Liberals in the 1970s and 1980s, however, was not that they did not believe in decentralisation but the fact that they seldom gained control of any local authorities within which to implement it. Most of the forms of decentralisation therefore occurred during this period under Labour councils whose Marxist-Socialist ideological influences supported the decentralisation of power at a local level.[54]

The first non-Labour council to experiment with decentralisation was Liberal-run South Somerset District Council in 1983. This was a big rural council with four major towns. It was divided into four area committees which had powers decentralised to them. The process seemed to work quite well in this rural district but what about an urban area?[55] This would have to wait another three years until 1986. In the May of that year, the Liberal Party (there were no SDP councillors there) took control of the London Borough of Tower Hamlets and held it until 1994. The Labour Party had controlled the council since local government re-organisation in 1965. Although the Liberals only had a majority of one seat, they immediately set about breaking up the council's existing administrative and political structures. This they did through a series of mini neighbourhoods, with the character of 'mini-town halls' over which were approximately five councillors.

In Tower Hamlets political campaigning by the Liberals was based around the Liberal Democrats' 'FOCUS' leaflets. They were seen as a means of promoting a form of 'popularism' within the new decentralised council structure. Local meetings involving council issues could at that time involve hundreds of people. In Tower Hamlets, the Liberals' concept of decentralisation also became based on the concept of rights and their relationship to territory and property. Therefore they stressed endorsement of council house sales and 'sons and daughters' schemes in the allocation of council housing. Such policies were enacted at the same time as an increase in racial tensions, and a rise in the popularity of the BNP in Tower Hamlets, which had a large Bangladeshi community.[56] This led to accusations of the Liberal Democrats taking on 'active racism' in order to compete with the BNP, and Paddy Ashdown ordered an inquiry from within the Party in 1993. The inquiry found evidence of 'misguided popularism' rather than 'active racial prejudice'. The report went on to define community politics as an 'ideology', rather than just being an election-winning tool. To this effect, it worked only when it reverted back to its original position of 'using power with and alongside local communities'.

It also led to the Association of Liberal Democrat Councillors (ALDC), making sure that there were model standing orders from which the Liberal Democrat councillors would now be able to regulate their community politics whilst both in council control and opposition.[57]

The failures at Tower Hamlets were the most serious challenge to the Liberals' notion that 'decentralisation should be at the heart of politics'. With the reasoning behind the failures identified it was the ALDC that now continued to develop policy ideas on the application of decentralisation in practice when the Liberal Democrats started to make impressive gains at county and district levels during the 1990s. Many of the most prominent ALDC central organisers or members were to find themselves elected to running councils or going to Westminster during this period. Their memories of being on local councils or closely connected with them were to reinforce their views on the continued need for the decentralisation of power.

The Liberal Democrats had spent some 18 years fighting, at a local level, against the centralisation of the state brought about by the Conservatives (1979–97). The New Labour Government introduced some forms of decentralisation with an allowance of area committees under its Local Government Act 2000. This means that most councils have since decentralised a number of non-contentious services such as refuse disposal and road maintenance. At the same time, however, they changed the way that local government was run to the more centralising cabinet system and away from the previous committee system. The 1997 General Election had not only seen New Labour elected, but it also saw the arrival of Andrew Stunnell (Hazell Grove) who had decades of council experience and was the former chief executive of the ALDC. He would now be one of the driving forces behind decentralisation in local government within the Liberal Democrats.[58] In 1999 the Liberal historian and ideologue Lord (Conrad) Russell produced his central thesis on British Liberalism: *An Intelligent Person's Guide to Liberalism*.[59] Russell traced the Liberal Democrats' desire for decentralisation, the autonomy of local government, devolution and pluralism back to the very roots of the Liberal Party and their predecessors the Whigs. Their resistance to the centralisation of power was something that had remained constant throughout the life of the Party.[60]

By the early 2000s, it was becoming apparent that, despite devolution in Scotland and Wales, at a local government level New Labour remained as big a centralising force as their predecessors. When, therefore, the 'new radical' Liberal Democrats produced their collection of essays in 2004 in their *The Orange Book: Reclaiming Liberalism*, Edward Davey dealt with the issue of decentralisation. Davey reinforced Liberal philosophy on decentralisation which was now referred to as 'localism'. Stronger local government and new regional assemblies were to be 'mechanisms for checking state power and for promoting quality and choice in public services for the individual'.[61] The follow-up to the *Orange Book*, *Britain After Blair: A Liberal Agenda* in 2006 had Simon Hughes (Federal Party President) writing the chapter related to decentralisation. Hughes simply reaffirmed the Party's commitment to pushing down power from the centre to the regions and local government.[62] There had been no radical change to this viewpoint.

Where Liberal Democrats are in power or the lead party they often continue to experiment with decentralisation. In Leeds City Council, Labour lost control in 2004 to a Liberal Democrat-led coalition. The Council then slowly worked towards a scheme to decentralise the whole city, dividing it into five wedges. Each had neighbourhood committees, with each subdivision being as big as a normal council. This is the largest attempt at decentralisation made by any UK council, with the city having a population approaching 750,000 people.[63] In 2006, the Liberal Democrat Group of the Local Government Association, in their submission to Sir Michael Lyons' *Inquiry into Local Government* continued to support decentralisation for local government and federalism for Westminster government as the central plank of any desired constitutional reform.[64] This was further supported by the Party's policy paper 79 which was endorsed by their September 2007 Brighton Conference.[65]

Conclusion

As stated at the outset, decentralisation had always been an accepted fact of Liberal and Liberal Democrat political thought stretching back centuries. Thus it isn't the ideology of decentralisation but the process of achieving it which has been the area for debate within the Party. Federalism and the means of its application have been a core policy of the Party since the late 1950s. In Scotland and Wales, devolution was seen to be clearly a method by which each nation's domestic parliaments could gain as many powers over domestic functions as was practicably possible within a federal United Kingdom. The Party's support in the devolution referendums there was essential in ensuring that the wider general public threw their support behind the concept of the Scottish Parliament and Welsh Assembly.

At an English level decentralisation was firstly about producing English regional government and secondly about decentralising local authority power to the lowest level. The challenges came to the Party in two ways. Firstly, when decentralisation occurred within a Liberal-run council such as Tower Hamlets the results could be both unexpected and controversial. These problems had to be ironed out. The second issue concerned adapting the whole Liberal philosophy about campaigning down to community level politics based around ward level 'FOCUS Team' campaigning. The two had long roots within the Liberal Party and evolved hand in hand with elements of decentralisation. Community politics was introduced incrementally and was controversial at first. This policy, however, became accepted practice by the late 1980s. Today, decentralisation has become so accepted within the Party that it is simply added to policy statements or ideological Liberal texts as a matter of fact, often without the rationale behind it seeming to need explanation. The sentiments behind this would perhaps have pleased the Grand Old Man – Gladstone – who supported and advocated these same views of decentralisation as a core Liberal philosophy nearly 130 years ago.

Notes

1 Cited in B. Keith-Lucas, 'The Liberal Party and local government', in V. Bogdanor (ed.), *Liberal Party Politics* (Oxford University Press, Oxford, 1983), p. 251.
2 R. Deacon and A. Sandry, *Devolution in Great Britain* (Edinburgh University Press, Edinburgh, 2007).
3 *20 Point Manifesto of the Liberal Party*, Liberal Party General Election Manifesto, 1945, p. 4.
4 *No Easy Way: Britain's Problems and the Liberal Answers*, Liberal Party General Election Manifesto, 1950.
5 *People Count*, Liberal Party General Election Manifesto, 1959, p. 4.
6 *Think for Yourself – Vote for Yourself*, Liberal Party General Election Manifesto, 1964.
7 *Power to the Provinces*, Liberal Party Local Government Committee, 18th April 1969.
8 *The Times*, 14th August 1969, p. 9.
9 Liberal Brighton Assembly, 17–20th September 1969.
10 'Liberal Policy Makers Spell Out Points for Negotiation with Government', Liberal Party Organisation Press Release, 2nd March 1977.
11 N. Bromley, R. Grayson, J. Liotta, M. Sharp and R. White, *Funding Federalism: A Report on Systems of Government Finance* (1999).
12 Constitution Unit, *Monitor*, Issue 12, September 2000, p. 2.
13 *It's About Freedom*, The Report of the Liberal Democracy Working Group, Liberal Democrats, Policy Paper 50, 2002.
14 Federal Policy Consultation Paper, No. 85, Liberal Democrats, 2007.
15 'The Power to be Different: Policies for Local and Regional Governance in England', Liberal Democrats, Policy Paper 79, 2007.
16 Jennifer Longford (daughter of Lloyd George) to author February 2007.
17 R. Deacon, *Devolution in Britain Today* (Manchester University Press, Manchester, 2006, 2nd edition).
18 D. Foulkes, J. Barry Jones, and R.A. Wilford, *The Welsh Veto: The Wales Act 1978 and the Referendum* (University of Wales Press, Cardiff, 1981), p. 25.
19 Welsh Liberal Party (1979), Liberal Programme for Wales.
20 The SDP–Welsh Liberal Alliance Manifesto, *The Priorities for Wales*, June 1983.
21 The word 'senedd' being the Welsh word for 'parliament', the reference to 'Beyond a Talking Shop' referring to the Wales Labour Party's own Executive Assembly without tax-raising or law-making powers.
22 Liberal Democrats Wales, *A Senedd for Wales: Beyond a Talking Shop: The Liberal Democrats Programme for Devolution for Wales* (1996).
23 *Scottish Self Government*, Scottish Liberal Democrat Publication, September 1964, 3rd edition.
24 W. Riddell, Vanguard No. 2, 'Towards Scottish Home Rule', Scottish Liberal Party, 1968.
25 D. Steel, Vanguard No. 3, 'Out of Control: A Critical Examination of the Government of Scotland', Scottish Liberal Party, 1969.
26 Scottish Liberal Party Press Release, 12th May 1971.
27 *The Times*, 31st July 1970, p. 2.
28 *The Times*, 1st November 1973, p. 5.
29 Deacon, *Devolution in Britain Today*, p. 102.
30 *The Times*, 3rd March 1979, p. 2.

31 Scottish Liberal Party Press Release, 8ᵗʰ March 1979.

32 B. Taylor, *The Road To The Scottish Parliament* (Edinburgh University Press, Edinburgh, 2002), p. 7.

33 *The Steel Commission: Moving to Federalism – A New Settlement for Scotland*, Scottish Liberal Democrats, 2006.

34 'Steel Commission Calls for New Powers for Scottish Parliament', 6ᵗʰ March 2006, Scottish Liberal Democrats.

35 J. Meadowcroft, 'The origins of community politics: new liberalism, Grimond and the counter-culture', *Journal of Liberal Democrat History*, 28, Autumn 2000, pp. 3–9.

36 C. Tyler, 'T.H.Green', in D. Brack and E. Randall (eds), *Dictionary of Liberal Thought* (Politico's, London, 2007), pp. 143–7.

37 Cited in Meadowcroft, 'The origins of community politics', p. 5.

38 A. Holmes, 'The idea of "community" in progressive politics', in *Community Politics Today: A Collection of Essays Including the Original 'Theory and Practice of Community Politics'* (ALDC, 2006).

39 R. Ingham, 'Community politics', in Brack and Randall (eds), *Dictionary of Liberal Thought*, pp. 73–5.

40 J. Meadowcroft, 'Community politics', Liberal Democrat History Group web site www.liberalhistory.org.uk/item_single.php?item_id=69&item=history (accessed 27ᵗʰ February 2009).

41 D. Walter, *The Strange Rebirth of Liberal England* (Politico's, London, 2003), p. 42.

42 Liberal Brighton Assembly, 11ᵗʰ September 1963.

43 D. Snowman and C. Layton, 'The Machinery of Government', Liberal Publication Department, October 1966.

44 *Power in the Provinces Report*, Liberal Party Organisation, 1968, p. 7.

45 Liberal Party Organisation Local Government Reform – Emergency Resolution Press Release, 19ᵗʰ August 1969.

46 Liberal Eastbourne Assembly, 24ᵗʰ September 1970.

47 *The Times*, 11ᵗʰ September 1970, p. 1.

48 Bogdanor, (ed.), *Liberal Party Politics*, p. 250.

49 B. Greaves and G. Lishman, *The Theory and Practice of Community Politics*, ALC Campaign Booklet No. 12, 1980.

50 Action Programme for the Counties, Liberal Campaign Manifesto County Elections, May 1981.

51 P. Knowlson, *Priorities for the Standing Committee*, Liberal Party Organisation.

52 I. Crewe and A. King, *SDP: The Birth, Life and Death of the Social Democratic Party* (Oxford University Press, Oxford, 1995), p. 196.

53 P. Hoggett and R. Hambleton, *Decentralisation and Democracy: Localising Public Services* (School of Advanced Urban Studies, University of Bristol, 1987).

54 R. Hambleton and P. Hoggett, *The Politics of Decentralisation: Theory and Practice of a Radical Local Government Initiative* (School for Advanced Urban Studies, London, 1984).

55 Sir David Williams to author, 27ᵗʰ April 2007.

56 D. Burns, R. Hambleton and p. Hoggett, *The Politics of Decentralisation* (Macmillan, Basingstoke, 1994), p. 219.

57 C. Copus, *Party Politics and Local Government* (Manchester University Press, Manchester, 2004), pp. 136–7

58 Sir David Williams to author, 27ᵗʰ April 2007.

59 C. Russell, *An Intelligent Person's Guide to Liberalism* (Duckworth, London, 1999).

60 D. Brack, 'Conrad Russell', in Brack and Randall (eds), *Dictionary of Liberal Thought*, pp. 351–3

61 E. Davey, 'Liberalism and localism', in P. Marshall and D. Laws (eds), *The Orange Book: Reclaiming Liberalism* (Profile, London, 2004), pp. 44–5.

62 S. Hughes, 'Democracy', in J. Astle, D. Laws, P. Marshall and A. Murray (eds) *Britain After Blair: A Liberal Agenda* (Profile, London, 2006).

63 Sir David Williams to author, 27th April 2007.

64 *Liberal Democrats in Local Government Submission to the Lyons Inquiry into Local Government*, The Liberal Democrat Group, Local Government Association, March 2006

65 'The Power to be Different'.

Political economy

The British Liberal approach to political economy has historically been rather different than that of other political parties. In clear contrast to the approach of the Labour Party, in particular – an organisation with its roots in the defence of a sectional economic interest, the organised working class – economic policy has been seen primarily as a means to an end, not as an end in itself. Indeed, the historian and Liberal Democrat peer Conrad Russell has argued that since Liberalism has its roots in the political and constitutional struggles of the seventeenth and eighteenth centuries, before the state could exercise any significant control over the levers of economic activity, 'the Party does not have an economic philosophy'.[1]

In that sense, 'political economy' – the inter-relationship of economics, law, and political science in explaining how political institutions, the political environment, and the economic system influence each other – is a more apt term than 'economic policy'. For Liberals, concerned centrally about the control and dispersal of power in society, the principal point about economics is that it affects the distribution of power, and can therefore enlarge, or diminish, the life-chances of individuals. The context in which economic policy is set, including international, constitutional and environmental policy, is as important for Liberals as the core economic policies themselves, and will be touched on throughout this chapter.

There have always been divisions within British Liberalism over the appropriate balance between the market and the state. 'Classical' or 'economic' liberals,[2] often harking back to the Party's approach throughout the nineteenth century, have tended to rank individual freedom above material equality and to argue that the state's sphere has to be very strictly limited. 'Social liberals', looking back in their turn to the New Liberal interventionist social policies of the early twentieth century, have argued that poverty, unemployment, ill-health, disability and a lack of education are serious enough constraints on freedom that state action, including redistributive taxation, is justified to redress them. Both groups have been aware of the dangers of the growth in the size of the state, including the increased power of bureaucracies, and the infringement on civil liberties that may entail, the tendency of elites to capture elements of state power, the growth of corporatism, a rising burden of taxation and so on. Whereas economic liberals have generally concluded that this should lead to an attempt to reduce the size of the state, social liberals have tended rather to argue that the state should be constrained (for example through a written constitution) and decentralised, to make it more accountable and participative.

Since this chapter is about political economy, it will tend to focus on this long-running disagreement between the different camps. It should not be forgotten, however, that except at a few specific points, the divisions between the two tendencies have never been hard and fast – it would be more accurate usually to think of a spectrum of views and positions, depending strongly on the economic and social circumstances of the time – and have only occasionally led to deep-seated disagreements over the future direction of the Party. Since, following Russell, for Liberals economics is about means rather than ends, other aspects of the Liberal approach – commitments to individual rights and civil liberties, for example, or to internationalism and European integration – have generally been more important, and have united social and economic Liberals more than economic policies have divided them.

As Russell went on to observe, this lack of a clear economic philosophy has been both a strength and a weakness to the Party. Its strength is that it has enabled the Party to adapt flexibly to new developments in economic thinking without having to undergo any major internal ideological struggle – unlike the Conservative switch to Thatcherite monetarism in the 1970s and 1980s, or Labour's abandonment of Clause IV in the 1990s. It has also enabled the Party to accommodate individuals with widely diverging views about economics. It has been a weakness in that in a period when economic policy has been a key electoral battleground in British politics it has not helped develop a clear Liberal or Liberal Democrat image. For example, although when the Liberal leader Clement Davies stated, in a speech on the Attlee Government's economic policy in 1945, that he was 'neither exhilarated nor frightened by the word "nationalisation"',[3] he was staying true to Liberal principles (in that for Liberals, ownership of the nationalised industries was not the point – it was how they were run that was important), but failing utterly to engage in what was then a key political debate.

Despite this, however, or perhaps because of it, Liberal – and Liberals' – thinking on aspects of political economy helped to define much of Britain's economic and social history throughout the nineteenth and twentieth centuries. The Liberal approach to free trade underpinned British economic success from the middle of the nineteenth century. The New Liberal belief in an interventionist social policy laid the foundations of the welfare state Labour was to build on after 1945. Even after the Party's fall from power, the country's post-war economic and social policy was largely framed by two Liberals, John Maynard Keynes and William Beveridge.

1945–56: Decline and dissension

Keynes and Beveridge may have been Liberals, but their proposals were implemented by governments of other parties. After the 1945 election, in which the

Liberal Party lost almost half its seats, including its leader's, it appeared doomed to terminal decline.

Free trade, the great cause of Victorian Liberalism, was still the central plank of the 1945 and 1950 Liberal election manifestos. However, by then it seemed the echo of a bygone age, particularly since from the mid-1930s the economy had recovered relatively strongly despite the introduction of protection by the National Government, a step which had caused the Liberal Party to leave the National coalition, ending its last peacetime involvement in government. Yet the Party could not abandon it, since it was virtually the only issue it could call its own – in 1942, according to Mass Observation, it was the only Liberal policy electors recognised[4] – and was vital to internal cohesion.

The proto-Keynesian programme on which the Liberals had fought the 1929 election, under David Lloyd George, had largely been abandoned during the 1930s; it was too radical for Lloyd George's successors to pursue in the face of the depression that followed Wall Street's Great Crash of 1929, and they stuck to the less controversial defence of free trade. Indeed, after 1945 the Party returned almost to a Gladstonian degree of fiscal rectitude, arguing for lower taxes and more thrift, particularly in reaction to high wartime expenditure and the Attlee Government's post-war reflationary strategy. In turn this helped to push the left of the Party out towards Labour.

Although the Beveridge Report had been endorsed by the Liberal Party, Liberals did not see it as creating a welfare *state*. As Beveridge himself put it, the aim of his report 'was not security through a welfare state but security by cooperation between the state and individual … The central purpose of the Beveridge Report was to ensure subsistence as of right in virtue of insurance and narrow the scope of assistance.'[5] The Report's proposed system of cash benefits financed by equal contributions from all sections of society – workers, employers and the state – embodied the Liberal dislike of class antagonisms and desire that all sections of society should work together in pursuit of the common good. The Labour Government's abandonment of the contributory principle for pensions, and the growing reliance on what became known as supplementary benefits, also not dependent on contributions, were criticised by Liberals as undermining individual self-reliance. Similarly, Beveridge's book, *Voluntary Action* (1948), was published partly as a reproof to the government's exclusion of friendly societies from the new social insurance scheme, increasing the power of the state at the expense of the voluntary sector. Liberals largely shared Beveridge's concern over the growth of the state, and hoped that the need for welfare provision would eventually disappear in the wake of rising material prosperity.

The right of the Party in particular also stressed the need for widening property ownership; the more that individuals owned property the more secure they would be economically, and also the more likely to participate in the civic society of their community. The Party's 1938 *Ownership for All* report had emphasised the role of property ownership as 'the bedrock of liberty',[6] encouraging greater initiative and risk-taking; it set out a variety of mechanisms by which property could be redistributed, including the rating of site values rather than buildings (a long-held Liberal belief, deriving originally from Henry George's proposals in the nineteenth century for the taxation of land values), and changes to inheritance tax.

The most innovative aspects of the *Ownership for All* report concerned profit-sharing, co-ownership and co-partnership in industry. This had been a long-running feature of Liberal policy; the 1928 'Yellow Book' had contained proposals for workers to have a say in the management of their firms. The 1945 and 1950 election manifestos contained pledges to improve the status and remuneration of the workers, set up works councils and sectoral joint industrial councils and encourage profit-sharing. In 1948 the Party committed itself to compulsory co-ownership for all firms other than the smallest. Although important to Party cohesion (it was one of the few Liberal policies the Party could really call its own), however, it did not strike a particular chord with the electorate.

In reality, to the outside world the Party lacked any coherent image: it was split ideologically between those in favour of greater state intervention and those opposed to it. As Malcolm Baines put it, 'different Liberal ideas co-existed not only in the same party, but often in the same person'.[7] He quoted Richard Acland, the Liberal MP who left in 1942 to found Common Wealth: 'the two attitudes even today seem to cohere often in one person. Mention any injustice and it's "the government will put that right"; mention any restriction imposed by government on anyone and it's "we'll set the people free".'[8]

Clement Davies, Party leader from 1945 to 1956, was unable to give any clear lead for fear of alienating one wing or the other. As a consequence Liberals tended to describe themselves in terms of the other two parties, as a moderating influence on the extremes of socialism and Conservatism; the 1951 manifesto referred to the need to 'strengthen the liberal forces in both parties'.[9] This was hardly an electorally appealing position, particularly since the defections of Liberal activists to both the other parties since the 1920s appeared to have made each of them more liberal in any case.

1956–67: Revival and innovation

In the 1950s, however, the divisions between economic and social liberals began to be resolved in favour of the latter. In the early part of the decade a determined attempt was made by a group of 'radical individualists' to return the Party decisively to its Gladstonian position of free trade, minimum government and individual liberty. Activists such as Oliver Smedley (who left the Party in 1962 in opposition to its support for entry to the Common Market) argued that the disasters of the 1950 and 1951 elections had been caused by a lack of adherence to these traditional beliefs.[10] In turn, however, this stimulated the establishment of the Radical Reform Group, an internal ginger group aimed at countering this rightward trend and stemming the haemorrhaging of left-wing Liberals to the Labour Party. Its early policy agenda focused on the proper funding of the welfare state and free health service, the maintenance of full employment, planned production in agriculture, and industrial reform, based on the pre-war Liberal approach of profit-sharing and co-ownership.

Partly because of the Radical Reform Group's activities, partly because the Party leadership was too cautious about moving away from the prevailing Butskellite consensus, and partly because the radical individualist programme appeared to be an old-fashioned dead end, these radical individualists' efforts were not successful, and the accession of the Radical Reform Group supporter Jo Grimond to the leadership in 1956 signalled their defeat. Some of them drifted into the Conservative Party and others to pro-market fringe groups, while Arthur Seldon helped to set up the Institute for Economic Affairs, which became an important source of economic liberal thinking and propaganda, helping to underpin, twenty years later, the emergence of Thatcherite Conservatism. (One of the many interesting counterfactuals in Liberal history is the question of whether Thatcherism would ever have existed if the radical individualists had won the internal struggle within the Liberal Party.[11])

Jo Grimond's accession to the Party leadership in 1956 heralded a period of policy innovation. He was charismatic, idealistic and imaginative, an inspiring speaker and a good communicator, especially to young voters. He was able to capitalise on the electorate's growing disenchantment with the other two parties, particularly after the Suez adventure of 1956 made it clear that the Conservatives were not Liberals in disguise. Furthermore, he was interested in ideas, and in his books and pamphlets he gave political Liberalism a new direction and purpose. He made the Liberals a respectable party to join once more, and attracted experts who contributed to a renaissance in Party thinking. Although ultimately unsuccessful, his political strategy – the realignment of the left, the uniting of Britain's progressive forces around the nucleus provided by the Liberal Party, basing politics on ideas rather than class interests – helped to attracted more radical and left-wing supporters, helping to cement the victory of the social liberals within the Party.

Free trade remained an important Liberal theme, though in a new guise. The international economic institutions created by, among others, Keynes, at Bretton Woods in 1944 were by the 1950s helping to trigger a significant expansion of international trade. To a large extent, support for trade liberalisation was shared by all three parties, though the Liberal Party generally argued for a faster and further removal of trade barriers. This was not without internal controversy, however, as the Party's parliamentary representation by now rested almost entirely on rural areas, where agricultural protectionism still held considerable appeal. After a 1953 Assembly vote for a policy of gradual abandonment of guaranteed markets and fixed prices for agriculture, Jeremy Thorpe seized the microphone and proclaimed that he and other candidates for rural seats would disown such an electorally damaging position.[12] In 1958 moves to delete the word 'unilateral' from a motion on free trade ended in uproar.[13] The 1959 manifesto, however, still demanded the dismantling of all protectionism within one parliament, and ended with the slogan: 'Exchange goods, not H-bombs'.[14]

The main innovation, however, came over Europe. In the second half of the

1950s the Liberal principles of support for European integration (part of the Party's general belief in the need for strong international institutions) and support for free trade began to come into conflict. Although in 1956 the Party had welcomed the proposal for the Common Market, it was uneasy about the exclusive customs union that was eventually formed under the Treaty of Rome in 1957. For a while, the Party officially preferred the proposal for a European Free Trade Association, which was eventually established in 1960 by countries outside the Common Market. In 1958, however, Grimond himself became convinced – partly by the arguments of his formidable mother-in-law, Violet Bonham Carter, a convinced member of the European Movement, and others of his supporters in the Party – of the need for change. A commitment to the European Economic Community fitted well with his drive to give the Party something new, distinctive and 'modern' to say.[15]

Support for British participation in the EEC became official Liberal policy in 1960. It was opposed by the purist free-traders within the Party, because of concerns over European protectionism against the rest of the world. But Grimond and his supporters had prepared well for the move, publishing statements and pamphlets in support, and by this point the purists had largely lost the argument; their remaining adherents mainly left the Party afterwards. In addition, and most importantly, for Liberals free trade was never solely an economic cause: the Cobdenite vision of trade building links between peoples was the key factor, and particularly relevant in Europe given the background of three major wars in the preceding ninety years. This commitment to European integration became, and remains, a defining feature of the Liberal Party and Liberal Democrats. In contrast to the other two main parties' reversals of position on the issue, the Liberals have remained committed to the European cause without significant internal dissent. In the 1960s and 1970s, this was an important factor in attracting new, pro-European, recruits to the Party, and in the 1980s a key foundation-stone of the Alliance with the SDP.

Membership of the EEC formed part of a broader theme of modernisation of the British economy, one which Grimond, which his aura of freshness, was well placed to exploit (Harold Wilson, with his 'white heat of the scientific revolution', did much the same). By the late 1950s concerns were growing over the relative strength of the economy in comparison to Britain's competitors. The Liberals identified the Conservative Government's foreign economic policy, based on an outdated view of Britain's imperial role, as the main problem. The strains of defending the value of sterling, seen as an international currency on a par with the US dollar, while at the same time maintaining the high levels of overseas military expenditure necessary to retain Britain's role as a world power, were producing chronic balance-of-payments deficits, provoking, in those days of fixed exchange rates, runs on sterling. In turn this forced the government periodically to deflate the economy, resulting in a stop–go cycle that undermined business confidence and long-term investment and growth. The Liberal solution was summed up in the title of a 1961 pamphlet, *Growth not Grandeur*.[16] It argued for a new international role for Britain, as part of the EEC, a reduction in military spending, and an economic policy geared to achieving a steady growth rate and featuring long-term planning stimulating higher capital expenditure.

Another plank of the modernisation strategy concerned industrial policy, where the Liberal aim was to heal the rift between the small owning class and the large working one, helping to reduce the conflicts plaguing British industry, establish consensus within firms round the overall growth target, and promote co-ownership and co-partnership. Grimond himself later became convinced of the value of co-operative enterprises, such as the John Lewis partnership in the UK or the Mondragon Cooperative Corporation in Spain (now the world's largest worker co-operative). These commitments sat well with the decentralist, community-minded ethos of Liberalism, which, in contrast to the social democracy of Labour administrations, was always sceptical of relying too much on centralised state solutions. Over-reliance on state action would enhance the power of bureaucracies, transforming those who received state services into the passive recipients of handouts, devaluing their humanity by depriving them of the ability to take decisions which affected their everyday lines.

For Grimond, these policies related back to his belief in the value of communities as the key social unit in which individuals could develop their full potential by sharing in the pursuit of common goals. Fearing the impact of the capture of the state by big business and big unions, and the development of the civil service into a self-serving oligarchy, he saw a possible answer in support for civil society: intermediate, non-state institutions providing a focus for individual citizens and a buffer between them and the central state. Thus the spirit of community and of localism was of cardinal importance; in his maiden parliamentary speech, in 1950, he expressed strong support for Scottish Home Rule, by which he meant self-government within the framework of a federal Britain. This was later extended, in Liberal manifestos, to Home Rule for Wales and regional government in England. Coupled with pre-existing commitments to electoral reform and a stronger framework for the protection of individual rights and civil liberties and the curbing of the power of the executive, this formed a package of sweeping reforms to the British constitution that has remained a key feature of Liberal policy to this day.

Co-ownership in industry, the spread of home ownership and the decentralisation of political and economic power were all ways to foster participation and an active citizenry. As Peter Barberis has put it, Grimond 'upheld a Millite position in advocating participation as an agent of improvement. In what he came to regard as an age of numbing conformity and moral turpitude he worried not that citizens would demand too much freedom but that they would be satisfied with too little.'[17]

1967–81: Centrism and environmentalism

The Grimond era rescued the Liberal Party from incoherence and near-oblivion. The internal left–right debates seemed to be settled, as Grimond's leadership, and the 1956 Suez debacle, brought a new generation of progressive activists into the

Party, and the 'radical individualists' departed. The Orpington by-election victory of 1962 and better (though still disappointing) results in the General Elections of 1964 and 1966 signalled that the Party was not going to disappear and that its views would be taken seriously by the media, if not on a par with the other two parties.

To a certain extent this had an inhibiting effect on the further development of Party policy. The more the Party seemed to be attracting votes, the less it was prepared to challenge the prevailing Butskellite consensus. In retrospect Grimond himself felt that the Party sacrificed ideas to psephological advantage. By the late 1970s he had become far more sceptical of state action and convinced of the values of small government and the market than he had been when leader; in a speech in 1980, for example, he even went so far as to claim that 'much of what Mrs Thatcher and Sir Keith Joseph say and do is in the mainstream of Liberal philosophy'.[18] Grimond's own political strategy of the realignment of the left, however, had made it much less likely that the Party would follow this path, and it remained broadly social liberal in character after Grimond's resignation in 1967.

Neither of his two successors, Jeremy Thorpe and David Steel, were as interested in ideas and policies as Grimond had been. New thinking *was* going on, but in contrast to the Grimond era it was concentrated at the grass-roots. An abortive revolt against Thorpe's leadership in May 1968 led to the establishment of the Liberal Commission, charged with translating the Party's principles into a coherent programme. Its report, *Liberals Look Ahead*, produced for the 1969 Assembly, revealed some innovative thinking, including proposals on environmental policy, then just emerging as a serious issue. This was developed subsequently, with the publication of a comprehensive *Report on the Environment* in 1972. The Liberal Party became the first of the major parties to call for a reduction in pollution and greater protection for endangered wildlife; it opposed the expansion of nuclear power, at least until the problems of waste disposal could be dealt with, and called for more energy conservation measures and the development of renewable sources of power. In 1979 the Assembly developed a more comprehensive critique of the aims of orthodox economic policy, adopting a resolution declaring that 'economic growth, as measured by GDP, is neither desirable nor achievable'. It was not until the late 1980s that this environmental critique of orthodox economic growth models was to become more widely accepted; in 1979 the Liberals were considerably ahead of their time.

The Party also began more seriously to consider the problems of the welfare state, as it was becoming more and more clear that the post-war implementation of the Beveridge Report had failed to eradicate poverty and need. Patterns of poverty had changed; in place of the mass unemployment and inadequate provision for childhood, sickness and old age on which Beveridge had focused, the new poor were increasingly low wage-earners, the chronically sick and disabled, and children in lone-parent families – in other words, those falling outside the social insurance system established by Beveridge (though some of this would have been dealt with by the subsistence-level family allowances he proposed but which governments never implemented). The Liberal manifestos of 1974 included commitments to a national minimum wage and a credit income tax scheme, combining income tax and social security to guarantee everyone a minimum income varied according to their circumstances.

In most other respects, however, the Party became more centrist in its approach, largely in response to signs of growing extremism in the other two parties, and in politics in general. This was the period of the breakdown of the post-war economic consensus, of major industrial strife, including the power workers' and miners' strikes of the early 1970s, and of the seemingly intractable problems of low growth and high inflation. The Liberal response in the 1974 elections was to stress the need to bring all sides together, 'to secure a new approach to our problems in which sectional and partisan interests are set aside in favour of the welfare of all … you, the elector, can help us in this task by rejecting the sterile class conflict of two discredited parties and voting in a new era of reconciliation'.[19] This was very much in the traditional Liberal approach, going back to Gladstone and before, of appealing to a wider interest than mere sectionalism. The detailed policies underlying this included a permanent prices and incomes policy, government-mandated caps on price and wage increases – not a particularly Liberal approach, but seen by all parties at the time as essential to deal with the inflation crisis. The earlier themes of decentralisation, industrial co-partnership and support for European integration were also present.

The Party finally gained an opportunity of putting its policies into effect under the Lib-Lab Pact, when Liberal votes kept Callaghan's minority Labour Government in power for eighteen months from March 1977. The outcome, however, was disappointing in terms of policy achievements, and all the Liberals could point to was some limited profit-sharing measures and – arguably – a reduction in inflation as a result of a greater degree of political stability.[20]

After the political disruption of the previous five years, it was not surprising that the 1979 election manifesto gave pride of place to constitutional reform, including decentralisation and electoral reform, presenting it as the essential prerequisite for the industrial and economic stability that the electorate clearly wanted. A statutory incomes policy still featured, though it caused some controversy within the Party, and environmental protection was given a major section. In the wake of the Lib-Lab Pact, the manifesto was reported more systematically in the press; *The Economist* complimented the Party on having once again produced strikingly the best party manifesto.[21] But it was not the programme the country wanted, as Britain voted decisively for Thatcher's Conservatives.

1981–88: Alliance and the social market economy

In 1981 the political scene was transformed by the launch of the Social Democratic Party in March, and the formation of the Alliance between the SDP and the Liberals six months later. The distinguishing features of the new party were opposition to extremism, either from Thatcherite Conservatism or militant socialism, and a commitment to Europe and constitutional reform. Although some Liberals warned against the centralist nature of the new SDP, for most it clearly made sense to enter into an electoral alliance with it.

The Alliance platform largely continued the 1979 Liberal themes. The 1983 election manifesto was broadly centrist, stressing the need to avoid extremism and confrontation politics and to promote 'partnership' and national unity. It also retained a clear commitment to comprehensive constitutional reform, and to a sweeping overhaul of the welfare state. The environmental section was toned down, the pro-technology SDP being far less sceptical of nuclear power than were the Liberals.

Although the Alliance won more than twice as many votes in 1983 as had the Liberals in 1979, the policy positions it took probably had little to do with it, and they were not notably in tune with the iconoclastic Thatcherite approach the electorate appeared to prefer. As noted above, the legacy of the internal Liberal struggles of the early 1950s had been the departure of the radical individualists and libertarians from the Liberal Party; by the 1970s they were located on the fringes of the Conservative Party and in the think tanks and policy institutes that Margaret Thatcher and Keith Joseph looked to for ideas when constructing their critique of the post-war economic consensus. The resulting association between the new economic liberalism and other aspects of the Thatcher style – authoritarian, nationalistic and socially reactionary – together with the growth in the importance within the Party of local activists and councillors, used to using the power of the state at local level, ensured that the Liberal Party stayed firmly in the social liberal camp, resisting any particularly pro-market move. This was reinforced by the association with the SDP, so that the Alliance ended up as the defender of the Butskellite consensus – as the *Financial Times* observed, to read the 1983 manifesto was to 'suffer something very like nostalgia'[22] – even while it was palpably breaking down.

The Thatcherite assault on the Keynesian approach of full employment and high welfare spending had a marked effect, however, on David Owen, who became SDP leader after the disappointment of 1983. Originally viewed as the most left-wing of the SDP's founding Gang of Four, he rapidly accommodated himself to Thatcherism, and indeed came increasingly to believe that strong leadership was what the Alliance needed – whereas, for Steel and most Liberals, Thatcherite Conservatism was the opposite of everything they stood for. In fact Owen had few firm policy principles, and used policy positions mainly as weapons with which to attack the opposition, whether that happened to be Labour, the Liberals or the Jenkinsites within his own Party. His approach included the development of the policy of the 'social market economy', a term that had in fact been introduced into British politics (from Germany) by Keith Joseph in 1975 as part of the construction of the case against state interventionism and high public spending.[23]

Joseph's social market meant restricting government intervention to the limiting of market distortions such as the abuse of monopoly power or restrictive practices. The 'social' aspect derived from the surplus produced by the more efficient and competitive economy that would emerge from the shackles of corporatism: higher profits, higher wages and higher employment all resulted in a higher tax yield, which could then be invested in education and welfare. Although David Owen's version differed from this at first – his early writings on the social market featured an incomes policy, industrial strategy and central planning – he steadily moved in a more pro-market direction. As the 1980s wore on he came to advocate privatisation of the nationalised industries even before the Conservatives started their large-scale denationalisation programme, argued for labour market reform to hold down real wages and increase international competitiveness, and supported selectivity in social security, while at the same time dropping his earlier proposals for an incomes policy and redistribution. He also called for the application of markets to public services, supporting the idea of an internal market within the NHS, again before the Conservatives did.

The Liberal response to Owen was to argue that there was no real difference from Liberal economic thinking. As Malcolm Bruce MP observed in 1985, many politicians of the left, faced with the dominance of the New Right, seemed to feel a need to express their understanding of and commitment to the operations of market forces – whereas Liberals had never questioned the role of the market, but, equally, had long been aware of its limitations.[24] The more Owen veered to the right, however, the more his views contributed to the growing tensions within the Alliance, at least at the centre (at the grass-roots the two parties generally got on well). But because Owen always opposed joint policy-making with the Liberals, and also because he never enjoyed total support within his own Party, the social market position did not feature in the 1987 Alliance manifesto.

Owen's political career effectively came to an end after he resigned the SDP leadership in 1987 after it voted to open merger negotiations with the Liberals. Although he attempted to continue to develop his social market thinking in his new third party, the 'continuing SDP', its rapid eclipse largely consigned the term to political oblivion. In any case, Owen never defined precisely what he meant by the phrase, and at different times he stressed different, and sometimes mutually incompatible, aspects (his 'Social Market and Social Justice' speech in January 1987, for example, contained a clear commitment to social justice, in contrast to the much more right-wing tone that he was generally adopting at the time). In hindsight, the debate around the social market can be seen as one facet of the broader trend, in Britain and in other Western democracies, towards more market-based and less interventionist approaches to economic and industrial policy; but the growing differences between Owen and the Liberals over the topic did little more than contribute to the image of dissension that became characteristic of the Alliance leadership.

1988–2005: Europe, environment and public services

The failures of the Alliance led, in 1988, to the merger of the two parties and the birth of the Liberal Democrats. The creation of a single party enabled the resolution of the issues that had divided the Liberals and the SDP – for example, nuclear power (and nuclear weapons) – and the departure of the Owenites ensured that there was little internal dissent, at least on policy issues. Although in organisational terms the merged party borrowed heavily from the SDP, in ideological and policy terms, the Liberal Democrats can be seen as a modernised Liberal Party, with a policy platform built around Liberalism. In practice, the social democracy of the SDP (excluding the later versions of Owen's social market) had not differed markedly from the social liberalism of the early 1980s Liberal Party. The main difference lay over attitudes to the state, where Liberals were more sceptical of the dangers of state power than the SDP tended to be, and more attracted to means such as decentralisation to constrain it.[25]

The first leader of the Liberal Democrats, Paddy Ashdown, was crucial in drawing together a coherent policy programme out of the wreckage of the Alliance. Unlike Steel and Thorpe, but in common with Grimond, Ashdown displayed a consistent interest in ideas, and his views largely helped to determine the direction and main themes of the Party in the 1992 and 1997 elections. Although this led to a few clashes with the Party's Policy Committee and Conference (who both tended to be less market-oriented than Ashdown in economic and social policy), he was able to stamp his ideas firmly on the Party largely because of the respect and admiration he enjoyed amongst members – 'ordinary party members will take things from him for which they would have lynched David Owen,' commented *The Economist* in 1991.[26]

Five main themes, three of them familiar from earlier periods, came to characterise the Liberal Democrat policy platform. In the early 1990s the European issue came to prominence once more, with the debates over the Maastricht Treaty of European Union in 1992–93. Liberal Democrats supported the treaty and also British entry to the single European currency. Also familiar from earlier manifestos was a comprehensive package of constitutional reform. Unlike in the 1970s and 1980s, though, the supporting arguments did not revolve around ending the confrontation between industry and the unions – which was far less relevant in the 1990s – but around the theme of giving more power to the individual, reducing the degree of centralisation in government which failed 'to make effective use of the talents and skills available across the country'.[27] This was a clear return to Jo Grimond's view of decentralisation as the route to participation and an active citizenry.

Building on earlier Liberal policies, environmental policies featured far more strongly in the Lib Dem platform. This fitted well with the growing concern over the environment exemplified by the 1992 'Earth Summit' in Rio, and the gradual understanding that environmental degradation was an inevitable consequence of the way in which Western economies were structured, culminating in the concept of environmentally sustainable development. The Party argued for a shift in taxation from income and employment to pollution and resource use, and called for much stricter national targets for reducing pollution. It also argued for some environmental constraints on free trade, recognising the impact that trade liberalisation could have on magnifying the effects of unsustainable patterns of production and consumption. Throughout the 1990s and 2000s the Liberal Democrats became widely regarded as the greenest of the three major parties, and are largely still seen so today, despite environmental policy developments in each of the others.

The two new approaches concerned economic policy and public services. In an important shift in economic policy (and one which, ironically, David Owen would probably have favoured), the Party called for independence for the Bank of England in setting interest rates and controlling monetary policy, removing these powers from politicians too vulnerable to electoral pressure, thereby helping to promote long-term stability. The need for greater competition, particularly in the privatised utilities, also featured. Although this was a distinct shift towards a more market orientation than the Alliance had displayed, it was not symptomatic of an economic-liberal non-interventionist approach to economics in general; the 1992 manifesto in particular contained an ambitious reflationary plan designed to bring down unemployment, and the 1997 document contained a commitment to increase the top rate of income tax, to make the system more redistributive.

The second new theme was the need to invest in public services, particularly in education, and the commitment to raise taxes to pay for it – the penny on income tax for education. Initially viewed by commentators as a risky move, the 1992 election campaign proved it to be a popular selling point, and the message was given a much higher profile in 1997. Again in a clear difference from the Owenite approach, the Party was critical of much of the Conservative Government's introduction of market mechanisms into public services.

This policy platform largely survived Ashdown's replacement by Charles Kennedy as leader in 1999. Unlike Ashdown, Kennedy was never interested in the details of policy; his skill lay more in being a communicator of others' ideas. Although Kennedy himself failed to give any particular lead to the direction of policy, some of his supporters had hoped he would place more of an emphasis on social justice, and injected some elements of this into the Liberal Democrat platform. Thus policy on taxation changed away from raising revenue for expenditure on public services – since the Labour Government was doing that in any case – and concentrated on being more fair, through replacing the Council Tax with a local income tax (a long-held Liberal policy) and raising the top rate of tax from 40 to 50 per cent. In 2005 the extra revenue this would generate was allocated primarily to pay for providing elderly and disabled people with free personal care and abolishing university tuition and top-up fees – a contributory factor behind the Party winning a string of university seats in the 2005 election.

Environmental policy continued to develop, with green policy points picked out in every major policy area in the 2001 and 2005 manifestos, in an attempt to demonstrate the sustainable development-led imperative of integration of environmental concerns throughout government and the economy. The commitment to Europe also remained clear, although as the EU developed and grew in size, and as Eurosceptic feelings spread throughout the UK, policy proposals tended to focus more on the need for reform of EU institutions, mainly to make them more democratic. British membership of the single currency was supported, but only subject to a referendum. The commitment to decentralisation also remained strong, although as Labour brought in limited devolution for Scotland and Wales, the Party shifted focus to decentralising the provision of public services, with less government interference such as central targets and more decision-making being made by professionals, with democratic oversight provided by local authorities.

2005 onwards: Economic versus social liberals?

The economic liberal–social liberal debate within the Party was not, however, over. In 2004, the publication of *The Orange Book: Reclaiming Liberalism*[28] triggered a debate over the future direction of the Party. Although in fact the book contained few specific proposals that were not already Party policy, its main message was clearly pro-market. One of its two editors, the former Party Policy Director David Laws MP, argued that the Party had too often veered towards 'a well-meaning "nanny-state liberalism"';[29] he cited the taxation of road travel and aviation as examples. Similarly, he complained that 'in the decades up to the 1980s, the Liberal belief in economic Liberalism was progressively eroded by forms of soggy socialism and corporatism, which have too often been falsely perceived as a necessary corollary of social liberalism'.[30] While being careful not to reject the social liberal agenda explicitly, Laws called for the Party to draw on its economic liberal heritage to address public service delivery, introducing more choice, competition and consumer power. He drew attention to the problems of inequality of opportunity, particularly as caused by child poverty, but failed to set out any proposals to deal with them, and did not discuss issues of redistribution.

The publication of the *Orange Book* led, three years later, to the appearance of an explicitly social liberal alternative: *Reinventing the State: Social Liberalism for the 21ˢᵗ Century*.[31] The book made the case for state action in a series of areas where market solutions were inadequate, including in particular the need to reduce income and wealth inequality and to tackle climate change. A major theme of the book was localism, and a series of chapters explored how decision-making and public service provision could be decentralised: 'It is about reinventing the British state so that it delivers social justice and environmental sustainability through a decentralised and participatory democracy.'[32]

The book dealt with the social liberal–economic liberal debate by arguing that Liberalism in Britain had been of the social variety since the late nineteenth century. Like their classical liberal forebears, social liberals believed that the state should as far as possible leave people alone to make their own decisions on how to live their lives, but they held in addition that freedom was not attainable without a fair distribution of wealth and power. Economic liberalism was not a distinctive and opposed strand of liberalism, but simply 'a preference for market mechanisms not in opposition to redistribution but as a method to be used in the detailed design of mechanisms for it',[33] and those party members who called themselves economic rather than social liberals were in reality both. The question of whether a particular public service could best be delivered by the market or the state had no general answer, but depended on circumstances. Differences between Liberals over the details of policy were more appropriately viewed as a continuous spectrum between maximalist and minimalist social liberals, who differed primarily over the extent of the redistribution they believed necessary to achieve the conditions for political freedom.

Although the two books were certainly different in tone and message, the extent of policy disagreement between them was limited, and several MPs contributed chapters to both. In practice the supposed divisions became a short-hand for all sorts of other disagreements within the Party, including the normal tensions that always exist between the parliamentary leadership and the grass-roots activists, but also differences of opinion over the leadership of the Party after the 2005 election. Although the election result had been good, many in the Party felt that it ought to have been even better, given the Party's high profile over opposition to the Iraq War and the failure of the Conservative Party to stage a significant revival; the period after the election saw several displays of unhappiness with Kennedy's lacklustre leadership. Journalists enjoyed identifying divisions between economic liberals and social liberals that did not exist to the extent they claimed, but there was no clear leadership on offer to damp down the divisions and take the Party in any particular direction. 'Economic liberals', or 'Orange Bookers', became equated with parliamentary 'modernisers', eager to short-circuit the Party's internal democratic structures and put more power into the hands of the MPs, while 'social liberals' were portrayed as the grass-roots activists unwilling to compromise the purity of their beliefs in the pursuit of power, happier to stay in opposition as a party of protest.

Although this picture was exaggerated, it had an element of truth. Certainly the bulk of the parliamentary party – who, through their constituency surgeries routinely saw those whom the state had failed – tended to be more sceptical of the use of state power than the bulk of the grass-roots activists, a high proportion of whom were councillors engaged in running local authorities, comfortable with using state power at local level to improve their constituents' lives.

Party policy development after 2005 gave a slightly confused picture. In two debates on tax policy, in 2006 and 2007, the commitment to a 50% top tax rate was dropped, on the grounds that it was too easy to represent as an attack on aspiration. The new policy, however, which abolished most exemptions and reliefs for top-rate taxpayers and reduced the basic rate of income tax sharply (paid for by much higher environmental taxes), was in fact more redistributive than the previous one – though it did not look like it very obviously; the scrapping of the higher top tax rate made it seem as though the Party was abandoning its position of the previous two decades and becoming a low-tax party. On the other hand, a major policy review exercise conducted in 2005–6[34] concluded that tackling the extent of inequality in British society should be one of the two top priorities for further Party policy development. This led in turn to the 2007 proposal for a 'pupil premium', providing extra resources for schools taking in children from disadvantaged backgrounds. The other top priority identified in the policy review was climate change, and in 2007 the Party also reaffirmed its environmental credentials, endorsing an ambitious programme for a zero-carbon Britain by 2050 and opposing the new generation of nuclear stations supported by the other two parties.

Like most Liberal leadership elections, that of late 2007 was not fought primarily on ideological grounds. Both candidates, Nick Clegg and Chris Huhne, had contributed chapters to both the *Orange Book* and *Reinventing the State*. After the election, the victor, Nick Clegg, argued in several speeches that he was both a social and an economic liberal. In his first major speech as Party leader, in January 2008, he spoke of 'marrying our proud traditions of economic and social liberalism, refusing to accept that one comes at the cost of the other. On that point, if not all others, the controversial *Orange Book* in 2004 was surely right.'[35]

Conclusions

Although the Party leadership, anxious to minimise the extent of internal disagreement, will always downplay the divisions between social and economic liberals, they nevertheless exist. As this chapter had demonstrated, differences of opinion over the appropriate balance of market and state power have been a consistent theme of internal Liberal debate since 1945 and before – and there is no reason to think they will cease. Yet as Conrad Russell argued, this does not represent a fundamental split in the Party; a debate about means and not ends, it is not a central feature of the Liberal philosophy. Indeed at times, as in the immediate aftermath of the 2005 election, the supposed divisions have become a shorthand for other disagreements.

Other features of Liberalism's approach to political economy have been of far greater importance in defining what it means to be a Liberal in post-war Britain. The political commitment to free trade, to the free flow of individuals and ideas as well as of goods and services, to building links between communities and nations, was inherited from pre-war Liberalism and developed in the 1960s to a consistent support for British participation in Europe. This was an important factor in the breakaway of the SDP's MPs from the Labour Party and continues to distinguish the Liberal Democrats from its rivals.

The belief in decentralisation, of economic as much as political power, and of the delivery of public services, is also a distinguishing feature, deriving from the Liberal belief in individualism and communities as the framework within which individuals can best live their lives. From the 1940s to the 1970s, an important aspect of this was support for the creation of communities at work, with proposals for co-partnership and co-ownership. For much of the post-war period, much of this was bound up with the perceived need to end the class-based confrontation that characterised British industrial relations and politics; Liberals tried to base their appeal on the fact that they were different from other parties in not deriving their support from a sectional class. At times, particularly in the 1980s, this risked degenerating into mere centrism, and in any case became less important in the

1990s, as New Labour increasingly converged on Thatcherite territory. Whether Labour's failure to reverse the dramatic rise in income and wealth inequality experienced since 1979 will lead to renewed class conflicts remains to be seen, as does the Liberal Democrat response.

Finally, the Liberal and Liberal Democrat commitment to environmentalism has helped inject a new dimension into British politics (and, incidentally, helped keep the Green Party weak, unlike the situation in some other European countries, where liberals' failure to take up the green agenda has facilitated the growth of green parties). No major party today can ignore environmental politics.

Out of power at Westminster since the war, all the Liberals, SDP and Liberal Democrats have been able to do is influence the political debate. Yet it is clear that in several ways they have done just that. 'The Liberal Democrat essay far outdistances its competitors with a fizz of ideas and an absence of fudge,' stated the *Guardian* in 1992.[36] In 1997 the *Independent* called the Party's manifesto the most challenging of the three, observing that politics without the Liberal Democrats would be 'intolerable'.[37]

Notes

1   C. Russell, *An Intelligent Person's Guide to Liberalism* (Duckworth, London, 1999), p. 57.
2   Both these terms, together with 'social liberal', are imprecise and have meant different things at different times in different contexts; this will be explored further in the text, but for a longer discussion, see D. Doering, 'Classical liberalism'; D. Brack, 'Economic liberalism' and D. Brack, 'Social liberalism', entries in D. Brack and E. Randall (eds), *Dictionary of Liberal Thought* (Politico's, London, 2007).
3   Edward Clement Davies MP, speech on motion of censure on government policy, House of Commons, 5th December 1945, in D. Brack and T. Little (eds), *Great Liberal Speeches* (Politico's, London, 2001), p. 335.
4   M. Baines, 'The Survival of the British Liberal Party, 1932–1959', unpublished PhD thesis (1989), p. 51.
5   Speech at the National Liberal Club, 1952, in ibid., p. 135.
6   Cited in R. Ingham, 'Elliot Dodds', entry in Brack and Randall (eds), *Dictionary of Liberal Thought*, p. 94.
7   Baines, 'The Survival of the British Liberal Party, 1932–1959', p. 123.
8   Ibid.
9   'The nation's task', Liberal Party Election Manifesto 1951, in I. Dale (ed.), *Liberal Party General Election Manifestos, 1900–1997* (Routledge, London, 2000), p. 81.
10 See W. Wallace, 'Survival and revival', pp. 43–4, and A. Gamble, 'Liberals and the economy', pp. 199–201, in V. Bogdanor (ed.), *Liberal Party Politics* (Oxford University Press, Oxford, 1983).
11 This possibility is examined in J. Parry, 'What if the Liberal Party had broken through from the right?', in D. Brack and I. Dale (eds), *Prime Minister Portillo … and Other Things That Never Happened* (Politico's, London, 2003).
12 Baines, 'The Survival of the British Liberal Party, 1932–1959', p. 94.
13 Ibid., p. 116.

14 'People count', Liberal Party Election Manifesto 1959, in Dale (ed.), *Liberal Party General Election Manifestos, 1900–1997*, p. 103.

15 See M. Baines, 'Liberals and Europe', *Journal of Liberal History*, 42 (Spring 2004), for more detail.

16 J. Grimond, *Growth not Grandeur* (New Directions, 1961), cited in Gamble, 'Liberals and the economy', p. 203.

17 P. Barberis, 'Jo Grimond', entry in Brack and Randall (eds), *Dictionary of Liberal Thought*, p. 150.

18 J. Grimond, 'The future of Liberalism', speech delivered on 29th October 1980 to the 80 Club, in Brack and Little (eds), *Great Liberal Speeches*, p. 359.

19 'Change the face of Britain', Liberal Party Election Manifesto February 1974, in Dale (ed.), *Liberal Party General Election Manifestos, 1900–1997*, pp. 147–8.

20 See D. Steel, *Against Goliath: David Steel's Story* (Weidenfeld and Nicolson, London, 1989), pp. 130–44, for an analysis (from a favourable viewpoint) of the Pact's outcomes.

21 D. Butler and D. Kavanagh, *The British General Election of 1979* (Macmillan, London, 1980), p. 159.

22 I. Bradley, *The Strange Rebirth of Liberal Britain* (Chatto and Windus, London, 1985), pp. 173–4.

23 For a full analysis, see D. Brack, 'David Owen and the social market economy', *Journal of Liberal History*, 47 (Summer 2005).

24 M. Bruce, 'The politics of economics', *New Democrat*, April/May 1985.

25 This argument is further developed in R.S. Grayson, 'Social democracy or social liberalism? Ideological sources of Liberal Democrat policy', *Political Quarterly*, 78:1 (2007), pp. 32–9.

26 'Paddy's people', *The Economist* 14th September 1991.

27 'Changing Britain for good', Liberal Democrat Election Manifesto 1992, in Dale (ed.), *Liberal Party General Election Manifestos, 1900–1997*, p. 316.

28 P. Marshall and D. Laws (eds), *The Orange Book: Reclaiming Liberalism* (Profile, London, 2004).

29 D. Laws, 'Reclaiming Liberalism: A liberal agenda for the Liberal Democrats', ibid., p. 24.

30 Ibid., p. 29.

31 D. Brack, R.S. Grayson and D. Howarth (eds). *Reinventing the State: Social Liberalism for the 21st Century* (Politico's, London, 2007).

32 Ibid., p. ix.

33 D. Howarth, 'What is social liberalism?', ibid., p. 3.

34 The outcomes were published as Liberal Democrat policy paper 76, *Trust in People: Make Britain Free, Fair and Green* (Liberal Democrats, London, 2006).

35 N. Clegg, speech at the 'Setting the Agenda' manifesto conference, 12th January 2008, available at http://www.libdems.org.uk/parliament/feature.html?navPage=features .html&id=13708 (acessed 17th February 2008).

36 Leader, *Guardian*, 19th March 1992.

37 D. Butler and D. Kavanagh, *The British General Election of 1997* (Macmillan, Basingstoke, 1997), p. 178.

Social morality

Liberty (in a political sense) is not only a negative but a positive conception. Freedom cannot be predicated, in its true meaning, either of a man or of a society, merely because they are no longer under the compulsion of restraints which have the sanction of positive law. To be really free, they must be able to make the best use of faculty, opportunity, energy, life. It is in this fuller view of the true significance of Liberty that we find the governing impulse in the later developments of Liberalism in the direction of education, temperance, better dwellings [and] an improved social and industrial environment.

Herbert Asquith[1]

Above all, Liberal Democracy is about liberty. That does not just mean freedom from oppressive government. It means providing all citizens with the opportunity to build worthwhile lives for themselves and their families and helping them to recognise their responsibilities to the wider community … That is the Liberal Democrat vision: of active government which invests in people, promotes their long-term prosperity and welfare, safeguards their security, and is answerable to them for its actions.

Paddy Ashdown[2]

These quotations, from the pens of two Liberal leaders from either end of the twentieth century, help illuminate the answer to the question of how Liberals believe society should deal with controversial moral issues. If, as they repeatedly contend, Liberalism is above all about liberty, an observer might imagine that Liberals would be able to provide a very simple answer to this question. This could follow from the 'very simple principle' enunciated by one of the foremost thinkers in Liberalism's history, John Stuart Mill: 'the only purpose for which power can be rightfully exercised over any member of a civilised community, against his will, is to prevent harm to others'.[3] Adhering to this principle, a firm believer in liberty could counsel simply that society should never interfere with individuals' moral choices, however distasteful they may be to anyone else, except if palpable injury to others is caused.

Yet this is not the position Liberals have always adopted. A crucial reason for this is that, even when professing liberty to be their most important value, modern

Liberals have contested its definition: what the arguments of Asquith and Ashdown reveal is that they do not believe that it means just being left alone. Consequently, as this chapter will show, British Liberals have embraced a far more interventionist approach to social morality than might be presupposed.

Liberty, morality and the state

To understand this, it is necessary to begin with a fuller discussion of Liberals' view of liberty, and specifically, Asquith's contention that there is a negative and a positive conception. The most famous explication of the distinction between these two is that presented by Isaiah Berlin. According to Berlin, negative liberty consists in the absence of external coercion: 'political liberty in this sense is simply the area within which a man can act unobstructed by others'.[4] By contrast, positive liberty means not the absence, but the presence of something, the ability to be the master of one's own destiny: 'I wish my life and decisions to depend on myself, not on external forces of whatever kind.'[5] The significance of these two concepts lies in the implications that have often been drawn from them for government: whereas the negative conception may be interpreted as suggesting a relatively minimal role for it, interfering as little as possible in individuals' lives, the positive can be used to justify it taking on many wide-ranging functions, to provide individuals with the opportunities and resources needed to be able to make autonomous decisions.

While this distinction has been subjected to numerous critiques (some questioning whether it is even logically coherent), it remains useful for understanding Liberals' views of freedom, not least because they themselves frequently cite it.[6] However, whereas Berlin worried about the susceptibility of the positive conception of liberty to being pressed into service for authoritarian ends – allowing dictatorial regimes to justify their rule in the name of advancing individuals' 'best interests' – most modern Liberals have regarded it more favourably. Rejecting the minimalist philosophy of government suggested by the negative conception, they have typically understood liberty as requiring, in Ashdown's words, 'active government', to promote a (liberal) vision of the good life. This means developing far-reaching policies in areas such as education, health and housing, with government thereby taking a very strong interest in how individuals lead their lives.

The lineage of this belief can be traced back to the 'new liberalism' of the late nineteenth and early twentieth centuries, when liberals such as T.H. Green and L.T. Hobhouse argued that true freedom is able to flourish only in specific social conditions, in which extremes of poverty and inequality have been ameliorated – a starving man may be free in the negative sense of not suffering from external constraints, but without food this freedom is of little use to him. For individuals to be able to exercise their freedoms in any meaningful sense, it is therefore necessary to address the most pressing social problems.

This social liberalism is arguably the most significant contribution Liberals made to British governance during the twentieth century. Even as Liberals found themselves increasingly marginalised politically, this philosophy played a part in the development of social and economic policy. In particular, the post-war consensus in British politics – founded on beliefs in an expanded welfare state and a mixed economy – owed much to social liberalism, seen most clearly in the fact that two of the most influential figures in its creation, John Maynard Keynes and William Beveridge, were Liberals rather than socialists.[7] Moreover, the enlargement of the state's role was for Liberals always about more than just economic growth and full employment; the robust moral sensibility that lay behind social liberals' convictions is well exemplified by Beveridge's description of the five social ills he sought to tackle – Want, Disease, Ignorance, Squalor and Idleness – as being the giant 'evils' of the age.

Another key inspiration for Liberals' social and moral agendas has been religion, especially via the influence of nonconformism. If the Church of England was once, as it used to be said, the Conservative Party at prayer, then in at least some communities, nonconformist churches were the Liberal Party at prayer.[8] Worth considering here is the active role played by nonconformist churches in temperance campaigns, with their demands for the strict control, or even prohibition, of the sale and consumption of alcohol. Fear of social disorder among the masses was a large part of campaigners' concerns, but as the Asquith quotation at the beginning of the chapter indicates, temperance can also be legitimated on the grounds of promoting positive liberty, since insobriety can be seen as an obstacle to individuals fulfilling their potential.

This issue provides a valuable illustration of how different conceptions of liberty can lead to divergent prescriptions regarding the regulation of morality. Whereas temperance advocates may wish much greater control to be exercised over individuals' personal behaviour, Mill's largely negative conception of liberty leads him to view efforts at the prohibition of alcohol as one of the 'gross usurpations upon the liberty of private life', and the puritanical crusaders for such restrictions as 'intrusively pious'.[9] Also of significance in Mill's critique is his analysis of the way in which temperance campaigners' understanding of rights goes beyond the traditional notion of individual rights to encompass the idea of 'social rights'. Upon this basis, he notes, regardless of whether any direct harm can be shown to be caused by the consumption of alcohol to anyone but the drinker, curbs can still be justified in terms of infringements on others' social rights – for example, because the social misery created by alcoholism may lead to a drain on the pockets of all taxpayers, as well as diminish the overall quality of life within society. Yet, Mill points out, similar arguments could be posited about almost any behaviour one finds objectionable, as infringing upon supposed social rights. The problem, therefore, with the idea of these rights is that 'there is no violation of liberty which it would not justify', making it a 'monstrous' one in the eyes of anyone concerned about individual freedom.[10] Even so, the concept of social rights lives on in contemporary Liberal discourses.[11]

Adherence to notions of positive freedom and social rights explains why many modern Liberals do not subscribe to Mill's very simple principle, or at least, interpret harm to mean more than solely direct injury to identifiable individuals. Of course, moving away from a negative, individualist conception of liberty leaves many Liberals sounding a lot like social democrats.[12] In order to maintain some distance from a more straightforwardly left-wing philosophy, Liberals' usual argument is that despite the affinities between their doctrines, Liberals are much more sceptical towards the state, preferring community-based approaches to state-centred ones.[13] Consequently, as well as recognising government's positive role in dealing with social problems, Liberals also express concern about the threat to freedom posed by an overbearing state; indeed, the same policy paper can cite with approval not only Keynes and Beveridge, but also Friedrich Hayek, the great critic of collectivist statism.[14] The expressed preference is therefore for an 'enabling state' rather than a heavily centralised one, which is 'creative and liberating, not sluggish and controlling'.[15]

One way that Liberals attempt to resolve any tension in these beliefs is by arguing for a concept of citizenship that strikes a balance between positive and negative liberty, by combining an emphasis upon both rights and responsibilities: individual rights help secure the realm of negative freedom, while responsibilities to the wider community do the same for that of positive freedom.[16] This implies a mixed set of attitudes towards the state, perhaps best summed up in the words of Charles Kennedy, who articulates his philosophy of government in terms of the twin propositions that it should 'do less in a few areas' and 'more in others'.[17]

How these ideas have played out in practice can be seen by turning to some key policy debates. Yet before doing this, it is necessary to recognise that any analysis is complicated by the fact that British Liberalism contains differing viewpoints, one important division being between social liberals and libertarians. As a result, at times there is relative unity, but at others there is not. For example, an article analysing the free votes of MPs on four private members' bills in 1994 relating to two contentious moral issues – capital punishment and the age of consent for homosexuals – concludes that, of the three main parties, Liberal Democrats were the most cohesive (and the most liberal).[18] However, later studies have shown that on free votes on many other social/moral issues – including euthanasia, gun control and hunting with dogs – the Party can be deeply split, possibly even more so than Labour or the Conservatives.[19] Further complexity arises when the views of the wider membership are additionally considered.

Nonetheless, by examining election manifestos, policy papers, conference resolutions and parliamentary activities, the dominant trends and perspectives within modern Liberalism may be discerned. Upon this basis, two sets of issues relating to social morality will be explored: crime and civil liberties, and the family and sexuality.

Crime and civil liberties

Even the most liberal of Liberals accepts the need for power to be exercised over individuals against their will when clearly identifiable harm is done to others. In these cases – such as when property is stolen or physical injury caused – Liberals do not dispute the necessity of legally enforcing society's moral norms. Yet this still leaves open the question of what philosophy of justice should be applied.

In general, modern Liberals tend to eschew a purely retributive approach to justice and may even display scepticism towards the efficacy of custodial punishments in preventing reoffending.[20] Instead, flowing from their understanding of positive liberty, they typically favour addressing the social causes of crime. Thus, crime should be tackled by pulling the whole range of social policy levers, not only conventional law and order ones: education, youth work, housing, health and childcare are just some that earn mention in policy discussions.[21]

Even when prison is required, rehabilitation rather than retribution is usually the stated goal.[22] Furthermore, a theory that has gained popularity in recent decades that has been embraced by Liberals is that of restorative justice, obliging offenders in some manner to make restitution to the victims they have harmed.[23] An especial appeal of this notion to Liberals is that they are able to link it to their focus on community, by seeking to have offenders compensate not just individuals who have been directly harmed, but the whole of their communities. For example, in their 2005 election manifesto, the Liberal Democrats endorsed the role of Community Justice Panels, which can set penalties such as requiring offenders to clean up graffiti or repair damage to property.[24] Using 'community' as a qualifier in discussions of crime policy is in fact common throughout Liberal discourses, 'community policing' and 'community sentencing' being two recurrent phrases.[25]

The other side of the coin for Liberals is resisting the argument that fighting crime, as well as terrorism, provides justification for eroding civil liberties. Indeed, the Liberal Democrats declare that they 'have the protection of civil liberties at the heart of [their] purpose and philosophy'.[26] Most notable in recent times have been attacks upon the authoritarian policies of New Labour, such as its anti-terrorist legislation, the limiting of the right to trial by jury and the plan for compulsory identity cards.[27] Liberals also have many well-established commitments to ideas such as a written constitution and a bill of rights. Moreover, they long campaigned for a Freedom of Information Act before one was passed in 2000; in 1978, the then Liberal MP Clement Freud tried to introduce freedom of information legislation by a Private Member's Bill, as did David Steel as Liberal Party leader in 1984.

Despite all this, there are definite limitations to Liberals' liberalism in relation to crime and civil liberties. In terms of crime policy, the real test of Liberals' credentials occurs with cases that are not clear-cut as to whether they meet the criterion of causing harm to others. While few would dispute that acts such as rape or murder evidently do, and thus warrant the curtailment of perpetrators' liberty, there are many acts that may attract moral disapprobation but which it is possible to argue directly harm only agents themselves, such as committing suicide; these are ones that Mill viewed as 'self-regarding'.[28] While it is not possible here to discuss the charge levelled by Mill's critics that there are no harmful acts that are ever purely self-regarding, more valuable insights into Liberals' beliefs can be gained from reflecting on cases that raise disagreements as to whether they are self- or other-regarding than those in which the harm caused is palpably to others. As such, a useful example to consider in detail is the taking of recreational drugs.

Drugs policy is an area where Liberal Democrats have earned a certain notoriety. In 1994, the Party Conference voted for the decriminalisation of cannabis (although all the Party's MPs voted against the motion) and it has remained Party policy to be against prosecuting individuals for the possession of cannabis for personal use and to keep its downgraded status since 2004 as a Class C drug.[29] Furthermore, the Party has argued for reducing ecstasy from a class A to a class B drug and, in arguing that criminal sanctions often make matters worse, education and treatment are presented as the preferred options for users of all drugs.

Liberal Democrats' opponents have gleefully seized upon these policies to label the Party as 'soft' on drugs.[30] However, most of the arguments deployed by Liberal Democrats in favour of a more relaxed drugs policy have little to do with any *laissez-faire* attitude to personal morality.

First, there is the pragmatic argument. For example, a 2005 policy briefing paper urging reform of the way in which drugs policy is approached takes as its starting point not the importance of respecting individual rights, but the recognition that the 'prohibitionist approach to drugs over the last 30 years has not worked', noting that there are around four million drug users in the UK.[31] In other words, a commitment to realism rather than libertarianism explains why the Party wants to review laws relating to recreational drug use, as a realist might any law that is flouted by a large section of the population for many decades.

Second, there is the crime reduction argument. Shifting the emphasis away from criminal sanctions, it is contended, would lower crime rates not only directly, but also by reducing the commission of other offences, since users become drawn into the criminal worlds of theft and violence when drug use is criminalised.[32] Whatever the merits of this argument, again it is not one about individual freedom, but about potential social benefits.

Third, there are health and welfare arguments. One such argument forwarded in relation to cannabis specifically is that its legalisation would be of benefit to sufferers of medical conditions like multiple sclerosis, because it can help in managing their pain.[33] Again, this may be true, but the invocation of these cases is more a way of sidestepping the issue of individual liberty than addressing it, since the vast majority of cannabis use is not for pain relief. Significantly, the main benefit of decriminalisation promoted for users of all recreational drugs is that it would be much easier to deliver education and treatment programmes to them if they were kept out of the criminal justice system, not that they would gain the freedom to be left alone to make their own choices.[34]

What also reveals that individuals' negative freedom is not of paramount concern is that there is a selective approach to which drugs' use should be treated more leniently; although ecstasy might be reclassified, the Party does not argue that the same should happen with 'harder' drugs like heroin and cocaine. Moreover, while incarceration may not be the preferred penalty for users, Liberal Democrats promise a crackdown on sellers of drugs, with the introduction of a new offence of 'dealing' to allow more effective action against long-term suppliers.[35] Yet as Mill recognised in relation to alcohol, clamping down on suppliers inevitably affects consumers – 'the state might just as well forbid [the individual] to drink wine as purposely make it impossible for him to obtain it'.[36] Consequently, targeting dealers of drugs rather than users may still entail infringements on the liberty of the latter.

Furthermore, it is not the case, even regarding 'soft' drugs like cannabis, that Liberal Democrats wish the state simply to step aside: the ultimate goal is 'to put the supply of cannabis on a legal, regulated basis'.[37] Thus, with education and treatment programmes bringing cannabis's consumers within the state's purview, and a regulated market bringing the drug's suppliers within it as well, major roles for the state would remain even if the sale and use of cannabis were made fully legal. Liberal Democrats have also been in the vanguard of demands for the greater regulation of a 'drug' that is already available legally, sponsoring the bill that became the 2002 Tobacco Advertising and Promotion Act, which bans the advertising of products that it is not illegal either to sell or to purchase. What this demonstrates is that the dominant view of liberty within the Liberal Democrats is one in which individual rights can be trumped by health and welfare concerns and, implicitly, notional social rights.

Beyond the area of drugs policy, Liberal Democrats are also quite prepared to compete with the other parties in using the fear of crime (according to their 1997 election manifesto, 'crime and the fear of crime affect almost every person and every community in the country'[38]) to justify support for expanding the powers of the state. Most notable is that they have repeatedly raised the stakes in the game of one-upmanship regarding police numbers. Their 1992 manifesto made the vague promise of 'putting more officers on the beat'; in 1997, this had become the specific pledge of three thousand more police officers; in 2001, they undertook to recruit six thousand extra officers, proclaiming this as two thousand more than the government planned; and by 2005, voters were being promised ten thousand police officers on top of Labour's plans.[39] The fact that policing is always discussed by Liberal Democrats in the context of user-friendly 'community' prefixed phrases – as if police officers are merely uniformed social workers – does not alter the fact that these proposals would mean strengthening the state's power. In none of the Party's manifestos is the possibility raised that fear of crime may not correspond to the real risks and nor is it considered that banging the drum of increasing police numbers may simply perpetuate moral panics about crime.

Of particular note about the 2005 pledge is how the Party intended to pay for ten thousand extra police officers, which was to be from the money saved by not proceeding with the government's plans for compulsory identity cards. This made the Liberal Democrats' opposition to identity cards appear less like a principled stand against the growth of the overbearing state than merely the result of a disagreement about how best to allocate spending to enhance its power.

In fact, many of the Party's criticisms of the illiberalism of its opponents are not as straightforward as they initially seem. A good example of this is shown by their attitude towards Anti-Social Behaviour Orders (ASBOs), introduced by Labour in the 1998 Crime and Disorder Act. On the one hand, Liberal Democrats criticise

ASBOs for the worrying implications they have from a liberal standpoint – by making those who break an ASBO liable to criminal sanctions, including prison, this effectively means criminalising non-criminal behaviour, since the antisocial activities they cover (which can include any vaguely-defined actions that cause alarm or distress to others) need not themselves be illegal.[40] Yet on the other hand, ASBOs are nonetheless deemed to 'have a place in tackling antisocial behaviour and [to] offer some short-term relief for residents who are plagued by it'. Moreover, this acknowledgment of ABSOs' utility is complemented by a proposal for the establishment of Orwellian-sounding Responsible Behaviour Panels within communities to deal with anti-social offences. Such proposals hardly suggest that Liberal Democrats do not similarly believe in penalising people for behaviour that is not itself illegal. What is also demonstrated is how community-rather than state-focused approaches may be just as oppressive of individual freedom.

As Mill understood, a crucial distinction for defenders of liberty should be drawn between a person's general character, which should not be the subject of punitive sanctions, and their specific actions, which may be if harm to others is caused; for example, 'no person ought to be punished simply for being drunk', only for any clearly identifiable harm that they cause while drunk.[41] The intrusively pious campaigners Mill condemns, who wish to control and regulate the activities of others merely because they find them distasteful, are today as likely to be found wanting to sit on 'responsible behaviour' bodies as preaching from church pulpits. In Mill's words, the response such figures deserve is to be told 'to mind their own business'.[42]

Liberals' record on civil liberties is also far from immaculate. Although they may criticise recent infringements in the wake of 9/11, the longer-standing issue of the Irish question shows that they clearly believe that there are circumstances in which upholding civil liberties should be subordinated to the demands of tackling 'terrorism'. Historically, Liberal governments were quite prepared to use repressive methods in Ireland to defend the British state's interests, which can be seen as the direct antecedents of those used in contemporary anti-terrorist efforts.[43] From the beginning of the modern 'Troubles' in Northern Ireland in the late 1960s, Liberals always supported the British military presence and accepted the 'emergency powers' granted by the various Prevention of Terrorism Acts passed from 1974 to 1989 (which, among others, allowed police to detain suspects for seven days without charge). Even when criticising encroachments on civil rights in Northern Ireland, Liberals have attacked the ways in which measures have been implemented more than the fundamental breaches themselves. For example, regarding the Diplock Courts established in Northern Ireland in 1972 – in which the right to trial by jury was suspended, in favour of trials conducted by a single judge – Liberal Party and Liberal Democrat manifestos never promised to reinstate jury trials, merely to have three judges presiding instead of one.[44] For these reasons, it is far from certain that were a Liberal Democrat government ever to be formed in future, it too would not be prepared to curb individual rights and liberties in the name of fighting terrorism.

The family and sexuality

In relation to the spheres of the family and sexuality, Liberals again lay claim to a stake in some of the most important changes of the post-war period. In the same way that they see the influence of Liberal ideas in the welfare reforms of the Attlee Government, so do they see it in the social ones of the next Labour Administration, the 1960s Government of Harold Wilson, in the liberal reforms promoted by Roy Jenkins as Home Secretary. Indeed, because Jenkins was one of the founding members of the Social Democratic Party (SDP) and subsequently a leading figure within the Liberal Democrats, his earlier political history is often co-opted as part of Liberalism's own. A typical judgement is that of Neil Stockley, one-time Director of Policy for the Liberal Democrats, who argues that even while a member of the Labour Party, 'Jenkins was, at heart, a modern-day Whig rather than a doctrinaire socialist'.[45]

Jenkins presided over reforms that made divorces easier to obtain and legalised abortion and homosexual practices between consenting adults.[46] As a result, he gained the sobriquet of 'the architect of the permissive society' (though he himself preferred to talk of 'the civilised society'). A further reason why Liberals associate themselves with the reforms of this era is that not all of the liberalising legislation was introduced as government bills; some resulted from the introduction of private members' bills, including the 1967 Abortion Bill sponsored by David Steel. One longer-term consequence of these developments was that, during the New Right's moral crusades of the 1980s, the parts played by Jenkins and Steel in the 'permissive' reforms of the 1960s made many moral campaigners suspicious of both the SDP and the Steel-led Liberal Party.[47]

When considering the role of the state vis-à-vis the family, Liberals frequently invoke the language of liberty, if not that of permissiveness, again attacking the authoritarian and intrusive policies of their opponents. For example, there is often disdain for the 'family values moralists' of the Conservative Party.[48] Similarly, Charles Kennedy argues that 'New Labour needs to realise that family life and the way we raise our children are private matters'.[49]

Contemporary Liberals also have more modest views of the family's significance. A useful illustration of this can be seen from a comparison of the three main parties' manifestos for the 1997 General Election, when Tony Blair's New Labour was making its first play for the votes of middle England. In the Labour Party manifesto, a section headed 'We Will Strengthen Family Life' asserts that 'families are the core of our society'.[50] Likewise in the Conservative Party manifesto, in a section entitled 'Choice and Security for Families', it is affirmed that 'the family is the most important institution in our lives'.[51] By contrast, the Liberal Democrat manifesto is much less fulsome in its assessment: under the simple subheading of 'Families', it is argued that 'families, in all their forms, are a basic building block of society'.[52] This much weaker contention implies that families are merely one of the important institutions of society, not necessarily the most; the claim is diluted even further by the evident desire not to privilege any one family model.

In fact, the social unit that enjoys most prominence in Liberal Democrat mani-festos is not the family, but the community (and not just, as examined earlier, in discussions of crime policy). This makes for an instructive contrast: in the Party's manifestos of 1997, 2001 and 2005, main sections are devoted to 'Secure Commu-nities', 'Action for Your Local Community' and 'Strong Local Communities' respectively, whereas policies relating to the family are either relegated to subsec-tions or simply dispersed throughout the documents.[53] What is also conspicuous is the virtual absence of statements about the family that suggest profound ideologi-cal commitments. Instead, the emphasis is upon pragmatic, welfare-related policies that are likely to arouse little in the way of principled controversy. Consequently, discussion tends to focus on measures aimed at making day-to-day family life easier – like strengthening rights to maternity pay and childcare, and encouraging 'family-friendly' employment practices such as flexible working – rather than staunch defences of the family as an institution.

A particular area in which Liberals see themselves as having a strong track record is that of 'alternative' sexualities, in terms of their support for lesbian, gay and transgender rights. The Liberal Democrats long opposed Section 28 – an amend-ment to the 1986 Local Government Act introduced by the Conservatives in 1988 to prohibit local authorities from promoting homosexuality – before its repeal in 2003; in both 1994 and 2000, the majority of Liberal Democrat MPs voted for the age of consent for homosexuals to be lowered from 21 to 16 (which was success-fully achieved on the latter occasion); in 2002, the Party supported the Adoption and Children Act, which legalised adoption by homosexual couples; and in 2004, it supported the Gender Recognition Act, giving transsexual people the legal right to live in their acquired gender. Furthermore, the Party proudly declares that it was 'the first to call for civil partnerships' for same-sex couples.[54] In fact, preceding the Labour Government's 2004 Civil Partnership Bill, the Liberal Democrat peer Lord Lester introduced a Civil Partnerships Bill as a Private Member's Bill in 2002.

However, Liberals' liberalism again has its limits. To begin with the reforms of the 1960s that Liberals acclaim, the freedoms gained were often heavily qualified or circumscribed – for example, even though homosexuality was decriminalised in 1967, the fact that the age of consent was set at 21 still left homosexuals in a posi-tion of inequality. Yet since it was the Abortion Bill that was sponsored by a Liberal MP, it is worth considering the issue of abortion in greatest detail.

The 1967 Abortion Act made abortion legal in the UK up to 28 weeks' gesta-tion (reduced to 24 weeks in 1990), with a termination requiring the consent of two practising doctors. What is important about this reform is that the main motive behind its introduction was not the desire to uphold individual rights, but health and social welfare concerns; in other words, again it was more a case of expanding positive rather than negative freedom. The immediate context of Steel's Private Member's Bill was a growing awareness that thousands of women every year were having illegal 'backstreet' abortions, at great risk to their lives and health. The Bill's introduction thus marked a pragmatic recognition of this fact, to bring these abortions within the realm of state regulation. As Steel himself puts it, his motivation in proposing the Bill was 'revulsion at the damage caused by criminal and self-induced abortion' and the benefits to public health that decriminalisation would bring.[55] Valuable as these might be, what is significant is what Steel did not emphasise in bringing the Bill forward, which is women's rights – indeed, Steel explicitly rejects the assumption that his Bill was based on the idea of 'a woman's right to choose'.[56]

Instead, what Steel sought was 'to create a positive state of law where medical practitioners could lawfully balance the rights and conditions of the mother against the assumption of the right to develop the full life of the foetus'.[57] This suggests a concern more for bolstering the power of doctors than with empowering pregnant women. What is also illustrated by this reform are the frequently paternalistic implications of the expansion of positive liberty, with the requirement that two doctors give their consent for a termination to take place indicating a clear lack of belief in the ability of women to make their own decisions without expert guidance. It is unsurprising that Steel has subsequently seen developments in medical technology, which have increased the viability of foetuses born prematurely, as implying the need to decrease the time limit in which women can secure an abortion even further (to 22 weeks) because his perspective was always a medical-centred rather than a women's rights one.[58]

Liberal Democrats' policies on gay rights also raise questions. For example, their pride in being the first to propose civil partnerships does not necessarily prove a genuine commitment to full equality. As gay rights campaigner Peter Tatchell argues in relation to the Act introduced by New Labour, by treating civil partnerships as exclusively for same-sex couples and marriage as for heterosexual ones, it effectively enshrines discrimination in law.[59] A policy of recognising same-sex marriage has not been so proudly trumpeted by the Liberal Democrats.

Furthermore, it is interesting to compare two of the 'mini-manifestos' the Party produced for the 2005 election, one entitled 'Focus on Families' and the other 'Focus on Lesbian, Gay, Bisexual and Transgender [LGBT] Rights'.[60] The former adopts a relaxed attitude to how families are constituted ('the modern British family comes in many different shapes and sizes'[61]) and expands upon the pragmatic measures highlighted in the main manifesto. Yet what is significant is what it does not mention. While in the manifesto for LGBT rights, the right to a family is explicitly asserted for gay and lesbian couples,[62] in the one devoted to the family, no mention of this appears at all. In fact, none of the words 'lesbian', 'gay', 'bisexual' or 'transgender' appears in either it or the main manifesto.[63] A cynic might believe that what this shows is that Liberal Democrats promulgate different policies to different audiences – one set to court the heterosexual vote, another the LGBT vote – rather than champion equal values universally.

In terms of attitudes to the family more broadly, in contrast to the anodyne tone of election manifestos, there are Liberal Democrat writings that do not exhibit the same indifference to how families are constituted, or share the belief that family life is largely a private matter. Indeed, in the libertarian-tinged *Orange Book*, a collection of articles by Liberal Democrat MPs and supporters, what is striking about the chapter on family policy is that it displays probably the least libertarian spirit of all the book's chapters, questioning the assumption that all family models are equally valid and rejecting the view that the state should adopt a 'laissez-faire approach' to how children are raised.[64] Consideration is thus given to using government mechanisms to encourage families headed by married parents (on the basis that this is what is best for children) and to the state actively promoting 'good' parenting.

Nor is official Party policy against major interventions by the state into family life. As already seen, the Party does not unambiguously reject ASBOs and it supports many other policies for expanding the powers and intrusiveness of the state into the family. For example, it wishes to encourage the use of Acceptable Behaviour Contracts, 'where children and parents are educated to take responsibility of unacceptable behaviour', and wants the Children's Commissioner for England to be given greater powers, to 'safeguard and promote the rights of children'.[65] Again, therefore, Liberal Democrats may be seen to want to go even further than New Labour in strengthening the state, especially when sanctioned by the idea of advancing children's rights. If Mill were writing today, he might well place these rights alongside social rights, in that they appear to allow almost any violation of parents' liberties to be justified.

Conclusion

With the ascendancy of ideas such as positive liberty and social rights, the prevailing disposition within modern Liberalism is to call for greater intervention in individuals' moral lives. This chapter has explored some of the ways in which this has structured policy discussions, often undermining Liberals' claims to be the spokespeople for freedom in British politics. Yet many other bases for this could be cited. In recent years, a particularly salient issue has become that of how far moral concern should be extended to include animals and the environment. In giving strong support to animal and environmental protection, many Liberals have been led even further down the path of abandoning liberal inclinations in favour of seeking to control, regulate and ban that of which they disapprove. The concomitant of the elevation of animals' wellbeing in Liberal thought has been the lowering of the status of human freedom, with Liberal Democrat Conferences having approved a whole range of resolutions calling for laws that would entail restrictions on individual liberty – to make the micro-chipping of dogs compulsory, to mandate the teaching of animal welfare in schools, and to ban animals in circuses and even giving goldfish as prizes at fairs.[66] Similar impulses are to be found in the Party's efforts to promote their wider environmental credentials. As such, the future is likely to mean the Liberal Democrats continuing to move in the direction of demanding more regulations and prohibitions, rather than in that of supporting greater moral liberty.

Notes

 1 H.H. Asquith, 'Introduction', in H.L. Samuel, *Liberalism: An Attempt to State the Principles and Proposals of Contemporary Liberalism in England* (Grant Richards, London, 1902), p. x.
 2 P. Ashdown, 'Introduction', in Liberal Democrats, *Make the Difference: The Liberal Democrat Manifesto 1997* (Liberal Democrats, London, 1997), p. 7.
 3 J.S. Mill, *On Liberty*, edited with an Introduction by Gertrude Himmelfarb (Penguin, Harmondsworth, 1974), p. 68.
 4 I. Berlin, 'Two concepts of liberty', in *Four Essays on Liberty* (Oxford University Press, Oxford, 1969), p. 122.
 5 Ibid., p. 131.
 6 Berlin's analysis specifically may even be acknowledged – see, for example, Liberal Democrats, *It's About Freedom: The Report of the Liberal Democracy Working Group – Policy Paper 50* (Liberal Democrats, London, 2002), pp. 12–13.
 7 This helps explain why Liberals often express positive views of the 1945 Labour Government's reforms – see, for example, Liberal Democrats, *Our Different Vision: Themes and Values for Social and Liberal Democrats* (Hebden Royd Publications, Hebden Bridge, 1989), p. 1.
 8 Even since the founding of the Liberal Democrats, there has remained an association with nonconformism – see A. Russell and E. Fieldhouse, *Neither Left nor Right? The Liberal Democrats and the Electorate* (Manchester University Press, Manchester, 2005), pp. 163–6.
 9 Mill, *On Liberty*, pp. 156, 155.
10 Ibid., p. 158.
11 For example, R. Grayson, 'Conclusion: A Liberal Democrat agenda', in R. Grayson (ed.), *Liberal Democrats and the Third Way* (Centre for Reform, London, 1998), p. 40
12 As one writer argues, 'the present policies of the Liberal Democrats are more recognisably social democratic than liberal' – J. Meadowcroft, 'Is there a Liberal alternative? Charles Kennedy and the Liberal Democrats' strategy', *Political Quarterly*, 71:4 (2000), p. 440.
13 See R. Grayson, 'Social democracy or social liberalism? Ideological sources of Liberal Democrat policy' *Political Quarterly*, 78:1 (2007), pp. 36–8.
14 Liberal Democrats, *It's About Freedom*, pp. 11, 12. As Liberals, neither Keynes nor Beveridge was an unalloyed advocate of collectivist statism.
15 Ibid., p. 24. See also Liberal Democrats, *Make the Difference*, p. 7.
16 P. Marshall, 'Introduction', in P. Marshall and D. Laws (eds), *The Orange Book: Reclaiming Liberalism* (Profile, London, 2004), p. 12.
17 C. Kennedy, *The Future of Politics* (HarperCollins, London, 2001), p. 94.
18 M. Read, D. Marsh and D. Richards, 'Why did they do it? Voting on homosexuality and capital punishment in the House of Commons', *Parliamentary Affairs*, 47:3 (1994), pp. 374–86.
19 P. Cowley and M. Stuart, 'Solidly against Labour: Liberal Democrat voting in the House of Commons, 2001–2005': www.revolts.co.uk/Solidly%20against%20Labour.pdf (accessed 2 April 2007)
20 Liberal Democrats, *Action to Reduce Crime: Liberal Democrats Policy Briefing 1* (Liberal Democrats, London, 2005).
21 Ibid.

22 Ibid.; SDP–Liberal Alliance, *Britain United – The Time Has Come: SDP–Liberal Alliance Manifesto 1987* (SDP–Liberal Alliance, London, 1987), p. 8; Liberal Democrats, *Freedom, Justice, Honesty: The Liberal Democrat Manifesto 2001* (Liberal Democrats, London, 2001), p. 7; M. Oaten, 'Tough Liberalism: a Liberal approach to cutting crime', in Marshall and Laws (eds), *The Orange Book*, pp. 211–34.

23 Liberal Democrats, *Changing Britain for Good: The Liberal Democrat Manifesto 1992* (Liberal Democrats, London, 1992), p. 37; Liberal Democrats, *Make the Difference*, p. 30; Liberal Democrats, *Together We Can Cut Crime: Policy Paper 78* (Liberal Democrats, London, 2007), passim; Kennedy, *The Future of Politics*, p. 47.

24 Liberal Democrats, *The Real Alternative: The Liberal Democrat Manifesto 2005* (Liberal Democrats, London, 2005), p. 9.

25 For example, Liberal Democrats, *Action to Reduce Crime*; Liberal Democrats, *Together We Can Cut Crime*, passim.

26 Liberal Democrats, *Protecting Civil Liberties: Liberal Democrats Policy Briefing 11* (Liberal Democrats, London, 2005).

27 Ibid.

28 Mill, *On Liberty*, pp. 71–2.

29 Liberal Democrats, *Honesty, Realism, Responsibility: Liberal Democrats Policy Briefing 10* (Liberal Democrats, London, 2005)

30 For example, see Conservative Party, *The Liberal Democrats' Little Yellow Book: Quotations From and On the Liberal Democrats* (Conservative Party, London, 2004), pp. 40–2.

31 Liberal Democrats, *Honesty, Realism, Responsibility*.

32 Ibid.

33 See, for example, Kennedy, *The Future of Politics*, p. 95.

34 Liberal Democrats, *Honesty, Realism, Responsibility*.

35 Ibid.

36 Mill, *On Liberty*, p. 157.

37 Liberal Democrats, *Honesty, Realism, Responsibility*

38 Liberal Democrats, *Make the Difference*, p. 29.

39 Liberal Democrats, *Changing Britain for Good*, p. 36; Liberal Democrats, *Make the Difference*, p. 29; Liberal Democrats, *Freedom, Justice, Honesty*, p. 7; Liberal Democrats, *The Real Alternative*, p. 9.

40 Liberal Democrats, *Together We Can Cut Crime*, p. 16.

41 Mill, *On Liberty*, p. 149.

42 Ibid., p. 155.

43 As one Liberal Democrat peer admits, New Labour's 'anti-terrorist legislation lies in a direct line with the similar initiatives of the Gladstone Cabinet's 1881 Coercion Bill, the Asquith Coalition's response to the Easter Rising [and] Lloyd George's use of the Black and Tans': Lord Alderdice, 'Liberals and Ireland: Introduction', *Journal of Liberal Democrat History*, 33 (2001/2), p. 5.

44 SDP–Liberal Alliance, *Britain United*, p. 7; Liberal Democrats, *Changing Britain for Good*, p. 50; Liberal Democrats, *Make the Difference*, p. 45.

45 N. Stockley, 'Biography of Jenkins': www.liberalhistory.org.uk/item_single.php?item_id=49&item=biography (accessed 5 April 2007).

46 Jenkins' own account of these developments is presented in his autobiography – R. Jenkins, *A Life at the Centre* (Macmillan, Basingstoke, 1991), pp. 180–1, 208–11.

47 See M. Durham, *Sex and Politics* (Macmillan, Basingstoke, 1991), p. 157.

48 M. Taylor, 'We always backed the free market', *Guardian*, 17th September 2004.

49 Kennedy, *The Future of Politics*, p. 95.
50 Labour Party, *New Labour – Because Britain Deserves Better: The Labour Party Manifesto 1997* (Labour Party, London, 1997), p. 21.
51 Conservative Party, *You Can Only Be Sure with the Conservatives: The Conservative Party Manifesto 1997* (Conservative Central Office, London, 1997), p. 11.
52 Liberal Democrats, *Make the Difference*, p. 51.
53 Ibid.; Liberal Democrats, *Freedom, Justice, Honesty*; Liberal Democrats, *The Real Alternative*.
54 Liberal Democrats, *Focus on Lesbian, Gay, Bisexual & Transgender Rights – General Election 2005: Liberal Democrat Manifesto for LGBT* (Liberal Democrats, London, 2005).
55 D. Steel, 'We need to rethink my Abortion Law', *Guardian*, 6th July 2004.
56 D. Steel, 'Abortion reform 1967', *Liberal Democrat History Group Newsletter*, 14 (1997), p. 12.
57 Ibid.
58 D. Steel, 'We need to rethink my Abortion Law'.
59 P. Tatchell, 'Civil partnerships are divorced from reality', *Guardian*, 19th December 2005.
60 Liberal Democrats, *Focus on Lesbian, Gay, Bisexual & Transgender Rights*; Liberal Democrats, *Focus on Families – General Election 2005: Liberal Democrat Manifesto for Families* (Liberal Democrats, London, 2005)
61 Ibid.
62 Liberal Democrats, *Focus on Lesbian, Gay, Bisexual & Transgender Rights*.
63 Liberal Democrats, *Focus on Families*; Liberal Democrats, *The Real Alternative*.
64 S. Webb and J. Holland, 'Children, the family and the state: a Liberal agenda', in Marshall and Laws (eds), *The Orange Book*, pp. 235–75.
65 Liberal Democrats, *Focus on Young People – General Election 2005: Liberal Democrat Manifesto for Young People* (Liberal Democrats, London, 2005); Liberal Democrats, *Focus on Families*.
66 For a fuller list of regulations the Party has proposed see Liberal Democrats, *Respecting All Animals: Liberal Democrats Policy Briefing 25* (Liberal Democrats, London, 2005).

Internationalism

The Liberal political tradition in the United Kingdom extends back at least to the eighteenth century, long before the Liberal Party emerged as a parliamentary force in the 1850s. This tradition, which acted as fore-runner to the modern Liberal Democrats, was associated with key personalities such as Charles James Fox, William Cobden and John Bright, as well as philosophers such as John Locke, the much misunderstood Adam Smith and John Stuart Mill.[1] Many of the causes they espoused had a strong international dimension, from welcoming the American and French revolutions, to support for free trade and campaigning against the slave trade. Early Liberals also believed in the virtue of democratic government limited by political systemic checks and balances, the extension of the franchise, and the replacement of monarchies supported by aristocracies and the doctrine of the divine right of kings by nation-states established with constitutions and legitimised by adherence to the principle of national self-determination.[2] It was a formula that triumphed in the Europe of 1848 and that reached its apex of influence in the Treaty of Versailles, which closed off the awful experiences of the First World War. Nor should we forget that the tradition of liberal interventionism in international affairs long pre-dates the arrival of Tony Blair at 10 Downing Street. It was indeed a Liberal Prime Minister, Lord Palmerston, who initiated the period of 'gunboat diplomacy'.

It was William Ewart Gladstone, four times Liberal Prime Minister between 1868 and 1894, whose invective against the Bulgarian atrocities (1876) not only electrified his election campaigning but also underlined the moral as well as political concerns behind much of British foreign policy. His biographer John Morley relays that Gladstone also said that 'indignation is froth except as it leads to action'.[3]

In addition, it is necessary to factor into the context from which Liberal internationalism springs the undeniable fact that Britain was a major colonial power and remained so well into the second half of the twentieth century. British politics could not avoid some of the consequences of this status – in terms of foreign, colonial and defence policy, and the involvement of British companies and traders in the exploitation and economic development of the colonies as well as in their governance. At the start of the twentieth century, the Liberal family found itself divided between 'imperialists' such as Asquith and Milner and 'pro-Boers' led by Lloyd George when confronted by issues of ethnic demands for autonomy in South Africa – and the guilt of having condoned racial segregation and discrimination there in earlier times was part of the driving force behind the close identification of the Liberal leadership with the championing of human rights in southern Africa from the 1940s to the present day.[4] The attrition of more conservative elements in the Liberal Party in the 1920s and 1930s (amid the rising tide of protectionism) probably made it easier for those who stayed loyal to the Party to be uncompromisingly in favour of decolonisation and of the extension of full civil and human rights to the whole population of all Britain's colonial territories.

When Britain emerged from the Second World War, the Liberal Party which had shared power in the wartime coalition under Winston Churchill was a shadow of its former self. Despite having intellectual giants like Maynard Keynes and William Beveridge in its ranks – giants who have made a huge difference to the course of economic and social policy ever since – the Party was short of leaders and leadership. Sir Archibald Sinclair, its leader and wartime Secretary of State for Air, had lost his seat in 1945 and his replacement, Clement Davies QC, was a reluctant successor and also occupied with his business career.[5] The Party had few unique selling propositions to put before the public but its passionate commitment to free trade and to human rights ensured that its members as well as its leaders were always open to taking a more international perspective than Britain's political mainstream. The pre-war Liberals had ploughed a lonely furrow, alongside the rebellious Winston Churchill, in demanding re-armament and a tough line against the rising tide of Nazism.[6] Post-war Liberals were keen supporters of new international institutions to solve the problems of the world – the United Nations, the International Monetary Fund, the General Agreement on Tariffs and Trade. They were also committed to the idea of 'collective security' which formed the central ideology of the new North Atlantic Treaty Organization and which successfully involved the USA and Canada as well as most West European democracies in its collective defence and mutual support arrangements. It was wholly in character therefore when British Liberals hosted the formation of the Liberal International in Oxford in 1947.[7] They drew strength and credibility from their continental European allies, many of whom formed part of post-war governments, and most of whom were well disposed to the emerging agenda of European integration. British Liberals in turn found that they and their forerunners were very respected by their continental colleagues and that, despite their parliamentary weakness, theirs was one of the largest Liberal parties (in terms of votes and membership) in Europe.

Early support for European integration

In some ways it may thus be seen as a small step for the post-war Liberals to embrace the notion of European integration – a view of a European future which was to become one of the Liberal Party's few unique selling propositions for many years. In the 1940s few opinion formers in the UK took European integration as a way forward to break the cycle of war between European nation-states. Apart from the Liberals no other political party and only a handful of politicians (such as Edward Heath, Duncan Sandys and Roy Jenkins) and the weekly magazine *The Economist* (owned by the Liberal Layton family) could be counted as pro-Europeans. Among Liberals too there were reservations about full-blown support for the emerging European Communities (EC). There were those who feared for Britain's future links with the Commonwealth once inside the EC tent and, more stridently, there were some – led by Oliver Smedley – who believed that the Party's traditional free trade position was being fatally compromised by signing up to a customs union.[8] Clement Davies as Liberal leader had no reservations, describing the formation of the European Coal and Steel Community as 'the finest step towards peace in the world which has ever been made'.[9] In 1948 the Party adopted at its annual assembly a resolution that called for the creation in Western Europe of a 'political union strong enough to save European democracy and the values of Western civilization, and a trading area large enough … to enable its component parts to achieve economic recovery and stability'.[10] When the Party leadership had to clarify its position in regard to the formation of the European Economic Community (EEC) under the Treaty of Rome 1957, its new leader, Jo Grimond, seems initially to have wobbled between support for the EEC or a broader but weaker free trade area.[11] This uncertainty however was quickly resolved in favour of the stronger form of European integration – the influence of Grimond's brother-in-law, Mark Bonham Carter,[12] allegedly proving decisive – and the Party thus embarked upon a consistently 'pro-European' approach to foreign policy with which no other British political party can compare.[13] This distinctive European line served not only to distinguish the Party's new recruits of some significance such as Lord Gladwyn, Lord Franks and, later, Christopher Mayhew,[14] but it was also a critical political position which was greatly to facilitate the alliance in the 1980s with the newly formed SDP, all of whose leaders were strongly pro-European. The Liberals, having been abused as 'mad' in the House of Commons in 1959 for pressing the claims of the EEC over the newly formed European Free Trade Association (EFTA)[15] went on to support the Macmillan-led application to join the EEC in 1961 and the Wilson Government's follow-up applications in 1966–67 and 1969–70. They were pleased to support Edward Heath's Conservative Government as it drove through the parliamentary legislation which enabled the UK finally to join in 1973. The votes of the Liberal MPs were critical to the passage of the European Communities Act 1972, although there was one dissident among the six MPs,[16] when Tory MPs who were 'Eurosceptic' voted with the Labour opposition.[17]

From an early stage the Liberal Party called for much stronger powers for the European Parliament and for it to be directly elected. This did not please Tory or Labour leaders in the pro-EEC camp when a referendum on maintaining the UK's membership came to be held in 1975. The pro-European mainstream wanted to suppress discussion of the possible supranational outcomes of a 'Yes' vote at the time, and though the referendum was won by a two to one margin, the emergence of a directly-elected European Parliament in 1979 could not be resisted. Liberal emphasis on a more democratic set of European institutions was to return in the 1990s. One of the by-products of the referendum campaign was that Liberal leaders such as David Steel and Jo Grimond came to work closely for the first time with pro-EEC Labour leaders such as Roy Jenkins and Shirley Williams, who were soon to be founders of the SDP which was later to merge with the Liberal Party in 1988 to form the Liberal Democrats.[18]

Another consequence of holding direct elections to the European Parliament (EP) was to raise a major political question about the use or not of proportional representation (PR) to elect the new British Euro-MPs. Despite the Labour Government's support for PR on this occasion, MPs as a whole refused to endorse PR by a large majority in 1978.[19] Another result of holding EP direct elections was the formation in 1976 of a pan-EC Liberal federation to which the British Liberals immediately affiliated. But the politics of some of the new federation's other members were to raise questions inside the Liberal Party about the suitability of this adherence.[20]

The Liberals later happily supported the re-launch of the single European market in 1985 and the resulting Single European Act in 1986, but they warned parliament that the significance of the change was being greatly underestimated and they railed at the absence of any national debate on this – a view which inadvertently they shared with the Eurosceptics.[21]

The electoral alliance between the Liberals and the SDP brought together two strongly pro-European political camps but was not without difficulties. The more Atlanticist SDP leaders were also keener to build defence policy into the EC framework. David Owen was highly dismissive of Liberal notions of a federal Europe, which sat well with the Liberal approach to devolution within the UK.[22] There were also some acrimonious internal battles over which Party should be designated to fight which Euro-constituency on behalf of the Alliance in the 1984 EP elections.

Liberal opinion has long supported economic and monetary union (as indeed did the Conservative Government from 1970–74) as the next logical step along the road to European integration. So it was no surprise that Liberal Democrat MPs supported the ratification of the Treaty of Maastricht in 1992–93. This time they warned that such a large step-change in the integration process demanded the most extensive public debate, but once again such warnings were ignored. Since that time the Liberal Democrats have continued to support UK adoption of the Euro, although subject to approval by referendum, and there has also been occasional debate about how quickly this would be practicable given the strength of the pound sterling.[23]

The Liberal Democrats have supported all the main developments of European integration since the start of the 1980s, especially enlargement of EU membership and the strengthening of EU environmental policies. Their support for the EU draft Constitutional Treaty (2004) was more lukewarm and, once more, to be subject to approval by a referendum. This enthusiasm for referenda on European issues, despite the traditional Liberal defence of parliamentary democracy, reflects a recognition by the Party that the European integration process has long progressed beyond the point where UK public opinion understands, let alone approves, what has been done in their name. Liberal Democrats think that a discrete referendum, both on the Euro and on the (failed) Constitution, would be needed to legitimise the transfer of sovereignty to Euro-institutions entailed and to give electors the chance to confirm the progress of the EC/EU well beyond what was publicly recognised at the time of the 1975 referendum. It is also a measure of the difficulty Liberals and now the Liberal Democrats have encountered where at least one-third of their voters in national elections do not support the Party's European policies. This had led the Party to play down its pro-European credentials at Euro-elections and to prioritise local council elections over Euro-elections if necessary.[24]

A continuing problem for Liberals and Liberal Democrats has been the reconciliation of their belief in strong parliamentary institutions at the level of the nation-state with their willingness to support strengthened supranational institutions like the European Union. There is no doubt that Europhile Liberal Democrats are well aware of the shortcomings of the EU in terms of its lack of transparency, accountability and democratic control.[25] Some, like Lord Dahrendorf, a former European Commissioner, doubt whether any form of democracy can be instituted successfully above the level of the nation-state.[26] The more mainstream approach has been to seek more powers for the European Parliament to act as a counter-weight to the Commission and the Council of Ministers. More recently there has been an acceptance of the value of increasing the scrutiny of national parliaments over EU business, a remedy that still evokes anger from continental liberal federalists.[27] Globalisation at many levels makes government at nation-state level increasingly ineffective. Liberal Democrats have long been ready to accept transfers of political power upwards and downwards on grounds of efficiency, greater autonomy and more local control. But as issues become more subject to government by international institutions, especially the EU, the effectiveness of traditional parliamentary instruments of scrutiny and control are challenged, and most often weakened. This is a dilemma that the Liberal Democrats have yet to resolve satisfactorily.

The UN and the role of the nation-state

British Liberals shared in the optimism after 1945 that spawned a plethora of new international institutions, particularly under the aegis of the United Nations. They saw the UN as the guarantor of human rights and international order and for many generations Liberals have argued for a strengthening of its power and authority. At local levels in Britain prominent Liberals were often active members of branches of the United Nations Association. Clement Davies who led the Party from 1945–56 was a passionate advocate of world government. Jeremy Thorpe, who was leader from 1967–76, repeatedly called for the creation of a standing UN disaster relief force and fund. The Liberal view was (and still is) that Britain's influence on world affairs would be maximised by supporting the authority of and taking action through the United Nations, especially once the UK had decolonised. Liberals argued consistently that a strong UN and other international collective security frameworks offered the best mechanisms for preventing international conflict and preserving peace.

In the 1980s Liberals were to suggest that Britain might give up its permanent membership of and veto power on the UN Security Council as part of a voting reform that recognised instead the position of the European Community. That kind of talk died with the Alliance and then merger of the Liberals and the SDP.[28]

Clearly the Liberals, and later the Liberal Democrats, were willing to present themselves as the least nationalist of the mainstream British political tradition, accepting faster than the rest of the political class and the general public that British power was in steep decline after 1945 as a result of war debt, loss of economic dynamism at home and the end of Empire abroad. The Liberal approach – often supported by leading international relations experts – was that Britain should rely on a strong commitment to international institutions, such as the UN and the EU, and collective security arrangements, especially through NATO. This approach has not always found favour with the Liberal electorate (notably in South West England on Europe) but it has given the Party the chance on several occasions to present itself as occupying political ground quite distinct from the other parties. Liberals supported the UN intervention, led by US troops, in Korea in 1950–51. They approved the participation of British troops in shoring up the South Korean Government from attacks by Communist forces from North Korea and hence guaranteed the autonomy of South Korea. In the Suez crisis of 1956, after some initial ambivalence,[29] the Liberal Party came out firmly against the Anglo-French occupation of the Suez Canal. Public opinion in Britain was highly polarised over the whole expedition, but a significant number of Conservative supporters were detached by the mixture of cynicism and gunboat diplomacy deployed by the Eden Government, which seemed both inappropriate and redolent of a bygone age. It is to this group that the Liberals were able to appeal as a progressive non-socialist, pro-UN, pro-European party. With a new charismatic leader in the form of Jo Grimond the Liberals were in a position to appear both fashionable and genuinely different.

A much less high-profile foreign policy and defence issue was to be taken up by the Liberals in parliament in the mid-1960s. They were the first Party to call for the withdrawal of all British troops based 'east of Suez'. This policy emerged in 1965 partly in response to the increasing financial and economic difficulties facing both the UK economy and its government, and partly as a result of coming to terms with the reduction of Britain's interests and capacity to influence events worldwide. For several years, Liberals alongside some defence experts were alone in making this realistic analysis, which eventually was accepted by the Labour Government in the late 1960s when they found that the cost of the necessary aircraft carriers to maintain an effective British presence east of Suez was no longer affordable.[30]

Unsurprisingly the Liberals were not in favour of providing help to the USA in its struggle with North Vietnam in the 1960s, but during this period neither was the Labour Government under Harold Wilson. There was no UN approval for such an intervention, and the increasing presence of US troops in Vietnam was widely perceived as serving American foreign policy interests rather than international peace or the protection of the sovereignty of a beleaguered state.

This does not mean that Liberal politicians had become more isolationist or completely Eurocentric in their approach to international affairs. Their continued support for international intervention, carrying on the Palmerstonian tradition, was now subsumed in demands for UN and/or NATO or EU joint actions. Just as the UN intervention in Korea in 1950–51 was fully supported, so were the much later NATO interventions in Bosnia (1994) and Kosovo (1999), which arose from the break-up of Yugoslavia and the orchestrated rise of Serb nationalism. The arrival of US and UK troops in Afghanistan in 2001 (soon to be followed by a UN peacekeeping force) was seen by the Liberal Democrats as essential to guarantee an orderly and stable democratically elected government after the ejection of the Taliban regime. Indeed the complaint from the Liberal Democrat camp over Yugoslavia was that intervention had come too late to avoid much of the 'ethnic cleansing' of the 1990s including such horrors as the massacre of 7,000 Bosnian Muslims by Bosnian Serbs at Srebenica. The Liberal Democrat leader, Paddy Ashdown, was constantly barracked as a warmonger by Labour and Tory MPs at Westminster for his appeals for early intervention to prevent conflict in the early 1990s.[31] This was an echo of the rough treatment in the Commons given to Jeremy Thorpe when he advocated the bombing of strategic rail links in Rhodesia in order to bring down the illegal white settler regime established in 1965 under the leadership of Ian Smith. This was a measure of the frustration Liberals felt at the inability of the international community to implement effectively economic sanctions against Rhodesia designed to achieve the same effect. Meanwhile the Liberal leadership was enthusiastic during the post-1945 period for international disarmament negotiations to succeed, especially in regard to the proliferation of nuclear weapons. They were generally willing to trade Britain's own independent nuclear deterrent as part of the process of international disarmament and became increasingly strident in their criticisms of the international arms trade, in which the UK was a major participant.

In the most recent times the Liberal Democrats have continued this notable legacy of being willing to break with the established parliamentary consensus on major issues of international policy. Their opposition to the Anglo-American intervention in Iraq in 2003 merits some analysis. Though there were many in the Party who opposed this intervention in principle on ethical or realist grounds, the declared policy of the Liberal Democrat leadership was that such intervention could only be supported, and with British troops, if there was a second UN resolution expressly supporting the timing of this intervention, following inspection of sites where weapons of mass destruction were alleged either to be stored or to be capable of being made. The Liberal Democrat leader, Charles Kennedy, was clearly disconcerted by the barracking he was to suffer on a daily basis for not waving the 'national' flag as British troops were being committed to Iraq. Only with difficulty was he persuaded to speak at the mass demonstration against this invasion of Iraq convened by the Stop the War Coalition in February 2003 and which succeeded in attracting at least one million marchers in London, the largest political demonstration ever to have occurred in British history. The political dividend for the Party's anti-Iraq-war position proved later to be significant, and was evident at the 2005 General Election. This may also have helped Sir Menzies Campbell, Kennedy's choice as foreign policy spokesman in the Commons, to capture the Party leadership in 2006.

Self-determination and human rights

On some issues of policy, however, where the de-colonisation process had stalled, the Liberal Democrats have adopted a more traditional stance. On the issue of Gibraltar and the Spanish claim of sovereignty over this British colonial outpost established after the Treaty of Utrecht in 1713, they have supported the principle of self-determination over the claim of sovereignty on territorial grounds. The Party also adopted the same stance in relation to the Argentine invasion of the Falkland Islands in 1982, defending the right of the 1,900 inhabitants, all of whom were of British descent, to be governed ultimately from London, as was the clearly expressed wish of the population.

Some discussion of the spectrum of Liberal opinion on matters concerning Palestine and the state of Israel is required given the central role of the Middle East in contemporary foreign policy debates. The Liberals had traditionally been much more open to Jewish participation in their Party than the Conservatives; and for a period from 1931–35 they had Sir Herbert Samuel, a prominent Jew, as Party leader. So the Party was always likely to give firm support to the creation of the new state of Israel in 1947, especially after the Jewish 'holocaust' in Europe under the Nazis and their allies. After the 1967 'six day war' in which Israel made territorial gains which were not recognised by the international community, much more criticism of Israel and more advocacy of Palestinian rights began to surface in the Party, especially among the resurgent Young Liberals. This has created continuing tensions between pro-Israeli and pro-Palestinian groups within the Liberal Democrats, which were more recently illustrated by the dismissal in 2004 of Jenny Tonge MP as a Liberal Democrat frontbench spokesperson in the Commons for openly challenging the values of a militarised and security-obsessed Israel which appeared to disregard entirely the rights of the Palestinians.[32]

A full understanding of the Liberal approach to international affairs is not possible without acknowledging that Liberal leaders and rank-and-file members have consistently argued for a liberalisation of trade to help solve the development problems of the poorest nations of the world. They have never resiled on the UN commitment made in the 1970s, requiring member states to devote 0.7% of their GDP to development aid. The Liberal commitment to free trade and the exploitation of comparative advantage between states has never overlooked Ricardo's warnings about the problems facing small states with nothing to trade.[33] Clearly that point has forced Liberals to be critical of the EU's agricultural policies over a long period, but such criticisms have often been downplayed because the general arguments for or against the EC or EU have still not been resolved in the UK. Equally, interest in the Commonwealth has waned over time within the Party as leaders and members have understood the deeper commitments and possibilities offered by the European integration process. That is not to deny that there has been a long-standing understanding within Liberal circles that better international relations and conflict resolution are not simply the product of diplomacy but must also be supported (if not pre-figured) by broader understandings of different cultures and values as much at the level of the individual as at the level of the nation or the state. One of the attractions of UK membership of the EC for Liberals was its commitment to 'an ever closer union of the peoples of Europe' rather than to a union of states. Liberals have frequently taken the lead at local levels to support and foster town twinning initiatives (which normally only involve European towns and villages) and which involve exchanges between ordinary citizens, not just their leaders. They have been happy to assert the legal and human rights of individuals as well as social groups anywhere in the world, sometimes regardless of negative political consequences. They vigorously opposed the UK Labour Government's overnight decision to withdraw the unrestricted rights of residence in Britain of Kenyan Asian UK Passport holders ejected in 1968.[34] Paddy Ashdown was keen to offer, unlike all other parties, all long-term Hong Kong residents full British passports, with rights of residence in the UK, ahead of the handover of the colony to the People's Republic of China in 1997. It is Liberals in both Houses of Parliament and Young Liberals who have led the protests from 1975 to date against Morocco's illegal occupation of the Western Sahara and have given backing to the Polisario. The modern Liberal Democrats have been just as keen on the more effective application of international law – for example in regard to war crimes in Rwanda or the former Yugoslavia, and more recently by means of the setting up of a new permanent international criminal court – to assist aggrieved or persecuted individuals and social groups in seeking justice and redress.

One emerging policy area where international agreements are becoming crucial to the safety and prosperity of the human race is climate change. Liberals and Liberal Democrats have supported strongly UN-inspired attempts to achieve international consensus and agreements on environmental questions from the early 1970s. In this policy field where Liberals long ago earned their 'green' credentials, the EU is seen by them as a key player in brokering enforceable international agreements as well as a uniquely effective institution for ensuring member-state compliance with commitments they have freely made to the rest of the world.

Conclusion

The long Liberal tradition of support for international action in defence of oppressed nationalities and ethnic groups remains as strong as ever – the refusal to support the invasion of Iraq in 2003 is exceptional. What has changed in 150 years has been the development of international institutions (such as the UN, the EU and NATO) through which multilateral rather than unilateral actions can be arranged. Liberals in Britain have been in the vanguard of support for such multilateralism, but in the 1990s they became concerned about the inability of the international community to prevent flagrant abuses of human rights within self-governing states or to deal with the spill-over effects of 'failed states': the collapse of Yugoslavia is a crucial example. Liberal opinion evolved to support international intervention in such cases where there were clear humanitarian objectives capable of being achieved.[35] Thus the Liberal inclination towards interventions, albeit on a multilateral basis, remains strong.

There would appear to be strong philosophical foundations, both political and economic, which have underpinned the internationalist perspective that Liberals have given to British politics and policy. This has often caused Liberals to stand outside the established political consensus at key moments of decision (as over EC membership in the 1950s and the invasion of Iraq in 2003) in British politics. Their commitment to the Atlantic Alliance has been much more balanced by willingness to become fully committed to the European integration process. They have refused to be dissuaded by domestic political pressures from defending the human rights of individuals and powerless groups all over the world, be they victims of apartheid, Kenyan Asians, the inhabitants of Diego Garcia, citizens of Hong Kong or asylum-seekers from anywhere. It is also evident that over time the claims of the European Union and the European integration process have increasingly dominated British Liberal and Liberal Democrat approaches to international affairs. There has long been frustration with the other parties who have preferred to hedge their bets in any tensions between the Atlantic Alliance and the European Union.[36] But while there has been clarity in the Liberal camp about prioritising Europe and seeking to maximise UK influence within the EU structures, this may well have accelerated a fading of interest in the rest of the world (especially the Commonwealth) and have curtailed their advocacy of the needs of developing countries.

Notes

1 See A. Bullock and M. Shock, *The Liberal Tradition from Fox to Keynes* (Black, London, 1956); also R. Falkner, *A Conservative Economist? The Political Liberalism of Adam Smith Revisited* (John Stuart Mill Institute, London, 1997) and A. Butt Philip, *John Stuart Mill and Modern Liberalism* (John Stuart Mill Institute, London, 2006).

2 Liberals in the early nineteenth century viewed the rise of nationalism and the replacement of aristocratic regimes by democratic governments as parallel and benign developments. It was the Liberal philosopher Lord Acton who spelled out that it was not

always practical to align the boundaries of states according to the principle of nationality and also that there was much to be said for democracies which encompassed a
diversity of nationalities. Acton concluded that 'the theory of nationality is a retrograde
step in history' while agreeing that the denial of nationality implies the denial of political liberty. See Lord Acton, *The History of Freedom and Other Essays* (Macmillan,
London, 1907) and G.E. Fasnacht, *Acton's Political Philosophy* (Hollis and Carter,
London, 1952).

3 J. Morley, *The Life of William Ewart Gladstone* (Macmillan, London, 1906), Book VII,
ch. 4, p. 161. Gladstone's last speech made in public was made in 1896 to denounce
massacres in Armenia and to support British armed intervention.

4 Notable for their involvement in African issues were three post-1945 Liberal leaders:
Clement Davies (1945–56) over the Seretse Khama affair in 1951; Jeremy Thorpe
(1967–76) over the revolt by white settlers in southern Rhodesia (later Zimbabwe); and
David Steel (1976–88) in his prominent leadership of anti-apartheid campaigns in the
1960s and 1970s. Leading Liberal lawyers such as Tom Kellock QC and John Macdonald QC also regularly took on court cases in Southern Africa of civil rights activists.
Macdonald also strongly defended the rights of the Chagos islanders whose whole population was removed from Diego Garcia in the Indian Ocean on the instructions of the
UK government to make way for a US base there in the 1980s.

5 See A. Wyburn-Powell, *Clement Davies: Liberal Leader* (Politico's, London, 2003).

6 Sinclair and Churchill formed a lifelong friendship when they met serving in the
trenches in France in the First World War. Their correspondence over forty-five years
has now been published in I. Hunter (ed.), *Winston and Archie* (Politico's, London,
2005).

7 See J. Smith, *A Sense of Liberty: The History of the Liberal International* (Liberal International, London, 1997).

8 See R. Douglas, *The History of the Liberal Party, 1895–1970* (Sidgwick and Jackson,
London, 1971).

9 House of Commons Debates, 21st February 1955, col. 899. See also Wyburn-Powell,
Clement Davies.

10 A. Butt Philip, 'The Liberals and Europe', in V. Bogdanor (ed.), *Liberal Party Politics*
(Oxford University Press, Oxford, 1983), p. 219.

11 Ibid., p. 221.

12 Mark Bonham Carter was briefly Liberal MP for Torrington from 1958 to 1959 at this
crucial period.

13 Butt Philip, 'The Liberals and Europe', pp. 217–40.

14 Lord Gladwyn, as Gladwyn Jebb, had served as senior UK diplomat and acting Secre-
tary-General at the founding of the United Nations; Lord Franks was a leading banker,
administrator and then head of an Oxford college; Christopher Mayhew was Labour
MP for Woolwich East from 1951–74 and defected to the Liberals in 1974.

15 The EFTA was proposed by the UK and formed by the Treaty of Stockholm 1960. Its
original signatories were the UK, Austria, Denmark, Norway, Sweden, Switzerland and
Portugal.

16 Emlyn Hooson QC, MP for Montgomeryshire (later Lord Hooson) took the view that
the EEC structure was not federal enough and so could not be supported.

17 See C. Lord, *British Entry to the European Community under the Heath Government of
1970–74* (Aldershot, Dartmouth, 1993).

18 See D. Steel, *Against Goliath: David Steel's Story* (Weidenfeld and Nicolson, London,

1989) and R. Jenkins, *A Life at the Centre* (Macmillan, Basingstoke, 1991).

19 See C. Cook, *A Short History of the Liberal Party 1900–1992* (Macmillan, Basingstoke, 1993); Steel, *Against Goliath*.

20 See Butt Philip, 'The Liberals and Europe'. The real issue was how far the new Liberal grouping in the EP would reflect the economic liberal rather than the social liberal tradition prevalent in the UK.

21 See Alan Butt Philip, 'A price on the European dream', *The Times*, 8th December 1989.

22 Personal knowledge as a member of the team formed to write the Alliance manifesto.

23 See Chris Huhne's arguments in J. Forder and C. Huhne, *Both Sides of the Coin* (Profile, London, 1999).

24 See Alan Butt Philip's 'European first and last: British Liberals and the European Community', *Political Quarterly*, 64:4 (1993).

25 See A. Duff, *Reforming the European Union* (Federal Trust, London, 1997); Alan Butt Philip, *Accountability and the European Union* (John Start Mill Institute, London 1996); Alan Butt Philip, *Reforming the European Union* (John Stuart Mill Institute, London 2005, 2nd edition).

26 R. Dahrendorf, *Democracy and the Nation State* (John Stuart Mill Institute, London, 1999).

27 The outburst by Guy Verhofstadt, Belgian Liberal Prime Minister, against the idea of strengthening the role of national parliaments in this way came close to breaking up the European Council meeting in June 2007 without agreement on the amending Treaty being proposed as a substitute for the failed Constitution.

28 See D. Owen and D. Steel, *The Time Has Come: Partnership for Progress* (Weidenfeld and Nicholson, London, 1987).

29 A. Watkins, *The Liberal Dilemma* (Macgibbon and Kee, London, 1966), pp. 83–6.

30 The Liberal Manifesto for the 1966 General Election stated: 'we reject the idea that Britain still has an independent peace-keeping role East of Suez ... We should cut our commitments East of Suez accordingly'.

31 Paddy (later Lord) Ashdown went on to be appointed the UN High Representative in Bosnia Herzegovina from 2002–5.

32 Dr Jenny Tonge had been the parliamentary party's international development spokesperson from 1999–2003 and spokesperson for children in 2003–4. She was given a life peerage in 2005.

33 D. Ricardo, *Principles of Political Economy and Taxation* (first published 1817).

34 See D. Steel, *No Entry* (Hurst, London, 1969).

35 See Sir A. Parsons, *Human Rights and International Intervention* (John Stuart Mill Institute, London, 1994) and E. Mortimer, *A Few Words on Intervention* (John Stuart Mill Institute, London, 1995).

36 See W. Wallace, *Europe or Anglosphere: British Foreign Policy Between Atlanticism and European Integration* (John Stuart Mill Institute, London, 2005).

Political strategy

This chapter concerns itself with the political and electoral strategy of the Liberal Democrats in a contemporary context and that of the Liberals since 1945. For a party like the modern Liberal Democrats, strategy is essentially about building credibility – demonstrating that the Party is worth voting for. The Party's main route to credibility can be through political leadership, the promotion of popular policies and electoral performance in local and national elections. The history of the post-war strategy of the Liberals, Alliance and Liberal Democrats is one of struggle; a struggle to 'break the mould' of British politics. There have been many false dawns and many setbacks. The mould has appeared to crack at times but for the most part has remained stubbornly resilient.

The Liberal Democrats occupy the political space between the two main parties in British politics. As Britain's third party they have to fight for every vote, every seat and every column inch and soundbite. They are condemned to struggle against the wasted vote syndrome and traditional third party squeeze. From a political marketing perspective this is an essential problem for the Party. The Liberal Democrats are consistently defined by their proximity to their competitors rather than to their own ideological attraction. And the Party is consistently condemned to combat the other parties on terrain that it would rather reject – the left–right axis.

Given the obstacles that the Party (and its predecessors) has had to face in the post-war era it might be deemed remarkable that the third party has survived at all. The state of the third party in Britain has improved dramatically since the end of the Second World War. They have seldom seemed likely to form a government but there have been times when they have threatened a significant breakthrough – and they remain a feasible coalition partner in the event of a hung parliament. Moreover as Table 10.1 demonstrates, the Liberal Democrats have prospered in recent years having increased their share of the vote in the last two elections and having tripled the Party's representation in parliament since 1992 (although not their vote share).

Table 10.1 Liberal* performance in UK general elections, 1945–2005

Election	Share of vote (%)	MPs	Election outcome
1945	9.0	12	Lab majority 146
1950	9.1	9	Lab majority 5
1951	2.5	6	Con majority 17
1955	2.7	6	Con majority 60
1959	5.9	6	Con majority 100
1964	11.2	9	Lab majority 4
1966	8.5	12	Lab majority 96
1970	7.5	6	Con majority 30
1974 Feb.	19.3	14	Lab largest party −33 seats short of majority
1974 Oct.	18.3	13	Lab majority 3
1979	13.8	11	Con majority 43
1983	25.4	23	Con majority 144
1987	22.5	22	Con majority 102
1992	17.8	20	Con majority 21
1997	16.8	46	Lab majority 179
2001	18.3	52	Lab majority 167
2005	22.0	62	Lab majority 66

*Refers to Liberal Party until 1979, the SDP–Liberal Alliance for the 1983 and 1987 elections and the Liberal Democrats from 1992 onwards.

Austerity and near oblivion

It is tempting to think that the intellectual reach of Liberalism was compromised as a result of being squeezed between the pragmatic realism of modern Conservatism and the gravitational pull of socialism in the post-war era. The Liberal Party's slow, but relentless, decline at the expense of Labour, fuelled by the onset of manufacturing trade unionism and universal male suffrage in the nineteenth century, may not have quite amounted to a 'strange death' but in the immediate aftermath of the Second World War the Party was almost pulverised by the continued expediency of the Conservatives and the rise of Labour.

In the post-war era, the Liberals were almost wiped off the electoral map of Britain, clinging to survival at geographic edges of the country and in the rural areas often associated with low-level agricultural union organisation and highly visible nonconformist church activity. Despite being routed in elections, the rump parliamentary party proved to be no less difficult to control than its predecessors and the Liberals struggled for a political identity distinct from the forces of Conservatism and socialism.

The 1945 election exposed the Party's weakness. The leader, Archibald Sinclair unexpectedly lost his Caithness and Sutherland seat (although only 59 votes behind the Conservative victor, he was actually placed third), and the party returned only a dozen MPs from 2.2 million votes. Clement Davies was installed as the new Party leader (although his leadership was probably destabilised by regular rumours of Sinclair's return). Davies' Party found it hard to capture the imagination of the public and had to rely on local electoral pacts with the Conservatives to survive in many parts of the country. The parliamentary party, despite – or maybe because of – its small size, proved difficult to manage as the proponents and opponents of state intervention fought over the body of the Party.

In truth, the tone of post-war politics in Britain was set by two Liberals – William Beveridge (the Liberal MP for Berwick-upon-Tweed, 1944–45, and made a Liberal peer in 1946) and John Maynard Keynes – (one of the authors of the 1929 Election Manifesto and Liberal peer from 1942). Together the works of Beveridge and Keynes became the blueprint for British post-war governance.

Labour's 1945 victory is commonly ascribed to their adoption of the Beveridge Report and its marriage to Keynesian demand management in their enthusiastic embrace of the social democratic paradigm via the combined public appetite for 'hope and public purpose'.[1] For their part, traumatised by defeat in 1945, Conservative recovery was conditional on their rapid acceptance of the Keynes plus Beveridge model.[2] Thus it might seem puzzling that the party of both Keynes and Beveridge fared so badly in the era of Britain's New Jerusalem. In fact the apparent influence of the Beveridge Report (the Report sold more half a million copies at a time of unprecedented austerity) on the 1945 election was insufficient to stop Beveridge himself losing the Liberal stronghold of Berwick-upon-Tweed to the Conservatives.

The Party that might have regarded itself as the natural heir to the intellectual reach of post-war settlement seemed strangely devoid of a firm ideological profile in post-war Britain. The Liberals continued to suffer from an evident split between interventionists and those who rejected state control as illiberal: a faultline that persists to this day in the contemporary Liberal Democrats with the distinction between social and economic liberals. In the post-war era this divide was not without electoral consequences. In the 1950 General Election the Party's representation fell to nine MPs, and in the 1951 election just six Liberals were returned (by some estimates the number might have fallen to two without the benefit of local pacts ensuring no Conservative opposition for Liberal candidates).[3]

Perhaps the key achievement of Davies was in simply holding the Party together in such traumatic circumstances. The Party found sufficient resolution to reject the come-hither advances of Churchill and the Conservatives who offered Davies a place in the new government after the 1951 election – which would surely have seen the Liberals absorbed into the greater Tory party in a short space of time.[4] Nevertheless, it is hard to absolve Davies – struggling with family tragedy and an ongoing personal battle with alcoholism – from blame for the apparent directionless period of Liberal political strategy.

Revival, realignment and community politics

Clement Davies was persuaded to stand down as Liberal leader in 1956 and was replaced by Jo Grimond whose leadership style was a welcome contrast to many in the Party.[5] As the Liberal Party was marched 'towards the sound of gunfire', it began to reassert itself a little more. Manifestos in the early 1950s had pledged to moderate the extremes of the other parties, but as Dutton (2004) notes, the Party could be fairly characterised as more of an anti-socialist than an anti-Conservative party.[6] Under Grimond and complete with a recharged grass-roots, the party offered a potential new strategy – realignment on the left.[7]

Grimond's first general election as leader of the Liberals saw the party double its share of the vote but fail to increase its number of MPs. The Party had already shown real signs of revival however, with Mark Bonham Carter's remarkable victory in the 1958 Torrington by-election and the long overdue start of a Liberal upturn at the local level. By 1960, Grimond was telling a Liberal rally that 'the Liberal Party should be the party to which people look for reforms which affect their daily lives ... Let us get things done and let us start in local government'.[8] By 1962 the Party had re-established itself in British politics with the spectacular victory of Eric Lubbock in the Orpington by-election.

The Grimond era became most synonymous with the theme of community politics, and is commonly credited with rescuing the Party from obscurity or oblivion through the rejuvenation of the Party's rank-and-file (although the famous Young Liberals' Community politics amendment to party strategy – 'a dual approach to politics, both inside and outside the institutions of the political establishment' – was adopted three years after Grimond had been succeeded as Party leader by Jeremy Thorpe). However the enduring force of community politics has been as an electoral tactic, allowing the Liberals to cash-in nationally on local success. Copus (2007) notes that the modern Liberal Democrats might be particularly adept at campaigning via 'Focus teams' but questions whether this is a sufficient grasp of the ideology of community politics.[9] McManus goes further, claiming that the Party's contemporary reliance on community electioneering has lost some of the philosophical coherence and intellectual force of Grimond's vision which 'was not merely about cracked pavements, but also about an entirely new, preventative, approach to social and community services, requiring a new attitude towards politics itself'.[10]

The rhetoric of community politics has played a lasting role in the building of third party credibility as the Party often has to establish itself as a local force before it can compete in the parliamentary constituency.[11] Since the heyday of the mid-1990s, the Liberal Democrat councillor base has diminished somewhat and the pathway from local election success to national success has narrowed rather in recent years. Nevertheless the language of community politics and the narrative of constant campaigning of local parties has remained a critical feature of political strategy for the Liberal Democrats.

Living with the enemy? Pacts and plans

Jo Grimond had allowed the Party to glimpse a future of mounting a challenge to Labour but Labour's 1966 election victory – despite an increase in Liberal MPs to 12 – precipitated another change of tack. Jeremy Thorpe succeeded Grimond as Party leader in 1967 and his leadership was constantly controversial. The 1970 election was a disaster; the Party had fallen into abeyance in too many constituencies and subsequently lost half its MPs and its share of the vote deteriorated further. The Party's fortunes seemed to revive thereafter – not least because the parlous state of governance in Britain saw the Party as the natural receptacle of protest in much of the country (although the Liberals were under pressure from the Nationalists in Scotland and Wales). By-election victories in Rochdale and Sutton and Cheam were followed by local election success in Liverpool which boosted the confidence of the Party. In the February 1974 General Election the Liberals fielded an impressive slate of candidates and received six million votes – nearly 20 per cent of the national vote share. Nevertheless, the vagaries of the electoral system hurt the Liberals as only 14 MPs were returned.

The stalemate after the February election gave the Liberals an opportunity to be seen wielding influence. Conservative leader Edward Heath was keen to explore the possibility of coalition with the Liberals to keep out Labour (who had won the most seats but taken fewer votes than the Conservatives). As Russell and Fieldhouse observed:

> To the outside world, Thorpe had got closer to power than any Liberal since Lloyd George. He entered Number 10 through the front door in the full glare of the media and was quick to spot that 'we're all minorities now'. Yet even this moment of glory was illusory ... many Liberal activists were unhappy at the prospect of upholding the Heath regime (a problem exacerbated by the lack of dialogue between Thorpe and the Party before his arrival at Downing Street).[12]

The October General Election saw the Liberals stand candidates in almost every seat but the momentum of February was trickling away. By 1976 Thorpe had resigned as leader, his career wrecked by scandal and some complacency. After a brief return of Grimond as caretaker, David Steel became the next Party leader. Within a year the Labour administration (now headed by James Callaghan) had lost its majority and was in deep trouble with the economy. Seizing a chance to be involved in government, Steel managed to negotiate a Lib-Lab Pact. In reality the Liberals might have bargained for more concessions from Labour than they received and the Party paid a penalty for being associated with an unpopular regime.[13]

The election of the first Thatcher administration in 1979 was emphatic and signalled a barren time for the Liberals (who had lost a million votes since October 1974). In fact the third party fortunes were revived by the formation in 1981 of the Social Democratic Party from the ranks of Labour's disillusioned senior elite.

As a result the prospects for the third party were focused for a generation on the possibility of usurping Labour rather than the Conservatives.

The formation of the Liberal–SDP Alliance had a tremendous impact in by-elections. After the SDP narrowly failed to take the Labour stronghold of Warrington in the 1981 by-election, the breakthrough result for the Alliance came in Croydon North-West as the Liberal candidate, Bill Pitt, romped to victory. Subsequent returns to parliament for SDP founders Shirley Williams and Roy Jenkins in by-elections in Crosby and Glasgow Hillhead, gave the impression that the Alliance was unstoppable. However the beginning of economic recovery and the rehabilitation of the Conservatives after the Falklands War did much to dilute the Alliance's potential.

As it turned, out the 1983 General Election was a vivid demonstration of the strategic obstacles facing a third party in a system designed to sustain only two. The Alliance secured nearly eight million votes and more than a quarter of the vote share but failed to get parliamentary rewards. The vagaries of the simple plurality electoral system saw the Alliance come second in far too many constituencies and first in far too few. Despite coming within two percentage points of Labour's vote share, the Alliance received 186 fewer seats.

A similar story was told in 1987 as the Alliance's return of 22 MPs seemed scant reward for a creditable electoral performance in terms of votes (22.5%). The aftermath of the 1987 election saw the long and painful formal merger between the Liberals and most of the SDP. The new Party – the Liberal Democrats – would be forced to contend with the same structural obstacles and strategic dilemmas as the old Liberals and Alliance.

Dealing with the era of New Labour

The Alliance had obviously been predicated on the Party's ability to take on and replace Labour as the main opposition to the Conservatives. However, the Liberal Democrats had promoted an official position of 'equidistance' between both Conservative and Labour parties. In 1992, at the Liberal Democrats' first general election contest, the new Party found it hard to establish why defectors from the Conservatives and Labour should vote Liberal Democrat. In particular the Party's refusal to rule out electoral pacts after the election was used by their opponents to dissuade potential defectors. A vote for the Liberal Democrats could act as Labour's Trojan horse according to the Conservatives and Labour stressed that even if the electorate voted for change, the Liberal Democrats could uphold a Tory government after all in a post-election coalition. For some this refusal was Ashdown's fatal mistake and was said to have cost the Party votes and seats.[14]

By the time of the next election however, things had changed dramatically. John Major's Conservative Government was mired in allegations of sleaze and the New Labour opposition – led by Tony Blair – had found significant common cause with the Liberal Democrats. The third party abandoned equidistance in the mid-1990s acknowledging that it had become a fiction.[15] Paddy Ashdown admitted in May

1995 that 'everyone knows that a vote for the Liberal Democrats is a vote to remove this Conservative Government'.[16] As a result, the Liberal Democrats became part of an unofficial anti-Conservative alliance with New Labour.

The Liberal Democrats more than doubled their representation at the 1997 election, but their national share of the vote actually fell slightly. The Party had learnt a significant lesson about winning seats under first-past-the-post and had prioritised, targeting resources on winnable seats rather than on the national campaign. As a result the electoral gains for the Liberal Democrats in 1997 were exclusively at the expense of the Conservatives.

The Blair–Ashdown nexus had encouraged close co-operation between the two parties. Indeed Ashdown's diaries make clear that the scope for such co-operation was remarkable.[17] Moreover the public had noted that the political landscape had changed. Russell and Fieldhouse (2005) demonstrate that public opinion had usually placed the third party as closer to the Conservatives than the Labour Party from the 1970s until 1992, but by the 1997 election the electorate had decided that the Liberal Democrats were much closer to Labour than the Conservatives.

Labour's landslide victory in 1997 and the haemorrhage of Conservative support overshadowed the Liberal Democrat performance – and may have fore-stalled a potential coalition between Labour and the Liberal Democrats – but it did not spell the end of the anti-Conservative alliance. There was collaboration between the two parties in joint consultations on constitutional matters (although Labour failed to deliver the promised referendum on the electoral system) and the parties actually formed coalitions in the newly devolved parliament in Scotland and assembly in Wales. If the Ashdown–Blair project cost the Liberal Democrats a few Conservative voters, it benefited the Party's overall credibility by making the Party look like a major player on the stage of British politics.

Ashdown's resignation in 1999 after 11 years as Party leader may be seen as the informal closure of the project – but the joint consultative committee formally continued until September 2001. In truth, although the Party's credibility had not been harmed by its proximity to Labour, Ashdown's credibility in his own Party had begun to suffer – especially after the report of the Jenkins Inquiry into reform of the electoral system was disregarded by the Blair Government. The election of Charles Kennedy as new leader of the Liberal Democrats was an acknowledgement that the close relationship between the two parties was changing, but the co-habiting partners were yet to go their separate ways.

Indeed in the 2001 election, the Liberal Democrat position remained one of competing with Labour but fighting the Conservatives.[18] Representation in parliament increased again (including taking Chesterfield from Labour) but in a welcome development for the Party so did Liberal Democrat vote share.

Kennedy was never as comfortable as Ashdown with the New Labour project. The aftermath of the attack on New York on 11th September 2001 provided the cue for the Liberal Democrats to decouple from the Blair premiership. Although cautiously supportive of the war in Afghanistan, the Liberal Democrats became the united party of opposition to the 2003 invasion of Iraq. Coupled with deep-seated reservations about the future of student finance and the protection of civil liberties, and opposition to identity cards, hostility to the war allowed the Liberal Democrats to manoeuvre themselves into a clear political space – at the radical edge of British politics.

Thus the Party entered the 2005 General Election with a clear critique of the New Labour project fighting on two fronts against both the Conservative and Labour parties. The Party had not revisited the tactic of equidistance but Kennedy had declared in September 2004 that the Liberal Democrats would not seek a post-election pact with either of the other two parties – there would be, he claimed 'no nods, no winks, no deals, no stitch-ups'.[19] The Party's hope was that it could continue to erode Conservative support in the south of England while setting its sights for the first time on making significant in-roads into the Labour heartlands in the north.

The essential problem for the Party was that this tactic was particularly difficult to maintain in a national contest. The unofficial (but often quoted) 'decapitation strategy' which had targeted senior Conservatives under challenge from Liberal Democrats was a complete failure. Michael Howard, Theresa May, David Davis and Oliver Letwin all increased the majorities over their Liberal Democrat opponents as the Conservatives made their first recovery at the expense of the Liberal Democrats since 1992, and three seats gained from the Conservatives were offset by five victories by the Tories in Liberal Democrat seats.

Dissatisfaction with Labour's actions in government was crystallised by the Liberal Democrat campaign which capitalised on opposition to the Iraq war, and plans to introduce student top-up fees. The Party felt that these messages could play well with sub-electorates such as Muslim voters and students who had traditionally given their votes to Labour. Indeed the Liberal Democrats did make 12 gains from Labour's 2001 haul, and significantly narrowed the gap on them in many constituencies in Labour's heartlands in the 2005 election. But at what cost? As Curtice has pointed out, this constituted the first time that the third party won significant votes and seats from a Labour government – historically when Labour were in power, their losses transferred more directly to the Conservatives.[20] Even then however it is noticeable that the social profile of the Liberal Democrat vote was not dramatically transformed and the Party's northern England victories over Labour were in fairly gentrified areas rather than in the industrial heartlands of old Labour's core support. Much has been made of the Liberal Democrat attempts to attract Muslim support[21] and indeed this does seem to have been a successful tactic in 2005 – however most Muslim voters still chose Labour in 2005 and even where the Liberal Democrats won with the assistance of the Muslim electorate, the Party still has much work to do to establish itself as the natural electoral choice of British Muslims.

There is an important point to be made here about the strategic appeal of the Liberal Democrats and the party system. Actually a three-cornered fight is the electoral reality in only a very few seats. In truth there tend to be a series of two-party micro-contests and the Liberal Democrats tend to fare best in seats where they have supplanted one of the other two parties as the credible alternative. Thanks to the strategy of building credibility through local election success, by 2005 the Liberal Democrats had established themselves as the effective opposition to the Conservatives in large swathes of the south of England and to Labour in many cities and towns areas in the north and celtic fringe.

However, the very nature of the Liberal Democrat marketing strategy in 2005 presented a new set of problems for the Party. Having hitherto been a party that had prospered, almost exclusively, at the expense of the Conservatives since their inception, the Liberal Democrats had more relative success against Labour in 2005. To achieve this, they adopted a coherent set of economic and political arguments that may have played well with potential Labour defectors but less well with established Conservatives. Since the 1990s the Liberal Democrat tactic had been to entice votes from disaffected voters by claiming that the Conservatives had abandoned moderate ground and that the party that one-nation Tories wanted to support no longer existed. This strategy might persuade defection from both unhappy Conservatives and realist Labour supporters in seats where the contest was effectively between the Conservatives and Liberal Democrats. The problem arose however as the Liberal Democrats set their sights on more traditionally Labour seats. Establishing a full critique of New Labour in power was accompanied by the development of a set of policies that were geographically and ideologically skewed in their appeal. Proposals to introduce local income tax to replace the council tax and a 50p marginal rate of tax for the top earners in Britain may well have been less popular in the south of the country. Moreover the political appeal to those disaffected with Labour was off-centre. Rather than appealing to moderates unhappy with party extremism, it was directed to those firmly in the camp of traditional Labour support unhappy with the record of achievement of the government. As such the very tactics designed to appeal to Labour switchers may have been counterproductive in keeping one-nation Tories on board outside the Labour heartlands.

Popular leadership, populist policies?

Charles Kennedy's leadership of the Liberal Democrats came to an abrupt end in January 2006. The timing of his leaving was brought about by personal crisis, but a slow recognition that, despite returning the highest number of third-party MPs since the 1920s in the 2005 General Election, the Party had underperformed, probably made the change inevitable.[22] The potential to make real advance at the expense of a disliked government and a still unpopular opposition had not been realised and the lack of confidence in the leader from his parliamentary colleagues[23] – despite his residual high personal ratings in the opinion polls – would surely have brought about a change of leader before the next election.

The succession election was a disaster for the Liberal Democrats. The removal of Kennedy had brought poor publicity, but revelations about the private life of two candidates (one of whom withdrew due to lack of support, and one who had to apologise for having consistently lied about his sexuality) made matters worse. The victor, Sir Menzies Campbell, had looked like the leader in waiting for a number of years, but suddenly found himself uncomfortable in the limelight. His age (he was 64 when first elected leader – but somehow gave the impression he was older) seemed problematic as the Conservatives had just skipped a generation to elect David Cameron as their leader, and Gordon Brown was limbering up to take over the premiership from Tony Blair. Campbell's apparent infirmity was a gift for satirists and political cartoonists. Campbell found it impossible to recover from a poor start and an inability to match the personal appeal of his predecessor (see Figures 10.1 and 10.2 which compare the public approval ratings of Kennedy and Campbell as leader). After Gordon Brown cancelled the election that never was in October 2007, Campbell surprised the Party by announcing his resignation as leader. A second leadership election in 18 months was required, where Nick Clegg defeated Chris Huhne by the narrowest of margins (although fewer than two-thirds of registered party members voted and membership figures were down from 72,000 in 2006 to 64,000 in 2007).

The point here is that the third party has since the 1970s counted on popular leaders as a rallying point for electoral support. At various times in their leadership, Thorpe, Steel, Jenkins, Owen, Ashdown and Kennedy were all the most popular of all political leaders (or at least the least unpopular leaders) according to poll

Figure 10.1 Kennedy's approval ratings in his last year as leader

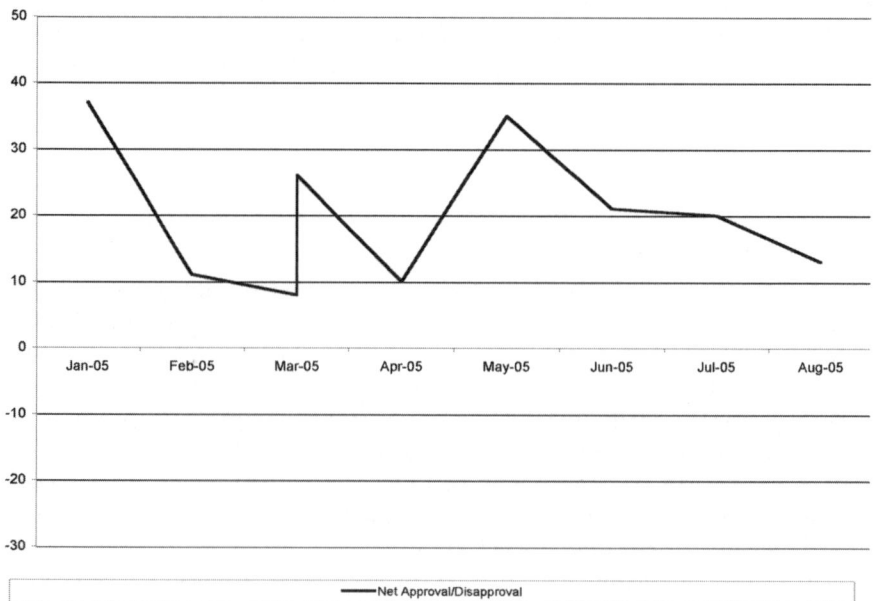

Source: ukpollingreport.co.uk

Figure 10.2 Campbell's approval ratings in his last year as leader

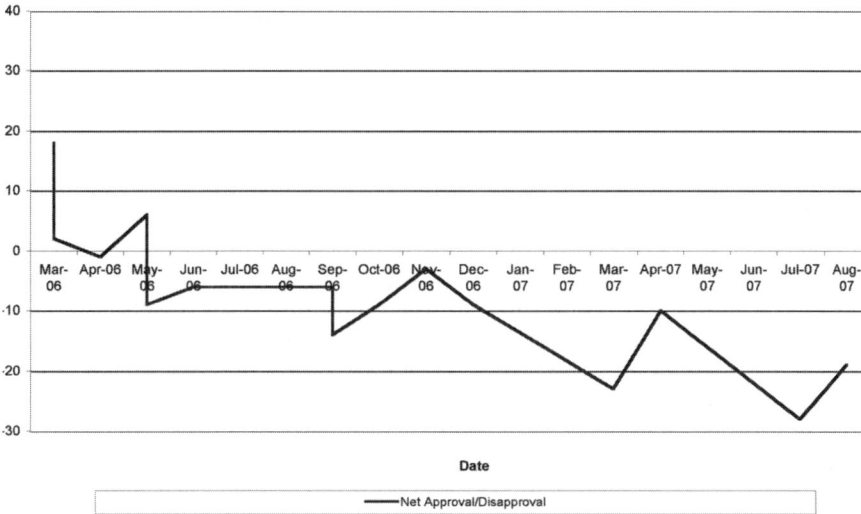

Source: ukpollingreport.co.uk

evidence, and yet the Party has yet to break the mould. Analysis of the Liberal Democrat vote has consistently shown that leader image has been a significant boost to the Party's support at election time (see for instance, Whiteley *et al.*, 2006).[24] New leader Nick Clegg will hope for a better approval rating than his predecessor but the harder task will be to convince the public that the Liberal Democrats are a credible force worthy of votes.

A key strategic challenge for the third party in Britain is to overcome the 'no-one knows what they stand for' syndrome. This is perhaps the reason why the Liberal Democrats seem especially keen on the process of policy review.[25] The Party is probably most identified with its hostility to first-past-the-post electoral systems and its commitment to the European Union. These are not insignificant policy platforms. The Party has twice – in 1972 and 1992 – refused to vote against a Conservative regime over key European legislation when a government defeat was not only likely but might have worked in the short-term interests of the third party. Nevertheless, the Party does tend to obsess with attempts to develop distinctive policy standpoints: no more so than on taxation where the Liberal Democrats have launched numerous initiatives in recent times covering – among many others – hypothecation (the penny on income tax to pay for education), local income tax to replace the council tax, a 50p marginal rate of income tax for top earners, and a green tax switch designed to be revenue-balancing and carbon-neutral. Moreover even when these standpoints have been well publicised and understood by the public, they have seldom benefited the Party. In 1997 only 21% of those voters who were in favour of directing tax money towards education voted for the Party actually proposing it. At the same time, 51% voted Labour and 23% voted Conservative.[26]

A further development in the Party's strategic communication is that it seems to have eschewed ideological standpoints for issues in recent times. In 1992 the Liberal Democrats designed their election campaign around five themes – broadly ideological topics where the Liberal Democrat standpoint was thought to be distinctive (these were the 'Five Es' – the Enterprise Economy, Education, Environment, Europe and Electoral and Constitutional Reform). In 2005 the Party was offering the public 'Top 10 reasons to vote Liberal Democrat' – a somewhat curious mix of the specific and the vague culminating in a list of policy preferences rather than distinctive ideological views ('Put patients first; free personal care when you need it; no tuition fees, no top-up fees; more investment in childrens' early years; 10,000 more police on the streets; £25 more on the pension every week; free off-peak local transport; axe the council tax; we should never have gone to war in Iraq; and take the environment seriously'). This move may have been the result of political research which shows that valence models of voting are increasingly useful in explaining electoral behaviour in Britain – so that social determinants of voting are less important than assessments of how parties would deal with particular issues.[27] And in order to demonstrate credibility in these valence issues party campaigning may begin to look rather esoteric at times.

Liberal Democrat kingmakers?

As the third party, the Liberal Democrats have to take account of their position relative to the other parties in British politics. As things stand, they are unlikely to form a majority government in the foreseeable future – as Table 10.1 illustrates, the Party's 2005 vote share was worse than that achieved by the Alliance in 1987 (and that result was thought so disastrous that the two partners were forcibly merged). Nevertheless, the party might be in a position to influence political outcomes – particularly if it were to hold the balance of power in a hung parliament. The key difference between third party performance in 2005 and 1987 however, was that the Liberal Democrats won 40 more seats at Westminster than the Alliance had done. This was the result of a keen campaigning machine which had decided some time earlier that the Party's key strategy was to increase its presence in the institutional heart of British politics.

The 2007 leadership election did little to alter this reality. In truth the distinction between the two leadership candidates was frequently overstated. Both wrote chapters for the *Orange Book*, both wanted to disregard the government's plans to introduce identity cards and both spoke of the need to reinvigorate British democracy through the empowerment of local communities. Both stressed their commitment to liberal ideals during the election campaign and Clegg even used his victory speech to claim he was 'a liberal by temperament, by instinct and by upbringing'.[28]

The clearest early distinction between the two was their respective strongholds in the party machine. The Liberal Democrats are a party of dual identities – granting leaders like Paddy Ashdown tremendous freedom to take the Party in a direction of their own choosing and yet constrained by a federal constitution and policy-making machinery designed to keep the Party elite in touch with the aspirations of activists. In the ousting of Kennedy the parliamentary party had demonstrated a power that was tangible if not quite located in the party rulebook.[29] Huhne, building on an impressive second place in the 2006 contest, was typically seen as the candidate of the grass-roots. Clegg was more identified with the parliamentary elite – he was able to claim the support of former leader Paddy Ashdown as well as the majority of Ming Campbell's former team. Both men entered the Commons in 2005 after stints in the European Parliament, both inherited seats that the Party had won relatively recently from the Conservatives, but while Huhne's Eastleigh seat is probably vulnerable to Conservative revival on the south coast, Clegg's Sheffield Hallam has become part of an emerging heartland for the Liberal Democrats where the opposition is Conservative but the surrounding area is solidly Labour.

The new leader may have to turn attention to post-election strategy well before the next election or risk a return of Ashdown's discomfort in 1992. Clegg's victory seemed to clarify that the Party will not move closer to the Conservatives in the near future, but the media attention on possible coalition partners will not diminish. In fact the most certain outcome of the leadership election was that Campbell's deputy and thus the acting leader, Vince Cable, was emboldened during his stint as caretaker. As a result even if the new leader was minded to change direction, the economic pathway for the Party is set to remain in the same hands for the foreseeable future.

The potential for the Liberal Democrats to be the kingmaker in a hung parliament does create a curious strategic dilemma for the Party. Given the current electoral mathematics it is possible that the Party would have more influence in a parliament where it had fewer seats – especially if it lost seats to the Conservatives and won seats from Labour in order to maximise its coalition potential. However, for our purposes we should assume that the Liberal Democrats' main strategic aim is to maximise their votes and seats. This is a reasonable assumption since the management of electoral fortunes is an inexact science and political outcomes often defy pre-election logic. Take for example the devolved elections to Scotland and Wales in 2007. In both the Scottish Parliament and the national Assembly for Wales the Liberal Democrats appeared to hold the balance of power, and yet the Liberal Democrats were excluded from power in both – the SNP outmanoeuvring the Scottish Liberal Democrats and managing to run the Scottish Government on their own, with Labour preferring a grand coalition with Plaid Cymru to a renewed partnership agreement with the Liberal Democrats in Cardiff. The failure to rebuild the Labour–Liberal Democrat coalition in Scotland and the determination of the SNP not to compromise their programme for the sake of partnership meant that the Liberal Democrats were excluded from the Scottish Government for the first time since 1999. Moreover, it began to look as if Labour were the only real coalition partner for the Liberal Democrats in the devolved institutions, but as Labour demonstrated in Wales they had other options. Having become accustomed to looking like a permanent fixture in Scotland, and the minor party partner in waiting for the Welsh Assembly Government, the Liberal Democrats were rapidly back to being the fourth party in both Scotland and Wales. With this in mind the Liberal Democrats would be well-advised to concentrate their efforts on maximising their own vote in the future – and this probably means continuing to fight on at least two fronts nationally against both Labour and the Conservatives.

Conclusions

The third party's struggle for credibility has epitomised the last 60 years. After flirting with oblivion in the aftermath of the Second World War, the Liberals' greatest influence came through the works of two of their grandees. Community politics and an energetic new leadership enabled the Liberals to revive but longer term the Party's fortunes continued to depend on their opponents' vision as much as their own. At times both Labour and Conservatives have looked vulnerable to Alliance and Liberal Democrat advance and both have fallen victim to spectacular by-election shocks at the hands of the Liberals.

That said, the overall appeal of the third party has not grown significantly since the 1980s – in fact the Alliance outperformed all other iterations of the third party in terms of vote share. It is indisputable however, that the Liberal Democrats have transformed their visibility in British politics by concentrating electoral resources into target seats which they pursue with professional rigour. The Party has usually benefited from popular leadership and has developed a consistent narrative of popular policies. However popularity appears to be a necessary but insufficient condition for Liberal Democrat success. The key to Liberal Democrat success is establishing credibility.

The Party's relative weakness in establishing an ideological bridgehead in public opinion has rather meant that the Liberal Democrats are a party of tactics and strategy, programmatic renewal but a curious lack of ideological cohesion. That is not to say that the Party is without its committed ideologues, but that the party has been forced to sacrifice the ideological, templates for electoral necessity. Moreover the success of campaign techniques in the local contexts of the constituency-based micro-contest has exacerbated the problem. The most pro-European party has established heartlands in regions dependent on fisheries and farming communities not known for their love of Brussels. The anti-Conservative alliance of the 1990s had begun to disintegrate by 2005 and subsequently a newly purposive Conservative Party threatened many of the Liberal Democrats' advances. Meanwhile the post-Blair Labour Party, under new leadership from the party that imposed student top-up fees and waged war in Iraq, might have the potential to reclaim some of the ground lost to the Liberal Democrats at the 2005 election. However the caretaker Liberal Democrat leader Cable's confident analysis of government mishandling of Northern Rock and missing data records did much to bring about the abrupt end of Premier Gordon Brown's honeymoon period and may have consolidated the Liberal Democrats' position as a credible party of opposition.

Again, the Liberal Democrats seem doomed to define themselves in terms of the other parties; the anti-Conservatives who are not the Tories, the social liberals who are not New Labour. The essential problem with trying to break the mould of politics is that the struggle is perennial. Although the building of party credibility is an ongoing process it can be a fragile one. Credibility begets credibility but a lack of credibility can spell obscurity for the Party. For the Liberal Democrats the struggle goes on.

Notes

1 P. Hennessy, *Never Again: Britain, 1945–51* (Cape, London, 1992).
2 See for instance K.O. Morgan, *Britain Since 1945: The People's Peace* (Oxford University Press, Oxford, 2001, 3rd edition).
3 D. Brack, 'Introduction', in I. Dale (ed.), *Liberal Party General Election Manifestos, 1900–1997* (Politico's, London, 1999).
4 A. Wyburn-Powell, *Clement Davies: Liberal Leader* (Politico's, London, 2003).
5 P. Barberis, *Liberal Lion: Jo Grimond: A Political Life* (Tauris, London, 2005).
6 D. Dutton, *A History of the Liberal Party in the Twentieth Century* (Palgrave, Basingstoke, 2004).
7 V. Bogdanor, 'The Liberal Democrat dilemma in historical perspective', *Political Quarterly*, 78:1 (2007), pp. 11–20.
8 A. Russell and E. Fieldhouse, *Neither Left nor Right? The Liberal Democrats and the Electorate* (Manchester University Press, Manchester, 2005), p. 23.
9 C. Copus, 'Liberal Democrat councillors: Community politics, local campaigning and the role of the political party', *Political Quarterly*, 78:1 (2007), pp. 128–38.
10 M. McManus, *Jo Grimond: Towards the Sound of Gunfire* (Birlinn, Edinburgh, 2001), p. 397.
11 See D. Dorling, C. Rallings and M. Thrasher, 'The epidemiology of the Liberal Democrat vote', *Political Geography*, 17, 1998, pp. 45–70, and I. MacAllister, E. Fieldhouse and A. Russell, 'Yellow Fever? The political geography of Liberal support', *Political Geography*, 21, 2002, pp. 421–47.
12 Russell and Fieldhouse, *Neither Left nor Right?*, p. 28.
13 V. Bogdanor (ed.), *Liberal Party Politics* (Oxford University Press, Oxford, 1983), p. 94.
14 P. Dunleavy, 'The political parties: The Liberal Democrats', in P. Dunleavy, A. Gamble, I. Holliday and G. Peele (eds), *Developments in British Politics 4*, (Macmillan, London, 1993), pp. 146–52.
15 A. Leaman, 'Ending equidistance', *Political Quarterly* 69:2 (1998), pp. 160–9.
16 P. Ashdown, *Diaries, Volume One 1988–1997* (Allen Lane, London, 2000), entry for 25th May 1995, p. 596.
17 Ibid. and P. Ashdown, *Diaries, Volume Two 1997–1999* (Allen Lane, London, 2001).
18 G. Hurst, *Charles Kennedy: A Tragic Flaw* (Politico's, London, 2006).
19 Charles Kennedy's conference speech, Bournemouth, Thursday 24th September 2004: www.guardian.co.uk/politics/2004/sep/23/libdems2004.liberaldemocrats5 (accessed 27th February 2009).
20 J. Curtice, 'New Labour, new protest? How the Liberal Democrats profited from Blair's

mistakes', *Political Quarterly*, 78:1 (2007), pp. 117–27.

21 See for instance, A. Russell, D. Cutts and E. Fieldhouse, 'National–regional–local: The electoral and political health of the Liberal Democrats in Britain', *British Politics*, 2, 2007, pp. 191–214.

22 For analysis of the nature of the Liberal Democrat 'underperformance' in 2005, see E. Fieldhouse, D. Cutts and A. Russell, 'Neither north nor south: The Liberal Democrat performance in the 2005 General Election', *Journal of Elections, Public Opinion and Parties*, 16, 2006, pp. 77–92.

23 A. Russell, E. Fieldhouse and D. Cutts, 'De facto veto? The parliamentary Liberal Democrats', *Political Quarterly*, 78:1 (2007), pp. 89–98.

24 P. Whiteley, P. Seyd, and A. Billinghurst, *Third Force Politics: Liberal Democrats at the Grassroots* (Oxford University Press, Oxford, 2006).

25 See for example, P. Dorey and A. Denham, '"Meeting the challenge"? The Liberal Democrats' Policy Review of 2005–6', Political Quarterly, 78:1 (2007), pp. 68–77.

26 Russell and Fieldhouse, *Neither Left nor Right?*, p. 124.

27 H. Clarke, D. Sanders, M. Stewart and p. Whiteley, *Political Choice in Britain* (Oxford University Press, Oxford, 2004).

28 Transcript online at http://news.bbc.co.uk/1/hi/uk_politics/7150595.stm (accessed 27th February 2009).

29 Russell, Fieldhouse and Cutts, 'De facto veto?'.

Part III

Commentaries

Classical liberalism in a modern setting

Whenever political activists and thinkers in the Liberal tradition get together, the surest way to generate an ideological punch-up is to divide them into 'economic' and 'social' liberals. The origin of this distinction probably lies in the days of the 1906 Liberal Government, a century ago, when there was a move towards greater state activism in social policy and away from the more austere approach of the classical liberals. Then in the 1980s the SDP–Liberal Alliance, and subsequent merger, brought together people from Labour's social democratic tradition and Liberals, whose individualistic values had been given articulate voice by the likes of Jo Grimond (who, it is now largely forgotten, was a strong advocate of such ideas as education and health vouchers). It is now difficult to disentangle who came from where in those parties but there are periodic echoes of former debates, as in the reaction to the *Orange Book* and the belated and muted intellectual response to it.

What these arguments fail sufficiently to register, however, is the extent to which the UK has been subjected to major experiments both in liberal economic reform and in large-scale social spending by government. Both have run into severe problems, some of which were not foreseen.

In a major social democratic experiment, Gordon Brown has increased the share of public spending (current and gross investment) in GDP from 37% (1999/2000) to 42% (2008/9 estimate). And while there have been undoubted improvements in health, education and policing, few would argue that these are commensurate with the costs. Specifically there has been a litany of government failures in large projects and complex benefit systems.

There has also been, at the same time, a major experiment in economic liberalism in the continuation of the Thatcherite reforms of the 1980s. Some of these changes – 'outsourcing' and marketisation of public services, building on labour market reform, deregulation and privatisation – have undoubtedly contributed to a decade and a half of sustained growth. But there have been some major failures: the spectacular growth of financial services since the Big Bang has now been overtaken by a major crisis; and there has been widening income and wealth inequality.

These experiences should be sufficient to give fundamentalists on both sides of the debate serious cause for self-criticism and for adapting their standard models.

The social democratic experiment

'Social democracy' embodies an essentially optimistic view about government. Governments can correct market failures through regulation; redistribute income and wealth efficiently and fairly; and provide tax-financed public goods competently which the market will under-provide. Democratic processes will establish clear choices while civil servants and public sector professionals and workers will deliver outcomes in a spirit of 'public service'.

The last decade has provided a big test of the act of faith involved in channelling large resource flows through government. Public spending is not, of course, an end in itself. Indeed, large sums have been consumed without producing significant service improvements. The Kings Fund has suggested that only a small percentage of health service funding has reached its destination. Much was swallowed up in salaries and administration. Salary improvements may be a necessary step towards service improvements if there is a recruitment and retention problem; and more professional administration may mean that clinicians are spending time on clinical work. But much of the public spending could not be tracked through to a socially beneficial outcome.

Another test is whether public spending has persuaded those with the discretion to choose alternatives, to stay with social rather than private provision. There has undoubtedly been a steady drift towards private education, and this has been a factor in driving education reforms especially in big cities, notably London. There has been 'privatisation' of law and order through 'gated communities'. And there has been an unambiguous shift from public provision in some areas (housing; the Post Office Counters network; dentistry) driven in part by a public preference for choice and quality.

It is, however, unhelpful to lump together public expenditure as an undifferentiated whole. There are, in fact, three broad categories. The first is 'social protection' – just under 30% – mostly transfer payments; a second is public investment; the third – the majority – being public services from the armed forces and the police to the NHS, education and centrally financed local government.

There is a strong social democratic case for redistribution through transfer payments between social classes, generations and regions, whatever view we take of the efficiency of public service provision. The earliest battles of the 'social liberals', in the early twentieth century, were over pensions and other forms of social insurance. Transfer payments do not – or should not – involve 'waste' or large administrative overheads. Nor do they pose any challenge to individual choice since recipients are, in theory, free to spend cash as they please.

One striking trend under the current government, however, has been a change in the nature of transfer payments towards more selective entitlements mainly based on income (pension and working tax credit; income-contingent student fees). One consequence has been a system of considerable complexity, prone to error and abuse, and with large administrative costs and perverse incentive structures.

The system of pension credit, working tax credit and other means-tested benefits has undoubtedly skewed resources towards the poorest groups in society; but at
a high price. Complexity has, moreover, deterred many applicants, with very low
take-up rates for some benefits – particularly working tax credit and council tax
benefit. There have been many errors including two million tax credit overpay-
ments which have, then, been clawed back, often creating considerable hardship.
There are severe disincentives to work because of high marginal rates of tax and
benefit withdrawal, and disincentives to save for retirement (and also arguably
disincentives to study). Complexity has generated a big expansion of administrative staff which has been curbed by crude headcount reductions resulting in poorer
service delivery, more errors and access only to a 'faceless state' of telephone
helplines which often fail to help even if they answer.

Then there are the government's weaknesses in managing large investment projects. The plan for Individual Learning Accounts was written off at the cost of £450
million. Attempts to reverse underinvestment in the public sector and to
modernise it with new technology have produced failed IT systems: Inland
Revenue tax credits; the magistrates' courts; the Post Office benefits swipe card; the
Passport Office; the Criminal Records Bureau. There are worrying reports of cost
over-runs and technical problems on the biggest project of all: the NHS national
IT scheme.

IT project disasters are not, of course, solely the prerogative of the public sector
but big public sector projects suffer from lack of accountability for cost over-runs
and other errors; a recourse to secrecy to disguise failure (as with the refusal to
divulge details of project performance under the Gateway Reviews); carelessness
with individuals' data (as with the loss of HMRC discs with material on 15 million
families); and a politically driven obsession with gargantuan scale and centralised
decision-making.

One factor undermining public services, particularly when there has been a
large injection of cash very quickly, has been the conflict between producer and
consumer (i.e. taxpayer) interests. Public sector workers, managers and professionals have their own interests which go beyond delivering 'public service': higher pay,
job security, prestige from empire building, status, risk aversion, professional recognition. It is a recognised phenomenon in all organisations – captured in what is
called 'agency theory' – for employees to subvert the aims of their organisation (as
with big private sector bonuses unrelated to performance). We have seen some
flagrant examples in the public sector in the last few years, one of the most costly
being the GPs' pay settlement. There has also been an enormous, self perpetuating
mushrooming of consultancies: often solutions looking for problems; and perpet-
uated by incestuous links between outside commercial interest groups, secondees
and civil servants lining up future job opportunities.

The government has tried to counter the self-serving or unfocused behaviour of
public sector staff by setting targets. But these targets have involved the creation of
a vast infrastructure of data collectors, inspectors, evaluators and reporters. Central
government agencies supervising local government alone cost over £1 billion to

operate. The administrative machinery of the NHS – Strategic Health Authorities, Primary Care Trusts and Foundation Hospital Trusts – has been substantially enlarged, much of it justified by the target culture. Quite apart from the administrative burdens, the proliferation of targets has created distorting behaviour: hospitals prioritising low priority, routine operations to meet waiting-time targets or to reduce the risk of failed operations; head teachers turning away children with special needs so as to boost their exam performance; police forces placing obstacles in the way of public crime reporting in order to reduce 'recorded crime'.

None of the above suggests that the experiment in social democratic spending was unjustified or has been a total failure, though it has been, at best, a very qualified success. We have, however, in parallel, been experiencing an experiment in economic liberalisation. What has that taught us?

The economic liberal experiment

There has been a continuation and enlargement of many of the 'Thatcherite' reforms introduced in the 1980s and 1990s: outsourcing of public services to private providers; competition in markets of former monopoly utilities (telecommunications, electricity); attempts to enlarge 'consumer choice' in relation to hospitals and schools; enlargement of the scope of the internal NHS 'market' with independent treatment centres and payment by results; attempts to eliminate cross subsidy (the Post Office); and introduction of fees in place of 'free' provision (universities). And the government has been resolute in economic liberalism: resisting traditional forms of industrial intervention, supporting 'free trade', welcoming inward investment and insisting on compliance with multilateral economic rules.

Yet the liberalisation of markets has had some serious negative consequences in some sectors.

One example is financial services and, specifically, banking. The 'Big Bang' of the 1980s opened up competition in the City of London, making it easier for individuals to invest in a wider range of products; increasing efficiency via a wave of takeovers and mergers; and giving a stimulus to the City in its efforts to be the leading international financial centre. But there have been serious market failures.

There has been a series of mis-selling scandals: private pensions, endowment mortgages, Equitable Life products, split cap trusts, share appreciation mortgages, equity release and payments protection insurance. Large numbers of people were sold products which they did not fully understand and which underperformed against promised returns. Millions of others have been angered by unfair, opaque charges on credit cards and bank accounts. There is a common market failure, 'asymmetry of information': producers, and sellers, of financial products know far more than even the better-informed buyers, and exploit that knowledge for commercial advantage.

There are also two other respects in which a competitive market model simply does not work in the banking sector. The clearing banks operate a clearing network, a natural monopoly, which can push up prices (fees) or restrict supply (delay cheque settlement) for commercial advantage. The Cruickshank Report in 2000 identified the monopoly of the clearing system as one way in which 'excess profits' are earned by the commercial banks. A bigger problem, also identified in that Report, is that banks have 'regulatory privileges': they can enjoy 'lender of last resort' facilities with the Bank of England which other firms do not have access to when faced with liquidity (and solvency) problems. We have seen in the current banking crisis how dependent are the banks on taxpayer support and this may lead the banks to the conclusion that they can, with impunity, maximise the private pursuit of shareholder returns while simultaneously offloading losses and risks onto the taxpayer. Governments are then forced into acquiescence by shouldering losses or taking banks over – as happened with Northern Rock.

One of the lessons from experience has been that a fully liberalised banking market is not an option. There has to be stronger consumer protection; more effective counter cyclical regulation of bank reserves; intervention by competition authorities to prevent abuse of the network monopoly; intervention to ensure that remuneration and bonus arrangements do not create systemic risk; and a clearer recognition that either banks should be allowed to fail or they should be closely regulated as utilities.

Another major industry in which the continuation of the 1980s liberalisation model has run into severe difficulty is transport, particularly railways and aviation. In both cases there are major market externalities: network externalities from an integrated transport system – which favour and create national monopolies – and the negative externalities of pollution and congestion. The creation of a private natural monopoly in the railways – Railtrack – with perverse incentives to under-invest, to inflate maintenance costs and to pass on inefficiencies to operating companies, has been partially addressed through re-nationalisation of the network (as well as via London Transport).

But severe problems and distortions continue. There is a tension between encouraging competition for franchises – which requires short franchises and effective sanctions including franchise cancellation – and creating incentives for long-term investment in capacity expansion. There has been a big increase in rail passenger use (by 40% over a decade) but as a consequence of under-investment there are severe capacity bottlenecks manifested in overcrowding on peak hour suburban services and long-distance intercity services. Second, failure to understand the importance of network externalities has led to problems of lack of inter-operability between different rail companies over ticketing arrangements – being addressed, now, very belatedly. The same misunderstanding has also led to disastrous experience with bus deregulation where classic market failures arising from 'cream skimming' have led to the destruction of urban and rural networks except in London, where a publicly owned network sits astride competitive outsourcing of individual contracts. Third, the modal mix has been massively distorted by the absence of consistent pricing systems. Railways charge full cost pricing to cover infrastructure and operating costs, albeit with some explicit subsidy. Road use is charged for only indirectly (via petrol and vehicle taxation and a growing patchwork of parking and congestion charges). Aviation carries large hidden subsidies as a result of sub-economic landing charges (cross subsidised by airport facilities) and 'free' traffic control infrastructure and the absence of congestion charging or fuel taxation. A variety of legal, institutional and political obstacles stand in the way of rational pricing policies. Fourth, there is, as yet, no rational and consistent way of factoring in environmental costs and benefits beyond piecemeal and arbitrary charges (petrol tax) and more sophisticated but limited measures (CO_2 differentiated Vehicle Excise Duty).

There is undoubtedly scope for achieving more efficiencies from the traditional liberalisation route – competition between airports, open skies policies – and from the use of market-based systems – road user pricing, auctioning landing slots – but the main challenges now lie in addressing big market failures in the sector.

These examples highlight different degrees of failure in the privatisation and deregulation model which this government has, with a few qualifications, largely continued. There is an inherent difficulty in balancing different policy objectives. There is also a certain naivety in government about the interest groups involved. Just as a naive belief in 'public service' led to government overlooking the 'agency problem' of self-interested public servants; so also a naive belief in the virtues of private sector solutions will lead to an underestimation of the ingenuity and ruthlessness with which firms will subvert regulators, undermine competition and try to wrap their self interests in the flag of national interest. Thus, City banks and 'national flag carrier' British Airways manage to project themselves as some kind of manifestation of Great Britain Ltd. BAA (despite being Spanish owned) has managed to turn the Department of Transport into a vehicle of its corporate interests. Banks have persuaded government to allow their regulatory privileges and 'excess profits' to continue even in the face of manifest failures. It is not necessary to invoke conspiracy theory or corruption: regulatory issues are complex and the producers usually understand them better than anyone else, including the regulators.

New approaches

The central conclusion is comforting to neither economic liberals nor social democrats: there have been major failures both in large-scale public spending and in 'economic liberal' experiments in deregulation and privatisation. What is required is some redefinition of what we want the state to do and what we want it to look like.

My starting point would be the idea of a simple (or simpler) state. Simple is not the same as small, the traditional concern of classical liberals. The simple state addresses the criticism that government is far too complicated. A case can be made that taxes and public spending are too big or too small as a share of the economy though, as it happens, the UK is roughly mid-range amongst developed countries and none of the three major parties are promising to change the mix very much. What is clearer is the hideous complexity of the tax system and of state benefits;

the proliferation of regulators; and the relentless accretion of new government powers and databases.

To reverse this trend will not be straightforward since the expanding complexity of government reflects, very often, political demands that 'something should be done' about a widening range of problems, a growing intolerance of risk in everyday life and a preoccupation (not unreasonable in itself) with 'fairness', even if this involves elaborate mechanisms to compensate all losers and prevent all cheating. There are also some good reasons for government intervention. In an increasingly integrated world with growing opportunities but also growing vulnerability to external events, people look to government to provide economic and financial stability, basic safety nets, the basic building blocks of a competitive economy – education, infrastructure – and sufficient a sense of equity to maintain a sense of community and nationality.

A simpler state would aim to simplify the tax system. There would be fewer income tax allowances and reliefs (which disproportionately benefit the better off) and lower rates. Tax cutting should emphasise the removal of those on low pay, small pensions and small part-time incomes from the income tax system with all the bureaucracy currently involved. Capital gains would be taxed at the same rate as income. Corporation tax rates would be cut and reliefs abolished. All of these changes – and others – would produce howls of protests from those who perceive themselves to be losers, so reformers would have to be determined.

A simpler state would reverse the trend under the Labour Government to place greater reliance on complex means-tested benefits and tax credits. The emphasis, for example, would be on restoring the value of the basic state pension, at a later retirement age, rather than growing reliance on pension credits; and family tax credits would be less complex and not reach so far up the income scale.

Government should try to do less. Despite some disengagement from the heavily interventionist policies of the 1970s, there is still a wider range of support arrangements for industry and agriculture and through regional development agencies which should usefully be disbanded. The whole costly paraphernalia of the 'surveillance society' culminating in a universal ID card scheme should be cut back drastically. That is not to say that governments can afford to be flippant about terrorism, crime or illegal immigration. But projects like the ID card scheme are solutions looking for problems. And much of the complexity in the criminal justice and regulatory system stems from pointless, hyperactive, legislating – with 3,000 new criminal offences created since 1997 – designed to give the impression of firm government.

Another way for the state to do less is to decentralise. Localism has become a popular mantra but little has been done, so far, to strip away the costly, interfering infrastructure of central command and control which sits on top of local government. Greater devolution of decision-making may well result in greater local variation. Local experiment will produce failures as well as successes.

Simple government also involves using markets rather than cumbersome regulation to achieve policy goals. We described above how the absence of effective market instruments to reflect environmental externalities was a major factor in transport policy, especially aviation.

The government's approach to scaling back government is not to simplify its tasks but to strip out staff, making it faceless – by withdrawing frontline staff. Thus government becomes (a little) smaller but no less complex and certainly less competent. There should instead be much more emphasis on competent administration and changing the culture of the senior civil service. Top civil servants are usually very bright analysts who are good at helping ministers answer questions, providing advice and managing their daily routine. There is little prospect at present of good project and service managers reaching the top. A new breed of civil servants who have won their spurs running large organisations, or big projects, or managing the change process, should be in charge of the public service.

The machinery of government needs to be stabilised, not constantly reinvented, but with the emphasis on competence and value for money. This technocratic approach and the emphasis on simpler, more competent, less expansive government may seem dull but is almost certainly the best way of assimilating the lessons of three decades of ideological experiment.

Centre: *in medias res*

Liberal Democrats usually object to being asked to place themselves on a 'left–right' axis. They point out that the terms 'left' and 'right' are increasingly confused and confusing and that, since people in Britain increasingly refuse to classify their political views, especially on moral issues but even on economic inequality, as falling along a left–right scale,[1] there is no good reason for commentators to continue to do so. Similarly, many Liberal Democrats also object to being called 'centrist' or 'middle-of-the-road'. Liberalism is not a moderate ideology. It is radical and different.

What applies to the position of the Party within British politics also applies within the Liberal Democrats. The 'centre' of the Party is not a compromise between 'extremes' of 'left' and 'right', but is rather the Party's centre of gravity or its core. It is the political position within the Party that is least like that of any of the other parties, where the Party's Liberalism is at its most distinctive and where it has least common ground with both the conventional 'left' and with the conventional 'right'. It is also the position around which the Party can most readily unite.

The enduring core values of the Liberal Democrats are political, not economic. Liberalism concerns itself above all with the distribution of political power. It distrusts concentrations of power and despises the worship of power. It seeks a fair society, but not at the cost of handing arbitrary power to a few guardians, no matter how benevolent. Its aim is a political system that allows individuals to pursue their own plans of life as long as they respect the capacity of others to do the same. Modern liberalism recognises that rights to be left alone are not enough, for two reasons. First, individuals will not be able to pursue reasonable plans of life freely if they lack the practical means of carrying those plans into effect. And secondly, legal rights in themselves offer only feeble protection against political onslaught. Maintaining the conditions under which a state will show equal concern and respect for its citizens is an endless political task, one that requires active political participation by liberals and the promotion of a democratic and tolerant political culture.

The central characteristic of core liberal thought is that ultimately it refers all questions back to the political: in each case the question is what course of action would best help to create and maintain the conditions for a liberal polity? That question breaks down into a series of familiar points: What course of action most effectively breaks up untoward concentrations of power? What course of action most effectively promotes democratic participation? What course of action most effectively promotes a culture of tolerance and respect for the life plans of others?

The combination of the political question that lies at liberalism's core and the realisation that rights are empty without the material conditions for putting them into operation yields practically all of the Liberal Democrats' key positions of principle and policy: decentralisation of political power; defence of civil liberties and political freedoms and championing individuals in the face of state power and monopolistic private power; promotion of education – to help create a critically minded electorate rather than one obsessed with production; support for the welfare state, including a comprehensive health service – to help create the material conditions in which people can meaningfully choose their own plans of life. The Party's internationalism and international law reflects the same attachment to tolerance and variety and a rejection of power politics. Even the Party's long-standing green commitment – dating back to the 1970s – rests on a belief that protection of the environment is a condition of any meaningful choice of life. If the planet is wrecked, there will be little point in worrying about maintaining a wide variety of potential life plans, for very few, if any, will be possible.

It is precisely the dominance of the political in liberal thought that puts it outside the conventional left–right scale that dominated twentieth-century politics. Both the twentieth-century left and the twentieth-century right took economic issues to be central to politics. The battleground between them consisted of two conflicts about ideas and values and one conflict about interest. The two conflicts of ideas were about the degree to which the state should care about economic equality and the degree to which the state should attempt to control economic activity. The two were interconnected – the left wanted to use state control to promote equality, whereas the right, not caring about equality, preferred to maximise economic output by allowing the market to allocate resources – but the degree of interconnectedness was often obscured by arguments that centred solely on the efficiency or otherwise of state intervention or on the desirability or otherwise of central planning in itself. The result was that politicians of the left would celebrate market failures and politicians of the right would celebrate bureaucratic failures apparently for their own sakes. The conflict about interest was the identification of one party with organised labour and the other with employers – the 'two sides' of industry. The problem for Liberals in the twentieth century was that they seemed to give equivocal answers to the questions that divided the other parties and which seemed at the time to define politics itself. Liberals were in favour of a fair society but they distrusted the state, and they saw politics as about individuals, not organised groups. That position made perfect sense to Liberals, but to those whose minds could not escape the conventional wisdom of left and right, the liberal position seemed 'wishy-washy', 'neither one thing nor the other' or 'centrist'. Liberalism was in reality only 'centrist' to those whose 'centre' was midway between two essentially non-liberal, and arguably illiberal positions, but, as a result of the hegemonic view that politics was economics by other means, liberalism had difficulty making its voice heard at all.

The situation now is different. Since the end of Cold War the straightforward classification of political views on the basis of whether they were more or less in sympathy with US-style capitalism has collapsed. Politics is increasingly concerned with a very different set of questions: how to maintain the possibility of peaceful, democratic politics in the face of furious passions about identity – whether religious, ethnic, national or at the level of civilisations; how to deal with the threat of climate change and more generally with the question of whether a society based on material consumption has any future; whether terrorism justifies the destruction of civil and political liberty; how to respond to the massive increase in the capacity of both states and private organisations to gather and process information; what to do about the double movement of, on the one hand, growing concentrations of media power – which amounts in effect to growing control over the means of mental production – and, on the other, the apparent decay of all political discourse into smaller and smaller soundbites, not to mention the inanities of radio phone-ins and of blogs; and how to cope with the potent and vicious circle of fear between classes, races and generations and rising levels of segregation – from gated communities to closed borders. As a result of the changing agenda, the other parties' positions on issues such as individual freedom, the environment and the distribution of political power are the ones that now seem equivocal and wishy-washy.

Some of those who cannot wean themselves from the twentieth-century view of politics tell themselves that politics has come to an end, that the only issues between the parties now are managerial and technical, matters of competence alone. That is because many of the issues that defined twentieth-century politics really have been reduced to technicality. The efficiency of different ways of organising economic activity is essentially a practical question with no absolute or timeless answer. As applied to the public services, it is little more than a question of human resources management. The issue of economic equality does remain, and is important to core liberalism, but its relationship with questions of economic organisation, as opposed to redistribution by more direct means, is far from clear. But politics has not really come to an end. What has ended is the relevance of the twentieth-century view of politics. The big political questions of the twenty-first century are ones that the old left–right scale ignored and now cannot cope with. Core liberalism, in contrast, can and does engage directly with those questions.

In simple terms, political views should now be classified on the basis of whether they are more or less in sympathy with the views of Rupert Murdoch – chauvinist, punitive, fearful, authoritarian, materialistic. On that basis, Liberal Democrats should be proud to be the Party least like Rupert Murdoch. On the major issues of the twenty-first century, liberalism's perspective is clear, and extremely challenging.

Core liberalism, for example, rejects identity politics. It sees individuals as capable always of abstracting away from their differences towards seeing themselves as simply human. At the same time, it demands respect for the choices other people make about how to live their lives, as long as those choices do not impinge on the capacity of others for choice. That makes liberalism a possible, perhaps the only possible, basis for a society characterised by religious and ethnic differences. Attempts to create identities to compete with religious and political identities, such as 'Britishness', cannot resolve the problem of exclusive identity because they are either exclusive themselves, and thus sow the seeds of future problems, or they are not exclusive enough and thus lack the potency of the identities with which they are supposed to compete. Liberalism provides a basis for agreement about what identities are, and are not, in a way that aims to limit their danger and incorporate them within a functioning democracy.

The idea that individual plans of life should be permitted unless they impinge on the capacity of others to pursue their own plans provides precisely the right balance between freedom and the needs of the environment. Liberal environmentalism means radical environmental action but it does not fetishise the environment. It locates the value of the environment not in mysticism but in how it provides the basis for individual human beings to make choices about their lives. But core liberalism, because it is at heart about the distribution of power rather than about economic interests, is also compatible with a decline in materialism as the driving force of western societies, a decline that will ultimately prove necessary if we are not only to cope with the climate crisis but also to ward off future environmental crises. If leading obsessively materialistic lives undermines the ability of all to make any sort of choice about their lives in the future, it is not illiberal to consider how materialism might be curbed, either by looking to the motives for it (often fear of powerlessness) and seeking other ways of satisfying them, or by recognising and encouraging other forms of success. Moreover, because Liberal Democrats are not the political representatives of specific economic interests (unlike both the other parties) they are well placed to tackle one of the central problems of the politics of the environment, namely corporate lobbying power. The other parties accept the view, which is structural for their own existence, that political action is a form of economic action, whereas the liberal instinct is that politics should as far as possible be liberated from purely economic motives.

Core liberalism is also unequivocal about the need to retain, and restore, civil and political liberties despite the threat of terrorism. A society founded on political liberty is what liberalism strives for. Sacrificing liberty for the sake of security is both self-defeating (since political liberty is the ultimate guarantee of security) and cowardly. Political and civil liberty is what we want our society to stand for. It is not an optional extra, or a nice-to-have tradition like folk dancing or stodgy puddings. It is the bedrock of the social contract itself, without which the state lacks all legitimate authority, including the authority to make us safer.

The growing ability of both state and private actors to control and to manipulate the populace through information-gathering and processing is a modern version of the old liberal theme of the problem of power. Power is necessary to achieve collective goals, but its abuse is a constant threat, especially where it is overconcentrated. That is ultimately why Liberals oppose identity cards and DNA databases. It is not a technical issue, about whether security systems are sound or whether officials are well-enough trained, but an issue of principle.

Similarly liberalism treats media ownership as a matter of the concentration of power, and not as just another market. It might be politically courageous to take on the power of News International, but the bile already directed at the Party by its newspapers means that the Liberal Democrats are not just the only party ideologically inclined to take such a step but also the only party with little or nothing to lose if they do. As for the inanity of the media and the internet, liberalism's fundamental commitment to freedom of expression rules out any interventionist approach, but the underlying problem is arguably the lack of face-to-face discussion about political decisions for which people have real responsibility. The obvious liberal cure is the devolution of democratic decision-making to the lowest possible levels, levels at which wide and effective participation become possible.

Localism also forms part of liberalism's response to the vicious circle of fearfulness and separation that lies near the centre of issues such as crime and immigration. Seeing others as part of the same community with similar problems, and thus not to be feared, is a potential result of reviving local politics. But localism by itself is not enough. Communities can be oppressive and exclusive rather than empowering and inclusive. The most important element of Liberal community politics that tended to be forgotten as community politics tended towards the condition of pure electoral tactic, was that the object of the exercise was the creation of liberal communities, not just any type of community. Liberal Democrats should not repeat that mistake. The temptations of cheap populism are especially strong in the areas of crime and immigration, but its effects are especially disastrous, as the fact that nearly 1% of the entire population of the United States now resides in prison testifies. Liberalism's contribution to these debates must recall its commitment to Enlightenment values – not just to rationality and acting on the basis of evidence rather than prejudice, but also to refusing to treat people merely as instruments.

Liberals no longer believe, if they ever did, in the inevitability of progress. The twentieth century put paid to that idea, as it almost put paid to liberalism itself. But liberalism has survived to become the best hope for ensuring that the century we are in will be at least not quite as catastrophic as the one we have just left. The views at the centre of the Liberal Democrats – 'centre' in the sense of the centre of a circle rather than the mid-point of a line – are not cocktail recipes for mixing this or that policy from one 'side' with this or that slogan from the other 'side'. They are simply liberalism itself.

Note

1 See C. Cochrane, N. Nevitte and S. White, 'Value change in Europe and North America', in J. Kopstein and S. Steinmo, *Growing Apart: America and Europe in the Twenty-First Century* (Cambridge University Press, Cambridge, 2008), pp. 69–70.

13 *Steve Webb MP*[1]

Social liberalism

The twin cores of social liberalism are freedom and fairness. This translates as a belief in the freedom of individuals to live their lives without undue interference from the state, alongside a recognition that freedom is not attainable without a fair distribution of wealth and power, which aims to enable each person to achieve their full potential in life.

Elsewhere in this collection, Richard Grayson has traced the main traditions and thinkers in the Liberal and Liberal Democrat parties that have given strength and impetus to these principles. He also makes the important point that occasional media stirring about the 'divide' between social and economic liberalism within the Party is a red herring. In fact, to quote him and fellow editors of *Reinventing the State*, David Howarth MP and Duncan Brack, 'economic liberalism is simply "a preference for market mechanisms not in opposition to redistribution but as a method to be used in the detailed design of mechanisms for it", and those party members who journalists like to identify as economic rather than social liberals are in reality both'.[2] These differences within the Party are not 'trivial', and they may on occasions imply different policy solutions. However, they largely relate to different views about means rather than ends, and ultimately they are all compatible with the core values of liberal democracy.

My aim in this chapter is to expand upon the themes outlined by Grayson, and to demonstrate how they are guiding the Liberal Democrats as we prepare for the next general election. It will be my task to demonstrate that the ideas and philosophy of the Party – reflecting the broad traditions within it – have a vital contemporary relevance to our society today. We must communicate to the British people a compelling narrative about what kind of party we are and what kind of society we would like to see, locally, nationally and globally.

It is commonly asserted that in British politics today there is a clustering of all the main parties around the 'centre ground'. It might be thought that Labour and the Conservatives have taken many traditional Liberal policies for their own.

For example, all main political parties now talk the language of environmentalism, just as sustainability and a concern for the environment have long been strands of Liberal thought, absorbed into social liberalism. It is recognised that we can no longer simply take our natural environment and its continual production of resources for granted.

But in reality, the other parties are paying lip service to the sustainability agenda. The Liberal Democrats are the only party that has pledged to make Britain entirely carbon neutral by 2050. Labour's policies are full of contradictions – for example, they simultaneously plan to expand airports and build more roads but see no contradiction between this strategy and serious action on carbon emissions. The Tories meanwhile are strong on 'polar bear-hugging' publicity stunts, but weak on substantive policy. The history of liberalism has always been about long-term solutions to deep-seated problems, and applying these principles to the major problem of climate change therefore comes most naturally to today's Liberal Democrats.

New politics emerging

The Tories and Labour represent the old politics of the establishment. The old politics is centralised, unaccountable and short-termist. People have disengaged because they do not believe that politics is relevant or significant in their everyday lives. The challenge for the Liberal Democrats in this climate is to introduce a new politics of openness and accountability. We need to be able to demonstrate the values of freedom and fairness, along with the increasingly important principle of sustainability, and re-engage people in the kind of active citizenship that means that they feel in charge of running their country. In the next section I consider how these three core themes of freedom, fairness and sustainability can be applied in practice in developing Liberal Democrat policy.

Link between theory and practice

Freedom

Recent reorganisations of the NHS have highlighted the centralised, unaccountable nature of national government today. Local hospitals have been threatened with downgrading and closure. Wards have been closed and budgets have been cut. And all the decisions have been made by unelected health authorities, accountable only to the Secretary of State in Whitehall. Local people have argued fervently in public forums, they have demonstrated on the streets with banners and marches, and they have been largely ignored by the decision-makers.

Without good health, the freedom to achieve your full potential is greatly restricted. A good local NHS is vital in helping to enable this, and the instincts of a social liberal are to ensure that the state has a role in guaranteeing good quality healthcare, which reflects and is shaped by the local circumstances of individuals and communities.

The state is a tool in the battle against inequality and ill-health, and decentralisation of government powers to a local level means that people can help to shape the services that they use. As well as a locally accountable NHS, cutting centralised bureaucracy and giving local authorities greater autonomy in levying taxes are both

ways that Liberal Democrats propose to give local communities the freedom to
govern themselves.

As I have said elsewhere, 'effective state intervention should be as local as possible and as accountable as possible – it should be the "state with a human face". The
state, as big bureaucracy, does not know best about the diverse needs of individuals, even if it can be effective as providing the means to meet those diverse needs.
The justification for intervention is always in the name of the greater good of
enhancing liberty.'[3]

Our instincts are to presume in favour of openness and transparency, and we are
the only party defending traditional British freedoms such as the right not to be
detained without charge, and the right to trial by jury. In area after area it is the
Liberal Democrats who are the bulwark against constant government attempts to
erode our liberty, often egged on by a Tory party that dare not risk being accused
of being 'soft on terror'. Whilst we recognise that the world is changing we also
recognise that hard-won freedoms, once lost, can seldom be recovered. All too
often the demand is made that we should abandon a particular freedom with little
justification beyond a general reference to the 'war on terror'. For social liberals,
this simply will not do, and those who cherish our freedoms can know that we are
the only party which can be relied upon to be consistent on these issues.

Fairness
But it is not just on traditional issues of freedom that the Liberal Democrats are
distinctive. We also have exciting proposals on tackling inequality which is still at
historically high levels despite ten years of a Labour Government. We are used to
Tory governments presiding over an increasingly divided society, but it is shocking
that under Labour so little progress is being made in reversing those trends. Recent
statistics showed that for all the government's talk of eliminating child poverty, this
is actually on the increase.[4]

More shocking still is the way in which social mobility is actually declining in
this country. Recent research has shown that the influence of social class on your
chances in life is actually more pronounced for those born at the start of the 1970s
and now well into their careers than it was for those born in the late 1950s.[5]

Our policies on poverty and inequality include a range of measures designed to
tackle some of these deep-seated problems. In particular, we propose redirecting
some of Gordon Brown's tax credits away from high earners. Instead we will introduce a new 'pupil premium' – around £1.5 billion of additional cash for the
education of children who need the most support. Not only will this obviously
benefit more deprived areas but it will also help children who have particular needs
in areas where no additional funding is available because the authority as a whole
is not considered 'deprived'. Instead of schools using backdoor methods to avoid
admitting children from deprived backgrounds, the 'pupil premium' will give
schools a financial incentive to admit such children and to make sure they achieve
their full potential.

Our fairness agenda also applies at the other end of the age scale, with plans to scrap the regressive council tax, and a long-term goal of a 'citizen's pension' which ends the scandal whereby so many women retire with wholly inadequate incomes in old age.

Sustainability

Our third policy strand is sustainability, and again we distinguish ourselves from Labour, who have seen green taxes fall in their role over the last decade, and the Tories, who set up a tax commission that decided environmental taxation was not important enough to include. We have set out a distinctive Liberal Democrat agenda on which we can campaign with confidence.

Some of our goals are bold in their scope, including a carbon-neutral domestic economy by 2050. We have looked systematically at every area of the economy to see what measures are needed to make substantial and rapid progress on reducing greenhouse gas emissions. On domestic emissions we want to see much better insulation and energy-efficiency standards, not just on new-build but on the existing housing stock that will be around for decades to come. On aviation we have a raft of measures to cut unnecessary emissions, including replacing air passenger duty with a tax based on the emissions of the flight, introducing new levies on air freight and on domestic flights where there is a credible rail alternative. On domestic transport we propose a much more steeply tiered vehicle excise duty, hitting gas-guzzlers hard, whilst a new levy on lorry freight will provide funds for a long-overdue investment in our railways.

This policy package was produced by a Liberal Democrat working group with a good representation of those sometimes described as 'economic liberals'. It has produced an agenda which not only promotes the freedom of individuals to earn and not to suffer pollution but which also substantially promotes fairness in the tax system. Rather than simply regulate or ban things, it harnesses the power of market forces to encourage energy efficiency and to penalise polluting behaviour. There is no inconsistency for social liberals in using market mechanisms as a servant, though not as a master.

Our 'free, fair and green' approach applies locally, nationally and internationally. Our attitude is strongly localist, giving local communities a real say over their public services and the decisions that affect their daily lives. We want to harness the power of national government in more effective ways, for example by ending the relentless prison-building programme and instead investing in new secure mental health facilities that will treat the causes of offending behaviour. And we are genuinely internationalist, recognising that so many of our problems can only be solved by working in constructive partnership with other nations, in contrast to the isolationism of the Tories and the US-dominated foreign policy of Labour.

The Liberal Democrat vision of a free, fair and green future is one that stems from a social liberal tradition, unites us as a party and clearly distinguishes us from the others. Our challenge now is to communicate that message at every opportunity and to bring the British public with us into that future.

Notes

1 This piece was written before the subsequent leadership election and Shadow Cabinet reshuffle, in which Steve Webb was moved from the manifesto team to shadow the Environment, Energy and subsequently Work and Pensions portfolios.

2 D. Brack, R. Grayson and D. Howarth (eds), *Reinventing the State: Social Liberalism for the 21ˢᵗ Century* (Politico's, London, 2007), pp. x–xi.

3 S. Webb and J. Holland, 'Communicating social liberalism', ibid., p. 364.

4 Households Below Average Income statistical release, Department for Work and Pensions, 22ⁿᵈ May 2007, Table 3.2, available at www.dwp.gov.uk/asd/hbai/hbai2006/first_release_0506.pdf (accessed 24ᵗʰ May 2008).

5 J. Blanden and S. Machin, Interim Findings from Sutton Trust Research 'Recent Evidence on Changes in Intergenerational Mobility', Centre for Economic Performance, London School of Economics, 2005.

Select bibliography

Ashdown, P., *Ashdown Diaries* vol. 1 (Allen Lane, London, 2000), vol. 2 (Allen Lane, London, 2001)

Astle, J., D. Laws, P. Marshall and A. Murray (eds), *Britain After Blair: A Liberal Agenda* (Profile, London, 2006)

Barberis, P., *Liberal Lion: Jo Grimond: A Political Life* (Tauris, London, 2005)

Bartram, P., *David Steel: His Life and Politics* (W.H. Allen, London, 1981)

Beith, A. *The Case for the Liberal Party and the Alliance* (Longman, Harlow, 1983)

Berlin, I., *Four Essays on Liberty* (Oxford University Press, Oxford, 1969)

Bogdanor, V., 'The Liberal Party and the Constitution', *Journal of Liberal History* 54, Spring 2007

Bogdanor, V. (ed.), *Liberal Party Politics* (Oxford University Press, Oxford, 1983)

Brack, D. (ed.), *Why I am a Liberal Democrat* (Liberal Democrat Publications, Dorchester, 1996)

Brack, D., R. Grayson and D. Howarth (eds) *Reinventing the State: Social Liberalism for the 21st Century* (Politico's, London, 2007)

Brack, D. and E. Randall (eds), *Dictionary of Liberal Thought* (Politico's, London, 2007)

Bradley, I., *The Strange Rebirth of Liberal Britain* (Chatto and Windus, London, 1985)

Bullock, A. and M. Shock, *The Liberal Tradition from Fox to Keynes* (Black, London, 1956)

Butt Philip, A., 'European first and last: British Liberals and the European Community', *Political Quarterly*, 64:4 (1993)

Campbell, J., *Roy Jenkins: A Biography* (Weidenfeld and Nicolson, London, 1983)

Cook, C., *A Short History of the Liberal Party 1900–2001* (Palgrave, Basingstoke, 2002, 6th edition)

Crewe, I. and A. King, *SDP: The Birth, Life and Death of the Social Democratic Party* (Oxford University Press, Oxford, 1995)

Cyr, A., *Liberal Party Politics in Britain* (John Calder, London, 1977)

Dale, I. (ed.), *Liberal Party General Election Manifestos 1900–1997* (Routledge, London, 2000)

Deacon, R., *Devolution in Britain Today* (Manchester University Press, Manchester, 2006, 2nd edition)

Deacon, R. and A. Sandry, *Devolution in Great Britain* (Edinburgh University Press, Edinburgh, 2007)

Douglas, R., *History of the Liberal Party 1895–1970* (Sidgwick and Jackson, London, 1971)

Douglas, R., *Liberals: A History of the Liberal and Liberal Democrat Parties* (Continuum, London, 2005)

Dutton, D., *A History of the Liberal Party in the Twentieth Century* (Palgrave, Basingstoke, 2004)

Fieldhouse, E. and D. Cutts, 'The Liberal Democrats: steady progress or failure to seize the moment', in Geddes and Tonge (eds), *Britain Decides: The UK General Election, 2005* (Palgrave, Basingstoke, 2005)

Freeden, M., *The New Liberalism: An Ideology of Social Reform* (Clarendon, Oxford, 1978)

Fulford, R., *The Liberal Case* (Penguin, Harmondsworth, 1959)

Grayson, R.S., 'Social democracy or social liberalism? Ideological sources of Liberal Democrat policy', *Political Quarterly*, 78:1 (2007)

Grayson, R.S. (ed.), *Liberal Democrats and the Third Way* (Centre for Reform, London, 1998)

Greaves, B. and G. Lishman, *The Theory and Practice of Community Politics*, ALC Campaign Booklet No. 12, 1980

Green, T.H., *Lectures on the Principles of Political Obligation* (first published 1883: Longmans, London, 1941 edition)

Grimond, J., *The Liberal Future* (Faber and Faber, London, 1959)

Grimond, J., *The Liberal Challenge* (Hollis and Carter, London, 1963)

Harris, J., *William Beveridge: A Biography* (Clarendon, Oxford, 1997)

Harris, P., *Forty Years In and Out of Parliament* (Andrew Melrose, London, 1946)

Hobhouse, L.T., *Liberalism* (first published 1911: Galaxy Press, New York, 1964 edition)

Hobson, J.A., *Confessions of an Economic Heretic* (Allen and Unwin, London, 1938)

Horabin, T.L., *Politics Made Plain* (Penguin, Harmondsworth, 1944)

Hurst, G., *Charles Kennedy: A Tragic Flaw* (Politico's, London, 2006)

Ignatieff, M., *The Needs of Strangers* (Chatto and Windus, London, 1984)

Jenkins, R., *A Life at the Centre* (Macmillan, Basingstoke, 1991)

Kennedy, C., *The Future of Politics* (HarperCollins, London, 2001)

Margo, J. (ed.), *Beyond Liberty: Is the Future of Liberalism Progressive?* (IPPR, London, 2007)

Marshall, P. and D. Laws (eds), *The Orange Book: Reclaiming Liberalism* (Profile, London, 2004)

McIver, D. (ed.), *Liberal Democrat Politics* (Harvester Wheatsheaf, Hemel Hempstead, 1996)

McManus, M., *Jo Grimond: Towards the Sound of Gunfire* (Birlinn, Edinburgh, 2001)

Meadowcroft, M., *Liberal Values for a New Decade* (North West Community Newspapers, Manchester, 1981, 2nd edition)

Michie, A. and S. Hoggart, *The Pact: The Inside Story of the Lib-Lab Government, 1977–8* (Quartet, London, 1978)

Mill, J.S., *Three Essays* (Oxford University Press, 1975; edited with an introduction by R. Wollheim)

Morley, J., *The Life of William Ewart Gladstone* (Macmillan, London, 1906)

Muir, R., *Future for Democracy* (Nicholson and Watson, London, 1939)

National Liberal Federation, *The Liberal Way* (National Liberal Federation, London, 1934)

Owen, D. and D. Steel, *The Time Has Come: Partnership for Progress* (Weidenfeld and Nicholson, London, 1987)

Pottle, M. (ed.), *Daring to Hope: The Diaries and Letters of Violet Bonham Carter 1946–1969* (Weidenfeld and Nicolson, London, 2000)

Russell, A. and E. Fieldhouse, *Neither Left nor Right? The Liberal Democrats and the Electorate* (Manchester University Press, Manchester, 2005)

Russell, C., *An Intelligent Person's Guide to Liberalism* (Duckworth, London, 1999)

Samuel, H.L., *Liberalism: An Attempt to State the Principles and Proposals of Contemporary Liberalism in England* (Grant Richards, London, 1902)

Samuel, H.L., *Memoirs* (Cresset Press, London, 1945)

Skidelsky, R., *John Maynard Keynes, 1883–1946* (Pan, London, 2004)

Smith, J., *A Sense of Liberty: The History of the Liberal International* (Liberal International, London, 1997)

Steel, D., *A House Divided* (Weidenfeld and Nicolson, London, 1980)

Steel, D., *Against Goliath: David Steel's Story* (Weidenfeld and Nicolson, London, 1989)

Thomas, G., *The Moral Philosophy of T.H. Green* (Clarendon, Oxford, 1987)

Thorpe, J., *In My Own Time: Reminiscences of a Liberal Leader* (Politico's, London, 1999)

Wallace, W., *Why Vote Liberal Democrat?* (Penguin, Harmondswoth, 1992)

Watkins, A., *The Liberal Dilemma* (Macgibbon and Kee, London, 1966)

Watson, G. (ed.), *The Unservile State: Essays in Liberty and Welfare* (Allen and Unwin, London, 1957)

Watson, G. (ed.), *Radical Alternative* (Eyre & Spottiswoode, London, 1962)

Whiteley, P.P. Seyd and A. Billinghurst, *Third Force Politics: Liberal Democrats at the Grassroots* (Oxford University Press, Oxford, 2006)

Wyburn-Powell, A., *Clement Davies: Liberal Leader* (Politico's, London, 2003)

Index